GOD IN CHRIST.

THREE DISCOURSES

DELIVERED AT

NEW HAVEN, CAMBRIDGE, AND ANDOVER,

WITH A

PRELIMINARY DISSERTATION ON LANGUAGE.

By HORACE BUSHNELL.

NEW YORK
CHARLES SCRIBNER'S SONS
743 AND 745 BROADWAY

Trow's
Printing and Bookbinding Company,
205-213 *East 12th St.*,
NEW YORK.

PUBLISHERS' PREFACE.

There has hitherto been no uniform edition of Dr. Bushnell's works. Appearing at wide distances of time, they have taken such shape as suited the occasion; and it has for some time seemed very desirable that they should be brought together in a more permanent and serviceable form. It was Dr. Bushnell's own wish that this should be done; and he has largely revised his books in preparation for this end. It is only to be regretted that it was not reached during his lifetime and under his supervision; but his failing health compelled him to relinquish the task, which his death has left to other hands to complete.

In the present volume we offer to his readers the first of the proposed uniform edition, in which most of his works will be included. The other volumes will follow this as rapidly as possible, not in the original order of their publication, but rather in that of their relative importance to the public; and it is hoped that the edition, when finished, may prove so compact and attractive in form, as to fulfill the design so long entertained, and satisfy the expectation that has awaited it.

ADVERTISEMENT.

This volume, though appearing as the last of the present Series, was almost the first of Dr. Bushnell's published works, and owes to that fact something of its interest. To the Preliminary Dissertation on Language he attached special importance; and it is so truly the key to his method of approaching truth, that it may almost be said to be impossible thoroughly to comprehend him, without having read it. The Discourses which follow were delivered in 1848, and contain his earliest public utterance on the nature and work of Christ. They were the first costly steps of that prolonged but most remunerative struggle for more untrammeled thought and larger truth. The final discourse, on "The True Reviving of Religion," bears the same date; but is, in parts, singularly applicable to the present conditions of the question.

It is for these reasons, and in accordance with the author's own wish, that this book, now for a long time out of print, is committed anew to his readers, as the door through which those of them may pass, who desire a closer access to his mind and its history, as well as to the history of that somewhat memorable epoch of New England theology.—Ed.

CONTENTS.

I. PRELIMINARY DISSERTATION.

PAGE

Language as related to thought and spirit. Origin of Language. Formation of Grammar. Views of others. Two departments in language. Applications of the doctrine. Reason of types or figures. Words of thought indeterminate. A false element in words of thought. Etymologies to be studied. Opposing words necessary. The logical method deceitful. Interpretation. Language insufficient for the uses of dogma. Creeds and confessions. How a writer becomes intelligible. Facilities of perverse criticism. Effects of a right view of language. Introductory 9–117

II. DISCOURSE AT NEW HAVEN.

The Divinity of Christ. Orthodox views of Christ and the Trinity. Trinity involved in the process of Revelation. God Absolute. Incidents of the revealing process. The Logos or Word of God. Incarnation. Trinity. Conclusion 119–181

III. DISCOURSE AT CAMBRIDGE.

The Atonement. Doctrine stated from the scriptures. The Protestant views stated and discussed. Subjective

PAGE

doctrine. Christ a perfect character. Christ as the Word of God. Christ dissolves the law of social evil. Christ brings light, opens eternity, assists our struggles. Justification wanted. Assured to us in Christ. Prepared in us. How prepared. The double administration of law and grace. Sin finally vanquished by the submission of Jesus. The incarnation viewed in its objects. Subjective view concluded. Objective view and its grounds. Judaism externally objective. Christianity internally. Religion as in art. The subjective view translated into the objective, becomes a vicarious religion. The objective view instituted by God. Christianity incomplete without the Altar Form. Comprehensiveness of the doctrine. How to be preached. Conclusion 183–275

IV. DISCOURSE AT ANDOVER.

Dogma and Spirit; or the true reviving of Religion. Christianity displaces the Pharisaic dogma. Enters the world as spirit and life. Lapses next into dogma. Consequent discord and corruption. The Reformation a partial remedy. The reviving of revivals insufficient. Dogma and spirit distinguished. Province and uses of Christian theology. Causes of the lapse into dogma. Resulting benefits of the same. Theological capacities of dogma. The head and the heart. The Christian ministry. Platforms and Articles. Piety itself limited by dogma. The Holy Spirit as the Spirit of Christ. Conclusion . . . 277–356

PRELIMINARY DISSERTATION

ON THE NATURE OF

LANGUAGE,

AS RELATED TO

THOUGHT AND SPIRIT.

PRELIMINARY DISSERTATION.

When views of religious truth are advanced, which either really or apparently differ from such as are commonly accepted, the difference will often be referable to causes that lie back of the arguments by which they are maintained—some peculiarity of temperament, some struggle of personal history, unknown to the public, the assumption or settlement of some supposed law or principle of judgment, which affects, of course, all subordinate decisions.

Thus, if Hume or Blanco White had come, at last, into a settled belief in what is commonly called orthodox or evangelical truth, any man, who understands at all the philosophy of opinions, will see that he would have held all his points or articles of belief under forms and relations that had some reference, more or less palpable, to his own spiritual history, and the struggles through which he had passed. It must be so; it lies not in his choice to have it otherwise. This, too, most likely is, in the estimation of Providence, the real value of the man; that for which he exists, and for which his mental struggles have been appointed—which, if it were known, ought surely to secure him a degree of patience, or even a respectful hearing. But, meantime, until the internal relation between his spiritual history and his opinions is known, he is very nearly certain to be a suspicious character. He may seem, indeed, to be scarcely true or earnest in his professed belief, because of the peculiar type and form observed in his opinions. It may even be suspected that in assenting to standards, he is only willing to find some shelter of impunity for his aberrations. Perhaps he will also be observed, since consciously he was not a devil himself in the painful struggles of unbelief or misbelief through which he has passed, to have a certain warm and even fraternal interest in persons or classes of men similarly exercised; endeavoring, possibly, to accommodate himself to their point of view: and this will be to many, a sign yet more suspicious. Suspicious, not because of any malignant purpose in them, but simply because they have no such elements in their own personal experience as will enable them to understand or conceive the man. It is only to be hoped that possibly they may learn enough of him at last, by their friction against him and his opinions, to pacify their suspicions, and rectify their uncharitable judgments.

In offering these suggestions, it is not my design to lay open to the public, even by implication, facts of personal history. I have, doubtless, had my own course of mental and spiritual struggle, as other men have theirs. I do not say that the opinions to be advanced in this volume, on important theological subjects, are either to be received, or to be endured, or even to be forgiven. I only say, that to *me*, they are true—truths of the profoundest moment, such as I must violate my own well being, and my spiritual integrity before God, not to embrace, to profess, and, with what ability I have, to maintain by appropriate arguments. At the same time, if the public will believe it, there really does not seem to me to be anything so peculiar in these views, that any one need be alarmed or stumbled by them. I seem to myself to assert nothing which is not substantial orthodoxy,—that which contains the real moment of all our orthodox formulas unabridged. Indeed, I cannot see that there is really more of diversity between the views here advanced and those commonly accepted, than there is between Paul and John, or Paul and James. And as it was right that each of these sacred writers should present his truth in the forms of his own life and experience, and so as to accord with the type of his own thinking habit, so I only seem to have asserted the great Christian truths held by our churches, in forms truest to me, as they are likely to be to all, who have been exercised by similar difficulties.

There is, however, apart from all such experimental difficulties, of which it does not become me to speak, a single subject, in regard to which I was long ago led, in the way of self-extrication, to take up views somewhat different from those which seem more generally to prevail; and as I have been drawn, partly in this manner, into what may seem peculiar in the doctrines and argumentations of the discourses that follow, I deem it my duty to conduct my reader, if possible, into the views I hold of that subject, that I may assist him thus to understand my position more fully. The subject of which I speak, is language; a very different instrument, certainly, from what most men think it to be, and one, which if they understood more exactly, they would use more wisely. In the misuse or abuse of this instrument, a great part of our religious difficulties have their spring. We have misconceived, as it seems to me, both its nature and its capacities, and our moral reasonings are, to just the same extent, infected with error. Indeed, it is such an instrument, that I see not how any one, who rightly conceives its nature, can hope any longer to produce in it a real and proper system of dogmatic truth. He will doubt the capacity of language to serve any such purpose. He will also suspect that our logical or deductive processes under it, are more likely, in general, to be false than true. And yet, in the matter of Christian doctrine, or Christian theology, we are found committing ourselves most unsuspectingly to language and logic, as if the instrument were sufficient, and the method infallible.

I do not propose, in the dissertation that follows, to undertake a full investigation of language. I freely acknowledge my incompetence to any such undertaking. What I design is, principally, to speak of language as regards its significancy, or the power and capacity of its words, taken as vehicles of thought and of spiritual truth. What I may offer concerning other topics involved in the general subject, such as the origin of language; the phonology of words, or the reason why certain things are named by certain sounds, and not by others; letters and the written forms of words; laws of grammar;

questions of ethnology, and the like; will be advanced in a purely incidental way, and with no other design than to make my theory of the *significance* of words more intelligible and clear. I cannot promise that I shall fall into no mistakes which the learned philologists and grammarians will detect, though I have little fear that they will discover any important error in what I advance, in regard to the philosophy of words, taken as *instruments of thought*, which is the particular subject under discussion.

To understand the precise power of words, or the true theory of their power, without some reference to their origin, will be difficult or impossible; for it is, in fact the mode of their origin that reveals their power. And yet what we say of their power may be true, in general, if what we say of their origin should not hold in every particular.

It is undoubtedly true, as many have asserted, that human language is a gift of God to the race, though not, I think, in the sense often contended for. It is by no means asserted, in the scriptures to which they refer, that God himself pronounced the sounds, or vocal names, by which the objects of the world were represented, nor that He framed these names into a grammar. It is only implied in what is said that He first called into action the instinct of language in our father, by directing his mind to the objects round him, "to see what *he* would call them." He was, Himself, in this view, the occasional cause of the naming process; and, considering the nature of the first man to have been originally framed for language, he was the creative cause; still the man himself, in his own freedom, is the immediate, operative cause the language produced is as truly a human, as a divine product. It is not only *for* the race, but it is also *of* the race—a human development, as truly as knowledge, or virtue, or the forms of the social state.

But, if we believe the scriptures, there is far less depending on this particular history than many seem to suppose. For, in whatever manner the first language came into being, it is expressly declared, afterwards, to be in existence no longer. Thus when it is affirmed in the history of Babel and the dispersion, that God there confounded the language of the race, that they might "not understand" each other and might be "scattered abroad over the earth," it is plainly testified, howsoever the first language came into being, that it exists no longer. Accordingly, the attempt so eagerly prosecuted, in former times, to ascertain what living language is descended from the first language, is really an attempt, under countenance of the Bible, to prove the Bible untrue. And so, when our modern ethnologists undertake, as they say, in behalf of the scriptures, to establish the unity of the human race, by tracing all human languages to some common source, through a comparison of terms, or names, found in them all, they would seem to controvert the authority of the scriptures by their argument, quite as effectually as they sustain it. No fair construction can be given to the history of the dispersion, as recorded by Moses, without understanding him to affirm the virtual destruction of the one language of the race by a miracle. According to the representation given, they are here thrown back once more, on their linguistic instincts;

and we are to look for the development of new languages, radically distinct from each other, such as the free move ment of small families or circles, instigated each by peculiar circumstances and causes, may produce. Nor have our ethnologists been able, as yet, with all their supposed discoveries, to disprove, at all, the original distinctness of many of the existing languages. Within certain circles of language, they seem to have a degree of success; but when they pass to certain larger circles—from the Indo-Germanic languages, for example, to the American or the Chinese—they find the matter offered to their theories wholly intractable and unreducible. So, I will even dare to prophesy, it always will be. I will also venture, with as much deference to the great learning of our investigators in this field, as properly becomes one who is only a spectator of their works, to suggest the inquiry, whether it is not likely, sometime, to be discovered, that the very mode of the argument hitherto used is involved in mistake. For if common terms are found sprinkled through many languages, and are taken to indicate a common origin in the languages where they are found, do not the diverse terms, made use of as names of things in the same languages, indicate, quite as conclusively, and even more conclusively, the original distinctness of these languages? There would be common terms, of course, in languages radically distinct; such as have been conveyed by emigrations, wars, and the mixture of races; such as relate to objects, measures, numerals, and dates, employed in the intercourse of commerce. On the other hand, it is impossible to conceive how different names for the same thing, and that a thing every day spoken of by every body, could have come into use, after having once had the same name—how *oak* became *quercus*, for example, or *quercus*, *oak;* how *house* became *domus; cloud, nubes; light, lux;* or the contrary. What do such diversities indicate, in fact, and that on the broadest scale, but that some time or other, there have been distinct namings of things; or, what is nowise different, the existence of distinct original languages? It is often true, in the speculations of the philosophers and literati, as in medicine, and, I suppose I must add, in theology, that they go by a fashion. Have we no reason to anticipate that a contrary fashion will sometime come into vogue among them, and that we shall sometime find them arguing for original diversities of language, as strenuously as now for the original unity of language? This, I judge, is the view, in fact, of Adelung, and, in a less decided form, of William Von Humboldt, two of the most competent and most respected investigators in this field.

At the same time, it cannot be pretended, by those who are most sanguine in the hope of sometime reducing all existing languages to a common origin or parentage, that the investigations hitherto made have yielded any definite token of success, except within certain acknowledged limits of affinity. The fact that there are living languages, between which no real affinity can be discovered, still exists in its integrity. And therefore we must either admit the existence of races originally distinct, or else we must refer these languages to the scripture solution of a miracle.

And now the question rises, in what manner were these distinct languages produced? It is not a question about language in general, or some one language in particular, but about the languages. If we say that God, by direct pronunciation of words, taught man language, we must mean that he taught, in this manner, as many distinct languages as there are, else our solution is too narrow for the problem. And as probably no one will imagine that God has, at any time, pronounced to the different families of the race so many languages, we fall back, most naturally, upon the view just given of the formation of the first language, and take up the belief that all these different languages are so many free developments of the race; though all from God, in the sense that he has created in all human beings a certain free power of self-representation or expression, which is itself a distinct capacity for language, and, in one view, language itself.

Nor is there any so great impossibility or mystery in this matter of originating a language, as many seem to suppose. I hope it will not offend the romantic or marvelling propensity of my readers, if I affirm that a new language has been created and has perished, in Connecticut, within the present century. A very distinguished citizen, whose name is familiar to the country at large, himself a scholar and a keen philosophic observer, had a pair of twin boys, who were drawn to each other with such a mysterious and truly congenital fondness as to be totally occupied with each other, and thus to make little or no progress in learning the language of the family. Meantime, they were constantly talking with each other, in a language constructed between them, which no one but themselves could understand. In this language they conversed at their plays as freely as men at their business, and in a manner that indicated the most perfect intelligence between them. At an early age one of them died; and with him died, never to be spoken again, what, beyond any reason for doubt, was the root of a new original diversity of human speech—a new tongue. Nor is there any reason to doubt that incipient and rudimental efforts of nature, in this direction, are often made, though in cases and modes that escape attention. Indeed, to believe that any two human beings, shut up wholly to each other, to live together until they are of a mature age, would not construct a language, is equivalent, in my estimation, to a denial of their proper humanity.

Let us trace the manner in a supposed experiment; for, in this way, the true conception of language as a human product, and also as a vehicle of thought, will be exhibited with more clearness and facility than in any other. The experiment can be made only in a small circle, as in a family, or between two or three individuals; for the sounds of a new language could never settle into a current use and significance, where many persons, or a large community, are concerned; because they do not exist together in terms of sufficient closeness and mutuality to allow the growth of common uses. Perceiving this, even Cæsar confessed his inability, with all the authority he had, to give currency to but a single word.

We suppose, then, two human persons to be thrown together, who, as yet, have never heard the use of words, and, of course, have no language. Considered simply as human, they have a certain ground or preparation in their very nature for speech. In one view, language is in them potentially beforehand, only it is not developed into actual existence; they are linguistic natures, so to speak, only it is not yet clear what kind of tongue they are going to create. This, in fact, is the opinion of Humboldt, and also of many of the most competent philologists. "Speech," he says, "according to my fullest conviction, must really be considered as inherent in man: language could not have been invented without its type pre-existing in man." This being true, we are then to see it formed or developed afterward, and become a historical fact. As to the manner in which the process goes on, I find no conception of it given which is satisfactory, or which adequately explains a universal fact pertaining to the significance and power of language, as an instrument of thought and spiritual expression.

There is no difficulty in perceiving how our two unlanguaged men will proceed, when thrown together in the manner supposed, as far as the naming of sensations or physical objects is concerned. For the object is always present as a mediator or interpreter between them, so that when a sound is uttered as a name for it, or in connection with it, they may always know to what the sound or name refers. Thus all sights, sounds, smells, tastes, and touches, or feelings, or what is the same, their objects, are easily named, and their names will come into currency without difficulty, when sounded as representatives of the objects. As to the sounds adopted, they will generally be determined arbitrarily, or, at least, by causes so occult or remote that we must regard them as arbitrary. There may have been reasons why one says *tree*, and another *arbor;* one *rock*, and another *saxum;* one *star*, and another *stella;* one *sun*, and another *sol;* but if there are such reasons, they are too abstruse to be investigated. Sometimes when *sounds* are the objects named, they will very naturally be imitated; as in *hoarse* and *hiss*. Still, no theory of sound, as connected with sense, in the names of things, will be found to hold extensively enough to give it any moment. In the languages radically distinct, we shall find that the sounds or names which stand for the same objects, have generally no similarity whatever; whence it follows, irresistibly, that nothing in the laws of voice or sound has determined the names adopted.

We have now seen how our two language-makers will get on, in the naming of things or physical objects. In this manner they will make out a string of *nouns* or names, which may be called a noun-language. It will comprise the names of all physical objects and demonstrations, including, of course, the names of actions; for verbs, prior to the formation of grammar, are only the nouns or names of actions. Thus far we have generated only a physical language, or terms of physical import. And thus far, even, animals are capable of language: they can learn, though not as easily and on as large a scale as we, to associate names or sounds with outward things and actions.

There now remains to be formed another sphere of language, wholly distinct, which the animals cannot learn, viz.: the language of intelligence; that which, under an outward form, carries an inward sense, and so avails to serve the uses of mind. It has been easy for our language-makers to agree in the use of sounds standing for outward objects and acts, because these outward objects and acts can be so fixed upon, or the mind so directed towards them, that a mutual understanding may be had in regard to the object which it is designed to name, before the name to be adopted is uttered. But if, now, one of them has a thought or emotion in his mind, or wishes to speak of a spiritual being or world, this, it will be seen, is not capable of being shown or pointed at, because it lies out of sense. The thought or emotion cannot be taken out and exhibited to the eye: how, then, can the two parties come to any such understanding as will enable them to name it? Here is a difficulty, and it is the great difficulty to be surmounted, in the production of intellectual language. And if we are to understand the nature of language as an instrument of thought and spiritual truth, or to judge of its capacity for uses of this kind, it will be just here, in the solution of this difficulty relating to the genesis of language, that we shall get the desired key to its significance in such uses.

How, then, shall our experimenters proceed? Obviously they cannot advance at all, save through the mediation of things; that is, of objects and acts in the sensible world, which may come in to their aid as signs of thought, or interpreters between them. It is only as there is a Logos in the outward world, answering to the logos or internal reason of the parties, that they can come into a mutual understanding in regard to any thought or spiritual state whatever. To use a more familiar expression, there is a vast analogy in things, which prepares them, as forms, to be signs or figures of thoughts, and thus, bases or types of words. Our bodily mechanism, and the sensible world we live in, are, in fact, made up of words, to represent our thoughts and internal states;—they only want naming, and then, passing into sound, to be re-produced or have their images called up by sounds, they drop out, so to speak, their gross material quality, and become words of spirit, or what the poet calls "winged words;"—cursitating forms of life, that fly out in sound upon the air, as interpreters and messengers of thought between the minds of men.

Thus, if the mind of one of our two strangers is laboring with any thought or emotion, he will strike at some image or figure in the sensible world, that is itself a fit representation of his thought or emotion—a form prepared in nature to be its type. Turning the attention of the other party upon this image, and signifying by gesture, probably, that he is trying to mirror some internal state in it, he puts the other party on generating that internal state, or the conception of it. The image becomes, in fact, a common sign or conception of the same internal state—they understand each other. So that, now, the name, when it is sounded, will stand, not merely as the name of the object or image physically taken, but the name, also, of that thought which it represented. And thus an intellectual word is generated.

I do not mean by this to imply that our language-makers will be acting as philosophers in this process, reflecting on their own states, and then finding images to figure them, or stand as words for them. On the contrary, they will be struggling out into speech, in the simplicity of children, guided not by reflection, but more by instinct. A very large share of the signs by which they interpret their thoughts one to the other, will consist of bodily gestures and actions—all as natural to the internal activity as a blush, or any flush of passion, to the inner state, represented and depicted by it in the face. For the body is a living logos, added to the soul, to be its form, and play it forth into social understanding. It will also be found that a very large share of the words which represent our emotions and thoughts, are, in fact, as their etymology declares, derived from the psychological expressions or demonstrations made through the body. Or when thoughts and emotions are represented by figures drawn from the physical creation above us and around us, the principle is the same: it is not done artificially, but by the simple force of nature. The soul that is struggling to utter itself, flies to whatever signs and instruments it can find in the visible world, calling them in to act as interpreters, naming them at the same time, to stand, ever after, as interpreters in sound, when they are themselves out of sight.

It is hardly necessary to suggest, that, when a physical object or action has gotten a name beforehand, in the noun-language of physics, our two experimenters will, sometimes, recall the name or word, using it now as a figure, in a secondary sense, to represent a thought or feeling. But here the process of manufacture, philosophically speaking, is the same. If the word becomes devoted to the secondary use, it will stand, as in the cases above described—a name of some physical form or appearance, which form or appearance shadows forth a thought or truth of the mind—then, by use, the regular suggestive of that thought or truth, and its representative in the current utterances of speech.

We find, then, that every language contains two distinct departments:—the physical department—that which provides names for things; and the intellectual department—that which provides names for thought and spirit. In the former, names are simple representatives of things, which even the animals may learn. In the latter, the names of things are used as representatives of thought, and cannot, therefore, be learned, save by beings of intelligence—(*intus lego*)—that is, beings who can read the inner sense, or receive the inner contents of words; beings in whom the Logos of the creation finds a correspondent logos, or reason, to receive and employ the types it offers, in their true power.

For the benefit of the mere English reader, who is wholly unexercised in subjects of this nature, it may be important to say, that what is here advanced in theory, is fully supported by reference to the actual history of our words. We cannot always, or in every instance, show what physical object or act lies named in our intellectual words to give them their power; though in a great majority of cases, the words carry their origin in their face; and where they do not, it is only to be supposed that the physical history of the word or name is lost.

Thus, the word *spirit* means, originally, *breath*, or air

in motion; that being the symbol, in nature, of a power moving unseen.

The word *religion* is *re*, back, and *ligo*, to bind—the conception being that man is made to be free, but bound back in terms of obligation to his Maker.

In the same manner, *expectation* is a looking forth, and *hope* a reaching forth, in which we see how accurately the original physical meaning of the word governs and distinguishes the internal meaning; for we look out for [expect] the coming of things both good and bad, but reach after [hope for] only those that we desire.

In the same way we have *prefer*, to set before; *abstraction*, drawing apart; *reflection*, turning back; *obedience*, before-hearing, as when a servant stands before his master, listening to receive his commands; *glory*, brightness; *grace*, outward beauty or concinnity; *faith*, a tie or ligature; *right*, straight.

Or sometimes a word takes a historical origin. Thus, the word *sincerity* is supposed to be the same as *sine*, without, and *cera*, wax; the practice of the Roman potters being, to rub wax into the flaws of their unsound vessels when they sent them to market. A sincere [without-wax] vessel was the same as a sound vessel, one that had no disguised flaw.

The English reader is to understand that all the terms in language, which are devoted to spiritual and intellectual uses, have a physical or outward sign underlying their import, as in the cases here named. Of this the scholar has never a doubt, although he cannot always, or in every instance, trace out the physical sign or base of the word, so as to be certain of it. All things out o sense get their names in language through signs and objects in sense that have some mysterious correspondence or analogy, by which they are prepared beforehand to serve as signs or vehicles of the spiritual things to be expressed.

But as yet we have no grammar; we have only nouns to represent the objects, physical and intellectual, about which we may wish to communicate. We have what Klaproth calls, "the stuff or matter of language," and "grammar is to be the fashioning or form."

I do not say that grammar, or the framing of words into sentences, is to be a matter wholly subsequent in time; for we shall see, by and by, that the relations of things in space are such as must, by necessary consequence, give laws of grammar at last to the words by which they are named; and, of course, we are to suppose a rudimental tendency to grammar, in the first efforts of speech. But this tendency will complete its aim, or produce a complete grammar, only under conditions of time and use.

Thus a *warm,* that is, a sensation of warmth, being always spoken of in connection with some object in which the warmth resides, will become an appendant word, or ad-jective.

Adverbs will be formed, out of original nouns or names of things, in a similar way.

Prepositions and conjunctions, though indicating no such fact to the mere English reader, are all, originally, names of things or actions, and are reduced to their present humble condition of servitude, by the process which constructs a grammar. Thus the word *through*, and the word *door*, when traced historically, coalesce in the same origin. Nor could anything be more natural, in stringing nouns together, before any precise grammar is formed, to speak of going *door* any wall or obstacle; which, if it were continued, would shortly make the word *door* into a preposition, as we actually see in the word *through*.

In the same way the preposition *by* is supposed to be the relic of a verb or noun of action, which signified pressing close upon, or rubbing.

So the conjunction *if*, is known to be the imperative mood of the verb *to give*, and is written in the old English, *gif*, with the particle *that* after it. "I will do this *gif that* [if] you will do the other."

In the same way, it is discovered, to the satisfaction of Horne Tooke and other philologists, that the conjunction *and* is the same as the imperative mood of *add*, or *an-add* [*on-add*] contracted. "Love and [on-add] truth."

It would carry me too far, to go at large into illustrations of the process by which the original noun-words are wrought into grammar. My object in adducing these few examples, is simply to indicate the manner of the process far enough to remove any suspicion of mistake in the conclusion at which we had before come, that all the terms of language are originally names of things or sensible appearances. As regards the connection of subject and predicate in sentences, or, what is the same, the grammatical structure of sentences, it must suffice to say that verbs are originally mere names of acts, or phenomena of action, not distinguished from what are called nouns, or names of things, until use settles them into place in propositions or forms of affirmation. A *shine* and a *run* are names of appearances, just as a *sun* and a *river* are names of appearances. And when these names are strung together, in the use, the *sun* and the *shine*, the *river* and the *run*, the idea of subject and predicate becomes associated, and the grammatical relation of subject and predicate is developed as a law of speech between them. I speak not here of the order of subject and predicate in sentences, for the order will differ in different languages. I only indicate the manner in which the relative qualities of subject and predicate are developed in language. Nature having them in her own bosom, existing there in real grammatical relation, not only gives us the words, but shows us how to frame them into propositions. And in the same way, it will be observed, in the hints just given concerning other parts of speech or grammatic elements, that they really have their birth in the grammar of the world. The prepositions, for example, the *over*, the *under*, the *through*, the *by*, are all so many actual relations; and when the subjects and predicates are brought into speech, these come also with them. And then, when propositions are advanced which relate to thought or spirit, where, in one view, the *over*, the *under*, the *through*, the *by*, are totally irrelevant, thought and spirit not being under the laws of space, still there is a mysterious relation in these outward analogies of space to the workings of the mind, such that the external grammar of creation answers to the internal grammar of the soul, and becomes its vehicle.

As a further illustration of the same general view, I

would refer the reader to a beautiful theory, if it should not, rather, be called discovery, of Professor Gibbs, relating to case in grammar, or more particularly to "case in the Indo-Germanic languages." The exposition of this theory will be found in the Christian Spectator, Vol. IX. Here it is shown that, as words themselves, or the bases of words, are found in space, so they are declined or formed into grammar under the relations of space. Thus it is ascertained that there is one case which represents the *where* of a predicate, a second the *whence*, a third the *whither*, a fourth the *by, or through what place*. This, in regard to words taken in their most external and physical senses. And then, precisely as physical objects become types or bases o. words having an intellectual significance, so, or in virtue of the same kind of analogy, the relations of space under which we find these objects, ascend with them to partake in their elevation, and shape their fitness to the uses of the mind. Thus, in the department of mind or spirit, four cases are found answering to the four just named, employed no longer to denote external relations, but the internal relations of thought and action—an internal *where*, *whence*, *whither*, and *by* or *through what place*. Prof. G. does not undertake to verify these deductions, except in the particular families of languages under examination. Still, it is very obvious that such results in grammar do not take place apart from some inherent law or system pertaining either to mind, or to outward space, or to one as related to the other. Indeed, it is impossible, with such a revelation before us, not to take up at once, the sublime conviction just now named, that grammar itself is, in some sense, of the outer world—in the same way as the terms or names out of which language is constructed. In this view, which it is not rash to believe will sometime be fully established, the outer world is seen to be a vast menstruum of thought or intelligence. There is a logos in the forms of things, by which they are prepared to serve as types or images of what is inmost in our souls; and then there is a logos also of construction in the relations of space, the position, qualities, connections, and predicates of things, by which they are framed into grammar. In one word, the outer world, which envelops our being, is itself language, the power of all language. "Day unto day uttereth speech, and night unto night showeth knowledge; there is no speech nor language where their voice is not heard,—their line is gone out through all the earth, and their words to the end of the world."

And if the outer world is the vast dictionary and grammar of thought we speak of, then it is also itself an organ throughout of Intelligence. Whose intelligence? By this question we are set directly confronting God, the universal Author, no more to hunt for Him by curious arguments and subtle deductions, if haply we may find Him; but He stands EXPRESSED every where, so that, turn whichsoever way we please, we behold the outlooking of His intelligence. No series of Bridgewater treatises, piled even to the moon, could give a proof of God so immediate, complete, and conclusive.

In such a view of the world, too, and its objects, there is an amazing fund of inspiration elsewhere not to be found. The holding of such a view is, in fact, sufficient of itself, to change a man's intellectual capacities and destiny; for it sets him always in the presence of Divine thoughts and meanings; makes even the words he utters luminous of Divinity, and to the same extent, subjects of love and reverence.

The Christian public of our country are well aware that the very distinguished scholar, whose theory of "Case" I just now cited, has never been celebrated as a rhapsodist, or enthusiast; and I know not any stronger proof, therefore, of the inspiring force derivable from a full insight of this subject, than when he breaks out in the midst of a dry grammatical analysis, in the following truly eloquent paragraph:—

"There can be no exercise, in the whole business of instruction, more useful to the mind, than the analysis of sentences, in the concentrated light of grammar and logic. It brings one into the sanctuary of human thought. All else is but standing in the outer court. He who is without, may, indeed, offer incense; but he who penetrates within, worships and adores. It is here that the man of science, trained to close thought and clear vision, surveys the various objects of his study with a more expanded view, and a more discriminative mind. It is here that the interpreter, accustomed to the force and freshness of natural language, is prepared to explain God's revealed Word with more power and accuracy. It is here that the orator learns to wield, with a heavier arm, the weapons of his warfare. It is here that every one, who loves to think, beholds the deep things of the human spirit, and learns to regard with holy reverence the sacred symbols of human thought."

This paragraph, taken in connection with the illustrations of the article just referred to, has the inspiring force even of a lyric. Rightly spoken is it, when language is represented thus, as a "sanctuary of thought." For, in what do we utter ourselves, what are the words and the grammar, in which we speak, but instruments of a Divine import and structure? Such a discovery, received in its true moment, were enough to make a thoughtful Christian stand in awe, even of his own words.

We have now seen in what manner our two language-makers will proceed to construct a tongue. It is not my intention to say that the process will go on in the exact order here described—first, physical terms; second, intellectual; third, a grammar. The several departments of the work will be going on together, under the guidance of the Word or Divine Logos, in the forms, images, activities, and relations of the outward world. For He is in the world, and the world was made by Him, though it knows Him not. It speaks in words He gave, and under a grammar that He appointed, and yet it knows Him not.

I have suggested the fact that a very large share of our intellectual words are based on bodily gestures and demonstrations. I know of no method in which I can better indicate the simple, instinctive, inartificial process of word-making and grammar-making, than by calling upon the reader to conceive a human person charged with thought and passion—many thoughts and many passions—uttering himself instinctively by the voice, and at the same time, by pantomime, indigitation of symbols, and changes of look. The voice will attend cr follow the action, naming off its demonstrations as bases of words; the action will supply and interpret the voice; or pointing to signs in the inanimate world adjacent, summon these to act as interpreters, and become bases of words; and then, as all this transpires in space, the laws of space will be making a grammar for the words, and determining their law. The resulting tongue will represent, of course, both the man's own liberty and the world in which he moves. And then, as one or more persons beside must be concerned, at the same time, the process will be doubled or trebled; and between so many forces all concurring, a tongue or language will, at last, be matured that will represent the parties, their instincts, characters, and temperaments; all the circumstances and accidents, too, of the outward state.

If it be objected to this view, that some existing languages have no grammar, being nothing but a collection of monosyllabic names or sounds, I must be permitted to doubt whether any such language exists. It may be that no laws of inflection, or conjugation, or even of composition, have yet been discovered in the Chinese language, for example; nevertheless it must be clear that some law of relation, some condition of subject and predicate pertains to that tongue, more exact than tc have the words somewhere in the Chinese empire, and that law or condition, whatever it be, is in fact a grammar. And it will also be found, when philosophically investigated, that this Chinese grammar, whatever it may be, really represents the great universal grammar of the soul and the creation.

How far the views of language, here offered, coincide with theories advanced by distinguished modern philologists, I am scarcely able to say. They may have been wholly anticipated, or they may be already exploded. It would be singular, if the scholars who are spending their lives in philological studies, should not detect some mistakes or crudities in my illustrations.

The very distinguished scholar, Frederic Schlegel, if I rightly conceive his theory, traces not merely the forms or bases of words to the creative Logos, but also the names or vocal sounds themselves. Thus he speaks of "words which in the unsearchable interior of Deity are spoken, where, as in holy song expressed, depth calleth unto depth." Descending, then, to the account of language given in the second chapter of Genesis, he receives it as teaching that God gave to Adam, literally and vocally, the rudiments of speech. "But," he adds, "under this simple sense there lieth, as does through all that book of twofold import, another and far deeper signification. The name of any thing or living being, *as it is called in God*, and designated from eternity, holds in itself the essential idea of its innermost being, the key of its existence, the deciding power of its being or not being; and so it is used, in sacred speech, where it is, moreover, in a holier or higher sense, united to the idea of the Word. According to this deeper sense and understanding, it is in that narration shown and signified that, together with speech, entrusted, communicated, and delivered immediately by God to man, and through it, he was installed as the ruler and king of nature."

But, unfortunately, this very transcendental theory

will account for but one language, and we certainly know that there are more than one. Besides, what reasonable man can suppose that "names" taken as vocal sounds "are called in God," and that the discourse of divine thought is transacted by means of internal pronunciations! How plain is it, also, that "the name of anything holds in itself, the essential idea of its innermost being," and becomes "united to the idea of the Word," not as a sound, but simply as having in the sound, or named by the sound, a physical type or base, which is the real supporter and law of its meaning, and the reason of its connection with the Logos. In other words, the truth is here inverted by Schlegel; what he supposes to be from the name, is plainly communicated to the name.

Some of the Germans are endeavoring, in general coincidence with the scheme of Schlegel, to elaborate a theory of names, taken as sounds, by which they will be seen to represent the most interior qualities of the objects named. They go into philosophic experiments on sounds, and find reason, as they think, to believe that all objects express their true nature by means of the vibrations they impart to the air—that is by their sound. That precise sound, accordingly, is their name in language. This most subtle and beautiful theory, however, will be seen at a glance, to have no real countenance in facts What endless varieties of name or vocal sound are employed in the different languages of the world, to signify the same objects! How, then, do these vocal sounds represent the interior nature, or proceed from the interior nature of their objects? Indeed, where the objects named are themselves sounds, the names have yet, in most cases, no agreement whatever. Thunder, for example, is the same sound the world over, and it is such a sound as we might imagine would almost certainly be imitated in the name given it. And yet, if we turn only to the American families of language, we are surprised to find that thunder is called, in the Chickasaw, *elloha;* in the Creek, *tenitka;* in the Huron, *inon;* in the Cadoes, *deshinin;* in the Nootka, *tuta.* Before such facts, filling, I may say, the whole domain of language, all theories about the representative nature of names, taken as sounds, would seem to be idle, in the last degree.

Mr. Locke presents a view of language, which, if we regard the mere words in which it is given, would seem even to be identical with that which I have advanced. He says,—"*It may also lead us a little towards the original of all our notions and knowledge,* if we remark how great a dependence our words have on common sensible ideas; and how those which are made use of to stand for actions and notions, quite removed from sense, have their rise from thence, and from obvious sensible ideas are transferred to more abstruse significations, and made to stand for ideas that come not under the cognizance of our senses, *e. g.* to imagine, apprehend, comprehend, adhere, conceive, instill, disgust, disturbance, tranquillity, &c., are all words taken from the operations of sensible things, and applied to certain modes of thinking. Spirit, in its primary signification, is breath; angel, a messenger; and I doubt not, but, if we could trace them to their sources, we should find in all languages, the names which stand for things that fall not under our senses, to have had their rise from sensible ideas. By which we may give some guess what kind of notions they were, *and whence derived, which filled their minds who were the first beginners of languages ;* and how nature, even in the naming of things, unawares suggested to men *the originals and principals of all their knowledge ;* whilst to give names which might make known to others any operations they felt in themselves, or any other ideas that come not under the cognizance of the senses, they were fain to borrow words from ordinary known ideas of sensation ; by that means to make others the more easily to conceive those operations they experimented in themselves, which made no outward appearance."

It is remarkable that while Mr. Locke seems even to set forth, in these terms, the precise theory of language I have given, he is yet seen really to hold it in no one of its important consequences. He even denies, shortly after, that there is any "natural connection between words and ideas," and declares that the significance of words is given "by a perfectly arbitrary imposition,"—as if there were no analogy whatever between the bases or types of words and the thoughts they are seized upon to represent. Doubtless the true solution of this mixture of light and obscurity, in his notions of language, is to be found in the fact that he was too much occupied with his theory of knowledge as derived from sensation, really to notice the true import and scope of his own suggestions. This also seems to be indicated as a fact, by the clauses I have placed in italics.

The late Dr. Rauch, in his work on 'Psychology,' gives an account of language that is sufficiently acute, and is generally coincident with the view here advanced.

On the particular point, however, which is labored in this article, the significance of language, he is less satisfactory; coming, in fact, to no results that are of any great practical moment in determining the true method of moral and religious inquiry. He grounds the possibility of language on the "identity" of reason and nature, (p. 233,) not on the *analogy* or outward analogical relation of the latter to the former. And that he has not mistaken his English word, as some might imagine, appears, I think, from the important fact that he makes no distinction between the terms of mere sense, and terms of thought or intellectual significance. Nature appears, in his view, to be counterpart to reason, in such a sense that the names of sensation and the names of thoughts, or intellectual states, fall into the same category, to be interpreted by the same law. Whereas, if there be any importance in the view I would present, it consists in showing that all terms of intellect or spirit come under a wholly different law, both as regards their origin and their interpretation, from the terms of sense or the mere names of things. This will appear more fully in the illustrations that follow.

We pass now to the application of these views of language, or the power they are entitled to have, in matters of moral and religious inquiry and especially in Christian theology.

There are, as we discover, two languages, in fact, in every language. Or perhaps I shall be understood more exactly, if I say that there are, in every human tongue, two distinct departments. First, there is a literal department, in which sounds are provided as names for physical objects and appearances. Secondly, there is a department of analogy or figure, where physical objects and appearances are named as images of thought or spirit, and the words get their power, as words of thought, through the physical images received into them. Thus, if I speak of my *pen,* I use a word in the first department of language, uttering a sound which stands for the instrument with which I write. But if I speak of the *spirit* of a man, or the *sincerity* of a Christian, I use words that belong to the second department of language, where the sounds do not stand for the mental ideas as being names directly applied to *them,* but represent, rather, certain images in the physical state, which are the natural figures or analogies of those mental ideas. How it was necessary, in the genesis of language, that it should fall into this twofold distribution, has been shown already. The man who knows his tongue only by vernacular usage, is aware of no such distribution. Many, who are considered to be educated persons, and are truly so, are but half aware of it. At least, they notice only now and then, when speaking of matters pertaining to thought and spirit, that a word brought into use has a physical image in it. For example, when speaking of a good man's *heart,* they observe that the word has a physical image connected with it, or that it names also a vital organ of the body. Then they either say, that the word has two meanings, a physical and a spiritual, not observing any law of order or connection by which the physical becomes the basis or type of the spiritual; or, they raise a distinction between what they call the *literal* and *figurative* uses of the word. But this distinction of literal and figurative, it does not appear to be noticed, even by philologists, runs through the very body of the language itself, making two departments; one that comprises the terms of sensation, and the other the terms of thought. They notice, in the historical investigation of words, that they are turning up all the while, a subsoil of physical bases; and, though they cannot find in every particular case, the physical term on which the word is built, they attain to a conviction that every word has a physical root, if only it could be found; and yet the natural necessity, that all words relating to thought and spirit should be figures, and as such, get their significance, they do not state. They still retain the impression that some of the terms of thought are literal, and some figurative.

This is the manner of the theologians. They assume that there is a literal terminology in religion as well as a figurative, (as doubtless there is, in reference to matters of outward fact and history, but nowhere else,) and then it is only a part of the same mistake to accept words, not as signs or images, but as absolute measures and equivalents of truth; and so to run themselves, by their argumentations, with a perfectly unsuspecting confidence, into whatever conclusions the *logical forms* of the words will carry them. Hence, in great part, the distractions, the infinite multiplications of opinion, the errors and sects and strifes of the Christian world. We can never come into a settled consent in the truth, until we better understand the nature, capacities and incapacities of language, as a vehicle of truth.

In order, now, that I may excite our younger theologians especially to a new investigation of this subject, as being fundamental, in fact, to the right understanding of religious truth, I will dismiss the free form of dissertation, and set forth, under numerical indications, a series of points or positions inviting each their attention, and likely, though with some modifications, perhaps, to be finally verified.

1. Words of thought and spirit are possible in language only in virtue of the fact that there are forms provided in the world of sense, which are cognate to the mind, and fitted, by reason of some hidden analogy, to represent or express its interior sentiments and thoughts.

2. Words of thought and spirit are, in fact, names of such forms or images existing in the outward or physical state.

3. When we investigate the relation of the form, or etymological base, in any word of thought or spirit, to the idea expressed, we are able to say (negatively) that the idea or thought has no such form, or shape, or sensible quality, as the word has. If I speak of *right* (*straight, rectus,*) it is not because the internal law of the conscience, named by this word, has any straightness or lineal quality whatever. Or if I speak of *sin, peccatum,* αμαρτία, where, in so many languages, as I might also show in a great variety of others, the image at the root of the word is one of lineal divarication, (as when an arrow is shot at the mark, and misses or turns aside,) it is not because sin, as a moral state of being, or a moral act, has any lineal form in the mind. Thoughts, ideas, mental states, we cannot suppose have any geometric form, any color, dimensions, or sensible qualities whatever.

4. We can also say, (positively) in reference to the same subject, that there is always some reason in every form or image made use of, why it should be used; some analogic property or quality which we feel instinctively, but which wholly transcends speculative inquiry. If there is no lineal straightness in rectitude, no linear crookedness or divarication in sin, taken as an internal state, still it is the instinct of our nature to feel some sense of correspondence between these images and the states they represent.

Milton, I suppose, could not tell us why he sets any form in connection with any spiritual thought. He could only say that he has in him some internal sense of concinnity which requires it. And yet, when he speaks of sin, he makes everything crooked as the word is, when of law, everything straight as rectitude. Thus he writes: "To make a regularity of sin by law, either the law must straighten sin into no sin, or sin must crook the law into no law." Something, doubtless, may be said which, in a certain superficial and pathological sense, may be called an explanation of the uses of these symbols; for example, that in sin, a man divaricates bodily, or goes to his mischief in a manner that is oblique or awry; and that, when he is in the simple intention of duty, he lets his "eye look right on," and follows his eye. I accounted for the symbols chosen to denote *hope* and *expectation*, by a similar reference to the pathology of hope and expectation. But this, if we do not wish to deceive ourselves, is only a mediate, and not a final explanation. Still the question remains, why the form of outward divarication has any such original relation to sin as to have been made the natural pathological demonstration of it,—why a crooked line, which is the more graceful in itself, should not have been the natural instinct, and so the symbol of the right, as it now is of the wrong. Here we come to our limit. All we can say is, that by a mystery transcending in any case our comprehension, the Divine Logos, who is in the world, weaves into nature types or images that have an inscrutable relation to mind and thought. On the one hand, is form; on the other, is the formless. The first represents, and is somehow fellow to, the other; how, we cannot discover. And the more we ponder this mystery, the closer we bring it to our understanding, the more perfectly inscrutable will it appear. If we say that the forms of the reason answer to the forms of nature and the outward life, that is true; but then there are no forms in the reason, save by a figure of speech, and the difficulty still remains.

5. There are no words, in the physical department of language, that are exact representatives of particular physical things. For whether we take the theory of the Nominalists or the Realists, the words are, in fact, and practically, names only of genera, not of individuals or species. To be even still more exact, they represent only certain sensations of sight, touch, taste, smell, hearing—one or all. Hence the opportunity in language, for endless mistakes and false reasonings, in reference to matters purely physical. This subject was labored some years ago with much acuteness and industry, by one of our countrymen, Mr. Johnson, in a 'Treatise on Language, or the Relations of Words to Things.' The latter

part of his title, however, is all that is justified; for to language in its more comprehensive sense, as a vehicle of spirit, thought, sentiment, he appears to have scarcely directed his inquiries.

6. It follows, that as physical terms are never exact, being only names of genera, much less have we any terms in the spiritual department of language that are exact representatives of thought. For, first, the word here used will be the name only of a genus of physical images. Then, secondly, it will have been applied over to signify a genus of thoughts or sentiments. And now, thirdly, in a particular case, it is drawn out to signify a specific thought or sentiment which, of course, will have qualities or incidents peculiar to itself. What, now, can steer a word through so many ambiguities and complications, and give it an exact and determinate meaning in the particular use it is applied to serve? Suppose, for example, one desires to speak of the *bitterness* displayed by another, on some given occasion. In the first place, this word *bitterness*, taken physically, describes not a particular sensation common to all men, but a genus of sensations; and as some persons have even a taste for bitter things, it is impossible that the word, taken physically, should not have an endless variety of significations, ranging between disgust and a positive relish of pleasure. If, now, it be taken as the base or type of an intellectual word, it will carry with it, of necessity, as great a variety of associations; associations so unlike, that it will be impossible to clothe it with the same precise import, as a word of sentiment. Then, secondly

men are so different, even good and true men, in their personal temperament, their modes of feeling, reasoning and judging, that moral bitterness, in its generic sense, will not be a state or exercise of the same precise quality in their minds. Some persons will take as bitterness in general, what others will only look upon as faithfulness, or just indignation. And, then, thirdly, in the particular case to which the word is to be applied, different views and judgments will be formed of the man, his provocations, circumstances, duties, and the real import of his words and actions. Accordingly, as one declares that he was bitter, another will receive the declaration as no better than a real slander. And so it must of necessity be. It is impossible so to settle the meaning of this word *bitterness*, as to produce any exact unity of apprehension under it. And the same is true of the great mass of words employed in moral and spiritual uses,—such as love, gentleness, contentment, patience, wisdom, justice, order, pride, charity. We think we have the same ideas in them, or rather, (which is more likely,) we think nothing about it; but we find continually that, when we come to particular uses, we fall into disagreements, often into protracted and serious controversies; and whether it be said that the controversy is about words or things, it is always a controversy about the real applicability of words.

What, then, it may be asked, is the real and legitimate use of words, when applied to moral subjects? for we cannot dispense with them, and it is uncomfortable to hold them in universal scepticism, as being only instruments of error. Words, then, I answer, are legitimately used as the signs of thoughts to be expressed. They do not literally convey, or pass over a thought out of one mind into another, as we commonly speak of doing. They are only hints, or images, held up before the mind of another, to put *him* on generating or reproducing the same thought; which he can do only as he has the same personal contents, or the generative power out of which to bring the thought required. Hence, there will be different measures of understanding or misunderstanding, according to the capacity or incapacity, the ingenuousness or moral obliquity of the receiving party—even if the communicating party offers only truth, in the best and freshest forms of expression the language provides.

There is only a single class of intellectual words that can be said to have a perfectly determinate significance, viz., those which relate to what are called necessary ideas. They are such as time, space, cause, truth, right, arithmetical numbers, and geometrical figures. Here the names applied, are settled into a perfectly determinate meaning, not by any peculiar virtue in *them*, but by reason of the absolute exactness of the ideas themselves. Time cannot be anything more or less than time; truth cannot, in its idea, be anything different from truth; the numerals suffer no ambiguity of count or measure; a circle must be a circle; a square, a square. As far as language, therefore, has to do with these, it is a perfectly exact algebra of thought, but no farther.

It will, perhaps, be imagined by some, indeed, it is an assumption continually made, that words of thought, though based on mere figures or analogies in their original adoption, gradually lose their indeterminate character, and settle down under the law of use, into a sense so perfectly unambiguous, that they are to be regarded as literal names, and real equivalents of the thoughts they signify. There could not be a greater mistake. For, though the original type, or historic base of the word may pass out of view, so that nothing physical or figurative is any longer suggested by it, still it will be impossible that mere use should have given it an exact meaning, or made it the literal name of any moral or ntellectual state. The word *sin* is of this description, and most persons seem to imagine that it names a given act or state, about which there is no diversity of understanding. Contrary to this, no two minds ever had the same impression of it. The whole personal history of every man, his acts, temptations, wants, and repentances; his opinions of God, of law, and of personal freedom; his theory of virtue, his decisions of the question, whether sin is an act, or a state; of the will, or of the heart: in fact, his whole theology and life will enter into his impression of this word *sin*, to change the quality, and modify the relations of that which it signifies. It will also be found, as a matter of fact, that the interminable disputes of the theologians on this particular subject, originate in fundamental differences of view concerning the nature of sin, and are themselves incontestible proofs that, simple as the word is, and on the lips of every body, (as we know it to be) there is yet no virtual agreement of meaning connected with the word. The same, as just now intimated, is true of *hope*, *fear*, *love*, and other like familiar terms, which we fancy have a meaning so well settled. They have a dictionary meaning that is settled;

but yet, hope, fear, love, is to every man what his own life-experience, and his theories, and mental struggles have made it, and he sees it, of necessity, under a color quite peculiar to himself; so peculiar, that he will even advance concerning it, what another cannot find the truth of, or receive. And this is true of all the intellectual terms in language, with the exception of a class just named, relating to necessary and absolute truths. Besides these, there is no word of thought, or spirit, that exactly measures its ideas, or does any thing more than offer some proximate notion, or shadow of the thought intended.

What I have here advanced, is confirmed by a very judicious remark of Whately, who says,—"It is worth observing, that the words, whose ambiguity is most frequently overlooked, and is productive of the greatest amount of confusion of thought and fallacy, are among the *commonest,* and are those whose meaning the generality consider there is least room to doubt. Familiar acquaintance is perpetually mistaken for accurate knowledge."

7. Words of thought or spirit are not only inexact in their significance, never measuring the truth or giving its precise equivalent, but they always affirm something which is false, or contrary to the truth intended. They impute *form* to that which really is out of form. They are related to the truth, only as form to spirit—earthen vessels in which the truth is borne, yet always offering their mere pottery as being the truth itself. Bunyan

beautifully represents their insufficiency and earthiness when he says—

> "My dark and cloudy words, they do but hold
> The truth, as cabinets inclose the gold."

—only it needs to be added, that they palm off upon us, too often, their "dark and cloudy" qualities as belonging inherently to the golden truths they are used to express. Therefore, we need always to have it in mind, or in present recollection, that they are but signs, in fact, or images of that which has no shape or sensible quality whatever; a kind of painting, in which the speaker, or the writer, leads on through a gallery of pictures or forms, while we attend him, catching at the thoughts suggested by his forms. In one view, they are all false; for there are no shapes in the truths they represent, and therefore we are to separate continually, and by a most delicate process of art, between the husks of the forms and the pure truths of thought presented in them. We do this insensibly, to a certain extent, and yet we do it imperfectly, often. A very great share of our theological questions, or disputes, originate in the incapacity of the parties to separate truths from their forms, or to see how the same essential truth may clothe itself under forms that are repugnant. There wants to be a large digestion, so to speak, of form in the teacher of theology or mental philosophy, that he may always be aware how the mind and truth, obliged to clothe themselves under the laws of space and sensation, are taking, continually, new shapes or dresses—coming forth poetically, mystically, allegorically, dialectically, fluxing through definitions, symbols, changes of subject and object, yet remaining still the same; for if he is wanting in this, if he is a mere logician, fastening on a word as the sole expression and exact equivalent of a truth, to go on spinning his deductions out of the form of the word, (which yet have nothing to do with the idea,) then he becomes an opinionist only, quarreling, as for truth itself, with all who chance to go out of his word; and, since words are given, not to imprison souls, but to express them, the variations continually indulged by others are sure to render him as miserable in his anxieties, as he is meagre in his contents, and busy in his quarrels.

But it will be observed, that most men are wholly unacquainted with the etymologies or forms of their words; and, of those who are not, that very few have really any mental reference to them, in their choice or use of terms. How, then, is it supposable, when they do not even go behind the intellectual signification of the words enough to have any sense, at all, of their forms, that the forms are yet conveying to the mind mistaken or false impressions that belong to themselves, in distinction from the truths they represent? They do it, I answer, with the greater certainty, because they do it in a manner so subtle, as not to awaken suspicion; for there is a *latent presence* of the forms of words, which is not less real because it is less palpable. It is even wonderful to observe, with what pertinacity the original form of a word will stay by it, unobserved or hidden from ordinary inspection, to guard its uses, and preside over its fortunes. It will even be present, unawares, in sufficient power to control the meanings and applications of those who never heard of a type, or etymology, in their lives

The Latin word *gressus*, for example, is one that originally describes the measured tread of dignity, in distinction from the trudge of a clown, or footpad. Hence the word *congress*, can never after, even at the distance of thousands of years, be applied to the *meeting* or *coming together* of outlaws, jockeys, or low persons of any description. It can only be used to denote assemblages of grave and elevated personages, such as councillors, men of science, ambassadors, potentates. The original type of the word *gressus*, which denotes only a matter as evanescent as one form of gait or carriage, in distinction from another, stays by, causing it, in all future uses, to stand upon its dignity, and assisting it, in spite of all revolutions and democratic levelings, to maintain its ancient aristocracy. And it controls the speech of the ignorant not the less certainly, because it is itself unknown to them. On the contrary, its sway is even the more absolute, that it governs by a latent presence.

So, also, if a reader who is wholly ignorant of the Latin type of the word *humility*, [ground-ness] were to fall upon the incongruous jumbled line of Young—

> "Zeal and humility, her wings to heaven,"

he would almost certainly be conscious of some defect, or fault of concinnity in the language. Not that humility has in itself any low, groundling quality; for there is no virtue more truly elevated in its own inherent properties. The only reason why there would seem to him to be a want of harmony in the expression, is, that there is a latent quality of form associated with the word, even when a classic education has not revealed it to his view. For the same reason, I suppose, that many persons of only a common education, would be likely to have some sense of discord in the expression, "I *prefer* [set before] being behind." It might not seem to be a decided bull in rhetoric, they might even use the expression, and yet, for some reason or other, they would hardly be able to like it—really for the reason that there is a latent power of form present in the word *prefer*, which refuses assent to the marriage.

In the same way, though unconsciously to themselves, there is a certain power of form, I apprehend, associated or intermixed with the meanings of their words generally. When they use the words *ap-prehend*, *com-prehend*, *op-posite*, *di-vulge*, *amb-ition*, *re-flection*, though the original images or types, are historically unknown to them, the meanings do yet lie in their minds, not as formless, but in forms or conceptions. Hence, in fact, the word *con-ception* (*con-capio*;) because we take up, ever, with our thought, some image whereby to represent it to ourselves; for, in our thinking processes, or, in what the old writers call our discourse of reason, we get on with our activity only by the interior handling of these forms or images Thinking, in fact, is nothing but the handling of thoughts by their forms. And so necessary is this, that, if we make use of a word whose original form is lost or unknown, we shall be found, in every case, to give the word, instinctively, an outward representation ourselves: that is, we shall image it, or give a form to the thought, in order to bring it into mental contemplation, or under the discourse of the mind.

Therefore, we may lay it down as a truth, that the

forms of words are always present, either as palpable or latent powers. In every case, they are conceptions of the truths signified, and not naked vocal names of those truths. Being really images, therefore, of that which has no sensible quality, they do always impute or associate something which does not belong to the truth or thought expressed; viz., *form*. On which account, the greatest caution is needed, that, while we use them, confidingly, as vehicles, we never allow them to impose upon us anything of their own.

8. But if we are liable thus to be carried away by the forms contained in our words, into conclusions or impressions that do not belong to the truths they are used to signify, we are also to peruse their forms with great industry, as being, at the same time, a very important key to their meaning. The original type or etymology of words is a most fruitful study. Even when they pass into meanings that seem to be contrary one to another, it will yet be found, in almost every case, that the repugnant meanings are natural growths, so to speak, of the same vital root; as some kinds of trees are seen to throw out leaves having several different shapes. The etymologists have been hard pressed, often, by ridicule, and it is not to be denied that they have sometimes produced fancies in place of facts. As little is it to be denied that words do, now and then, present no aspect of agreement in their senses, with the types out of which they spring. They appear to have suffered some kind of violence—to have fallen among thieves, and been left, half dead from the injury they have suffered. And yet

there is a wonderful light shed upon words, in most cases, by the simple opening of their etymologies. Distinctions are very often drawn at a stroke, in this way, which whole chapters of dissertation would not exhibit as well. Sometimes a dark subject is made luminous, at once, by the simple reference to an etymology; and then we are even amazed to see what depths of wisdom, or spiritual insight, have been hid, as it were, in our language, even from ourselves.

The remark of Whately, touching this point, while it indicates a proper caution in accepting the light of etymologies, is yet far too negative to be justified even by his own illustration. He says it is worth observing, as a striking instance of the little reliance to be placed on etymology, as a guide to the meaning of a word, that "*hypostasis*, *substantia*, and *understanding*, so widely different in their sense, correspond in their etymology." But, admitting the difference of meaning, the Greek element (στασίς) *stasis*, the Latin *stantia* and the English *standing*, being all different inflections in the grammar of the several tongues, are really not grammatical equivalents, and, therefore, have not the same directing forces, as types of thought. Besides, it is not true that the etymology of these words is no guide to their meaning. On the contrary, all their meanings, however diverse, stand in exact harmony with their etymologies, and no one of them could be sufficiently understood, without reference to its root or type. The meanings, in fact, of these three words are not as wide apart as the meanings we find under the same word, in our own tongue, and yet, in the latter case, every one of the meanings will be seen tc have a clear historic reference to its radical type, and to grow out from it, by a perfectly natural process.

9. Since all words, but such as relate to necessary truths, are inexact representations of thought, mere types or analogies, or, where the types are lost beyond recovery, only proximate expressions of the thoughts named; it follows that language will be ever trying to mend its own deficiencies, by multiplying its forms of representation. As, too, the words made use of generally carry something false with them, as well as something true, associating form with the truths represented, when really there is no form; it will also be necessary, on this account, to multiply words or figures, and thus to present the subject on opposite sides or many sides. Thus, as form battles form, and one form neutralizes another, all the insufficiencies of words are filled out, the contrarieties liquidated, and the mind settles into a full and just apprehension of the pure spiritual truth. Accordingly we never come so near to a truly well rounded view of any truth, as when it is offered paradoxically; that is, under contradictions; that is, under two or more dictions, which, taken as dictions, are contrary one to the other.

Hence the marvelous vivacity and power of that famous representation of Pascal: "What a chimera, then, is man! What a novelty! What a chaos! What a subject of contradiction! A judge of every thing, and yet a feeble worm of the earth; the depositary of truth, and yet a mere heap of uncertainty; the glory and the outcast of the universe. If he boasts, I humble him; if he humbles himself, I boast of him; and always contradict him, till he is brought to comprehend that he is an incomprehensible monster."

Scarcely inferior in vivacity and power is the familiar passage of Paul;—"as deceivers, and yet true; as unknown, and yet well known; as dying, and behold, we live; as chastened, and not killed; as sorrowful, yet always rejoicing; as poor, yet making many rich; as having nothing, yet possessing all things."

So, also, it will be found, that the poets often express their most inexpressible, or evanescent thoughts, by means of repugnant or somewhat paradoxical epithets; as, for example, Coleridge, when he says,—

"The stilly murmur of the distant sea
Tells us of silence."

Precisely here, too, I suppose, we come upon what is really the true conception of the Incarnation and the Trinity. These great Christian mysteries or paradoxes, come to pass under the same conditions or laws which pertain to language. All words are, in fact, only incarnations, or insensings of thought. If we investigate the relations of their forms to the truths signified, we have the same mystery before us; if we set the different, but related forms in comparison, we have the same aspect of repugnance or inconsistency. And then we have only to use the repugnant forms as vehicles of pure thought, dismissing the contradictory matter of the forms, and both words and the Word are understood without distraction,—all by the same process.

Probably, the most contradictory book in the world is the Gospel of John; and that, for the very reason that it contains more and loftier truths than any other. No good writer, who is occupied in simply expressing truth, is ever afraid of inconsistencies or self-contradictions in his language. It is nothing to him that a quirk of logic can bring him into absurdity. If at any time he offers definitions, it is not to get a footing for the play of his logic, but it is simply as multiplying forms or figures of that which he seeks to communicate—just as one will take his friend to different points of a landscape, and show him cross views, in order that he may get a perfect conception of the outline. Having nothing but words in which to give definitions, he understands the impossibility of definitions as determinate measures of thought, and gives them only as being *other forms* of the truth in question, by aid of which it may be more adequately conceived. On the other hand, a writer without either truth or genius, a mere prosaic and literal wordsman, is just the man to magnify definitions. He has never a doubt of their possibility. He lays them down as absolute measures, then draws along his deductions, with cautious consistency, and works out, thus, what he considers to be the exact infallible truth. But his definitions will be found to hang, of necessity, on some word or symbol, that symbol to have drawn every thing to itself, or into its own form, and then, when his work is done, it will be both consistent and false,—false, because of its consistency.

10. It is part of the same view, that logic itself is a defective, and often deceitful instrument. I speak not here of logic as a science, but of that deductive, proving, spinning method of practical investigation, commonly

denoted by the term *logical.* It is very obvious, that no turn of logical deduction can prove anything, by itself, not previously known by inspection or insight. And yet, there is always a busy-minded class of sophists or speculators, who, having neither a large observation, nor a power of poetic insight, occupy themselves as workers in words and propositions, managing to persuade themselves and others that they are great investigators, and even discoverers of truth. It being generally known that John, James, and Peter, are men, they advance, by a strict logical process, to the conclusion that Peter is a man!—in which they seem to themselves, and, possibly, to some others, to have added a valuable contribution to the stock of human knowledge. They do not see that their premise contains their conclusion, and somewhat more, and that the only real talent of investigation lies in a power of insight by which premises are seen or ascertained. They impose upon themselves, too, the more readily, because it is so generally true, that their conclusion is not contained in their premise; hence, they seem to themselves to be really multiplying truths with great facility and rapidity,—only it happens, that, inasmuch as their conclusions were not in their premises, they are false! And so it turns out that these great investigators and provers, the men who think that nothing is really established until it has been proved, that is, deduced from something else, are generally the worst propagators of falsity in the world. If they had Julius Cæsar's grammar, it would be a sad abridgment of their discoveries, though not any very great subtraction from the world's knowledge. "I have formed in my thoughts," he says, "a certain grammar, not upon any analogy which words bear to each other, but such as should diligently examine the analogy or relation betwixt words and things."

It seems to be supposed, or rather assumed, by the class of investigators commonly called logical, that after the subject matter of truth has been gotten into propositions, and cleared, perhaps, by definitions, the faculty of intuition, or insight, may be suspended, and we may go on safely, to reason upon the forms ot the words themselves, or the "analogy the words bear to each other." And so, by the mere handling of words and propositions, they undertake to evolve, or, as they commonly speak, to *prove* important truths. They reason, not by or through formulas, but upon them. After the formulas are got ready, they shut their eyes to all interior inspection of their terms, as in algebra, and commit themselves to the mere grammatic laws or predications of theii words—expecting, under these, by inversion, evolution, equation, *reductio ad absurdum,* and the like, to work out important results. And this is popularly called *reasoning.* They do not seem to be aware that this grammatic, oı constructive method, while it is natural as language itself, having its forms in what I have called the grammar of the soul and of the creation, is yet analogical only to truth and spirit—a warp that is furnished out of form and sense, for the connecting into speech of symbols or types that lie in form and sense; on which account, propositions are called *formulas,* or little forms. Or we may represent the constructive method of logic and grammar as the iron track of speech, along which the separate cars of words, connected by iron copulas, are drawn out into regular trains, and determinate courses of motion; which iron track and copulas, however, we are not to fancy, are at all more intellectual, closer to the truth of reason, or less analogical than the separate cars themselves. And, therefore, whatever is wrought out by the combination of formulas, (of course I do not question the syllogism which really works out nothing,) having only a certain analogical or tropical force, must be received by insight, as all symbols are, not as any absolute conclusion, or sentence of reason.

In the pure algebraic process, the result is wholly different; because the terms all stand for exact quantities, and the predicates of addition, subtraction, multiplication, division, involution, evolution, inversion, equation, and the like, are all absolute; so that if the worker goes on to his life's end, producing his changes of formula, he will never come into one that is not true.

But suppose the algebraist had no fixed quantities out of which to make his formulas; that his terms were only tropes for certain ideas that have no definite measure, affirming, of course, something not true, as well as something true; suppose that definitions were impossible, save that one trope may sometimes help out another, and that paradoxes are quite as often needed to help out the infirmity, or displace the one-sidedness of definitions. Suppose that all his connective signs, his equations, his evolutions of formula, were indeterminate, and his process never true, save in a certain analogical and poetic sense—what figure, in such a case, would he make with his algebraic process? A glance in this direction suffices to show that the only real and true reasoning, on moral subjects, is that which never embarks on words and propositions, but which holds a constant insight of all terms and constructions—"diligently examining the analogy or relation betwixt words and things."

Observe, in a single proposition—the simplest affirmation that can be invented, I might almost say, pertaining to the intellectual life—how indefinite any mere formula must be. I assert that "*man thinks.*" Here the subject is man, of whom is predicated some causative agency, and some form of result. As regards the agency, it may be understood (1.) that the man thinks under a law of mechanical necessity, as a machine works; or (2.) that he thinks under a law of plastic self-determinating necessity, as a tree grows; or (3.) that he thinks under a law of mental suggestion, which he can only interrupt by his will; or (4.) that he wills to think; or (5.) that he thinks spontaneously. And then as to the product, *thought*, nothing is so difficult as to settle any definite conception of that; but we will suppose only five more ambiguities here—combining which, in as many pairs as they will make, with the five preceding, we have twenty-five distinct meanings. If, now, going back to the subject, *man*, it be asked whether the formula intends (1.) man as created in his natural freedom and innocence; or, (2.) man as under the power and bondage of evil; or (3.) man as illuminated and suggestively directed or swayed by the supernatural grace of God; or (4.) man as regenerated in good, and contesting with currents of evil thought still running in his nature—all of which are important distinctions—we have then just a hundred different meanings in our simple formula—*man thinks*. Or,

6

dismissing arithmetic as inappropriate, we may better say that the language is only tropical, and the meanings, of course, indefinitely variable. For all these, language provides only a single form of predicate—a single grammatic formula. And yet it seems to be imagined that we can saddle mere forms of words, and ride them into necessary unambiguous conclusions!

It will also be observed, that our mere reasoners and provers in words, in order to get their formulas arrayed for action, always rule out, or clear away, those antagonistic figures, paradoxes, and contrarious representations, by means of which only a full and comprehensive expression of the truth is possible. They are great in the detection of disagreements, or what they call contradictions; and the finding out of such elements, or the reducing of another to this bad dilemma, by their constructive process, they suppose to be a real triumph of intelligence—which is the same as to say that they can endure none but a one-sided view of truth.

It will almost always happen, also, to this class of investigators, that, when reasoning of man, life, self-active being, God, and religion, they will take up their formulas under the conditions of cause and effect, or space and time, or set them under the atomic relations of inorganic matter. Discussing the human will, for example, or the great question of liberty, the writer will be overpowered by the terms and predicates of language; which being mostly derived from the physical world, are charged, to the same extent, with a mechanical significance. And then we shall have a sophism, great or small, according to his capacity—a ponderous volume, it may be, of formulas, filled up, rolled about, inverted, crossed and twisted—a grand, stupendous, convoluted sophism—all a mere outward practice, however, on words and propositions, in which, as they contain a form of cause and effect in their own nature, it is easily made out that human liberty is the liberty of a scale-beam, turned by the heavier weights. Meantime, the question is only a question of consciousness, one in which the simple decision of consciousness is final;—to which, argument, whether good or bad, can really add nothing, from which nothing take.

As great mischief and perplexity is often wrought by raising the question of before and after, under the laws of time. The speculative, would-be philosopher wants to be able always to say which is first in the soul's action—this or that. What endless debates have we had in theology concerning questions of priority—whether faith is before repentance, or repentance before faith; whether one or the other is before love, or love before them both; whether justification is before sanctification, and the like. We seem to suppose that a soul can be taken to pieces, or have its exercises parted and put under laws of time, so that we can see them go, in regular clock-work order. Whereas, being *alive* in God when it is truly united to Him, its right exercises, being functions of life, are of course mutual conditions one of another. Passing out of mechanism, or the empire of dead atoms, into the plastic realm of life, all questions of before and after we leave behind us. We do not ask whether the heart causes the heaving of the lungs, or whether the lungs have priority, and keep up the beating of the heart; or whether the digestive faculty is first in time, or the assimilative, or the nervous. We look at the whole body as a vital nature, and finding every function alive, every fibre active, we perceive that all the parts, even the minutest, exist and act as mutual conditions one of another. And so it is in spiritual life. Every grace supposes every other as its condition, and time is wholly out of the question. But, the moment any one of our atomizing and mechanising speculators comes into the field, the question of priority is immediately raised. Perceiving that love seems to imply or involve faith, he declares that faith is first. Then, as another is equally sure that faith implies love, he maintains that love is first. A third, in the same way, that repentance is before both; a fourth, that both are before repentance. And now we have a general debate on hand, in which the formulas will be heard ringing as flails, for a dozen years, or a century. Meantime, it will happen that all the several schools of wisdom are at fault, inasmuch as none of the priorities are first, or rather all are first; being all conditions mutually of one another. Might it not have been better, at the first, to clear ourselves of time and the law it weaves into words and predicates—to perceive, as by a little insight we may, that, in all vital and plastic natures, the functions have a mutual play?

In the speculative deductive use of formulas, it sometimes happens, also, that the argument contains a law of degrees, and thus constructs, when fairly carried out, an infinite series. Thus, in the argument for a God, "an effect," we are told, "infers a cause; a design, a designer." The doubter assents: "but," he adds, "the supposed designer is one who is adapted, in his nature, to the making of designs, and therefore, I perceive, in this adaptation of means to ends in him, that following the same law, there is a designer back of him. Go with me, then, up an infinite series, as the argument legitimately requires, or else excuse me from the first step, as you excuse yourself from the second." By just this kind of process it was that Shelley, immersed in the logic of Oxford, became an atheist; as also all the scholars of that great university might properly be, and would, if they yielded implicitly to the drill under which they are placed, and forgot all the simpler wisdom of nature, in the learned wisdom that is taught them. But if we can think it any thing to *see* God—all formulas, inferences, degrees, out of the question—if we can say "God is expressed to us here on every side, shining out as a Form of Intelligence in every object round us," it will not be difficult to find the God our logic denies us. This, in fact, is the real virtue of Paley's argument; only, to give it a more imposing logical form, he has run it into a suicidal series by the statement.

In offering these illustrations of the value of the logical method in religious and moral reasonings, I have only hinted at some of the important issues involved. To set the subject forth in all its momentous relations would require a volume; and such a volume the world intensely needs.

11. In the reading or interpretation of an author, writing on intellectual and moral subjects, we are to observe, first of all, whether he takes up some given word or figure, and makes it a law to his thinking. If some

symbol that he uses to-day stands by him also to-morrow, rules his doctrine, shapes his argument, drawing every thing into formal consistency with it, then we are to take up the presumption that he is out of the truth, and set ourselves to find where his mistake is. Brown started a new theory of cause and effect, demolishing these first ideas, or we might even say, categories of the mind, and reducing all events to mere conditions of antecedence and consequence. It was a great discovery, and when it was drawn out into full form or complete system, setting, as one may say, a whole book revolving about these two words, it was too captivating to be rejected. Never was the grave world of philosophy more remarkably fooled, or at a cheaper rate. It did not occur to many of the learned professors to question the real import of these two famous words, *antecedence* and *consequence;* in doing which, it would have come to light that they are the loosest and remotest of all rhetorical figures applicable to the subject, having, in fact, no real applicability at all. They did not ask whether the antecedence spoken of is antecedence in space. Then, when a man follows a wheelbarrow, the causative agency of the motion is in the wheelbarrow. Or, not satisfied with this, they did not inquire whether antecedence of time is intended. Then, it follows, that if the cause be antecedent in time to the effect, there is, for just that length of time, a cause without an effect. And so, or by this brief inquest, it would have been seen that the whole scheme of antecedence and consequence is nothing but a very insipid blunder,—that there is in fact no real antecedence of any kind in the case—nothing to give color to the words, save that when we are going to *be* causes, or act causatively, we commonly make approaches and preparatory motions. I bring this illustration simply to say that a philosopher, taking up this theory, and finding it hung about the one simple figure of before and after, as being itself the very truth, and sufficient to rule all other truth, ought to have presumed a falsity. And how miserable the falsity that exchanged the word *cause*, naming an exact, eternal, and necessary idea, for a figure of time or space that had scarcely any intelligent relation to the truth whatever! So, in general, we are to judge of all moral and religious theories, hung about single words, or based on single definitions, and carried through whole lives of speculation.

12. If we find the writer, in hand, moving with a free motion, and tied to no one symbol, unless in some popular effort, or for some single occasion; if we find him multiplying antagonisms, offering cross views, and bringing us round the field to show us how it looks from different points, then we are to presume that he has some truth in hand which it becomes us to know. We are to pass round accordingly with him, take up all his symbols, catch a view of him here, and another there, use one thing to qualify and interpret another, and the other to shed light upon that, and, by a process of this kind, endeavor to comprehend his antagonisms, and settle into a complete view of his meaning.

What Goethe says of himself is true of all efficient writers:—"I have always regarded all I have done, as solely symbolical, and, at bottom, it does not signify whether I make pots or dishes." And then, what Eckerman says of him in his preface, follows of course: "Goethe's detached remarks upon poetry, have often an appearance of contradiction. Sometimes he lays all the stress on the material which the outward world affords, sometimes upon that which is given to the inward world of the poet; sometimes the greatest importance is attached to the subject, sometimes to the mode of treating it; sometimes all is made to depend on perfection of form, sometimes form is to be neglected, and all the attention paid to the spirit. But all these seeming contradictions are, in fact, only successive presentations of single sides of a truth, which, by their union, manifest completely to us its existence, and guide us to a perception of its nature. I confide in the insight and comprehensive power of the cultivated reader, not to stop at any one part, as seen by itself, but to keep his eye on the significance of the whole, and by that means, to bring each particular truth into its proper place and relations."

Is it a fault of Goethe that he must be handled in this manner? Rather is it one of the highest proofs of his genius and the real greatness of his mind. Had he been willing to stay under some one figure, and draw himself out into formal consistency, throwing off none of these bold antagonisms, he must have been a very different character—not Goethe, but some dull proser or male spinster of logic, never heard of by us.

What, then, shall we say of Christ and the Gospel of John? If it requires such an array of antagonisms to set forth the true idea of poetry, what does it require to set forth God and redemption? What should we expect, in such a work, but a vast compilation of symbols and of forms, which to the mere wordsman, are contrary to each other? And then what shall we do?—what, for example, with the trinity, the atonement, the bondage and freedom of sin? Shall we say, with the infidel, this is all a medley of contradiction—mere nonsense, fit only to be rejected? Shall we take up these bold antagonisms, as many orthodox believers have done, seize upon some one symbol as the real form of the truth, and compel all the others to submit to it; making, thus, as many sects as there are symbols, and as many petty wars about each truth as it has sides or inches of surface? Or shall we endeavor, with the Unitarians, to decoct the whole mass of symbol, and draw off the extract into pitchers of our own; fine, consistent, nicely-rounded pitchers, which, so far from setting out any where towards infinity, we can carry at pleasure by the handle, and definitely measure by the eye? What critic has ever thought of handling Goethe in the methods just named? We neither scout his inconsistency, nor drill him into some one of his forms, nor decoct him into forms of our own. But we call him the many-sided great man; we let him stand in his own chosen symbols, whether they be "pots or dishes," and do him the greater honor because of the complexity and the magnificent profusion of his creations.

There is no book in the world that contains so many repugnances, or antagonistic forms of assertion, as the Bible. Therefore, if any man please to play off his constructive logic upon it, he can easily show it up as the absurdest book in the world. But whosoever wants, on the other hand, really to behold and receive all truth, and would have the truth-world overhang him as an empyrean of stars, complex, multitudinous, striving antagonistically, yet comprehended, height above height, and deep under deep, in a boundless score of harmony; what man soever, content with no small rote of logic and catechism, reaches with true hunger after this, and will offer himself to the many-sided forms of the scripture with a perfectly ingenuous and receptive spirit; he shall find his nature flooded with senses, vastnesses, and powers of truth, such as it is even greatness to feel. God's own lawgivers, heroes, poets, historians, prophets, and preachers and doers of righteousness, will bring him their company, and representing each his own age, character, and mode of thought, shine upon him as so many cross lights on his field of knowledge, to give him the most complete and manifold view possible of every truth. He has not only the words of Christ, the most manifold of all teachers, but he has gospels which present him in his different words and attitudes; and then, besides, he has four, some say five, distinct writers of epistles, who follow, giving each his own view of the doctrine of salvation and the Christian life, (views so unlike or antagonistical that many have regarded them as being quite irreconcilable)—Paul, the dialectic, commonly so called; John, the mystic; James, the moralizer; Peter, the homilectic; and perhaps a fifth in the epistle to the Hebrews, who is a Christian templar and Hebraizer. The Old Testament corresponds. Never was there a book uniting so many contrarious aspects of one and the same truth. The more complete, therefore, because of its manifoldness;

nay, the more really harmonious, for its apparent want of harmony.

How, then, are we to receive it and come into its truth? Only in the comprehensive manner just now suggested; not by destroying the repugnances, but by allowing them to stand, offering our mind to their impressions, and allowing it to gravitate inwardly, towards that whole of truth, in which they coalesce. And when we are in that whole, we shall have no dozen propositions of our own in which to give it forth; neither will it be a whole which we can set before the world, standing on one leg, in a perfectly definite shape, clear of all mystery; but it will be such a whole as requires a whole universe of rite, symbol, incarnation, historic breathings, and poetic fires, to give it expression,—in a word, just what it now has. Finding it not a Goethe, but as much greater than he as God is greater than a genius of our own human race, when we think of ourselves trying to give out the substantial import of the volume in a few scant formulas, it will probably occur to us just to ask what figure we should make, in a similar attempt upon one who is no more than a German poet? And then, it will not be strange if we drop our feeble, bloodless sentences and dogmas, whether of belief or denial, and return, duly mortified, into the faith of those august and magnificent forms of scripture—incarnation; Father, Son, and Holy Ghost; atonement as blood, life, sacrifice, propitiation, ransom, liberty, regeneration, wisdom, righteousness, sanctification, and redemption—the great mystery of godliness.

13. The views of language and interpretation I have here offered, suggest the very great difficulty, if not impossibility of mental science and religious dogmatism. In all such uses or attempted uses, the effort is to make language answer a purpose that is against its nature. The "winged words" are required to serve as beasts of burden; or, what is no better, to forget their poetic life, as messengers of the air, and stand still, fixed upon the ground, as wooden statues of truths. Which, if they seem to do; if, to comfort our studies of dogma, they assume the inert faces we desire, and suffer us to arrange the fixed attitudes of their bodies, yet, as little Memnons touched and made vocal by the light, they will be discoursing still of the free empyrean, disturbing, and scattering, by their voices, all the exact meanings we had thought to hold them to, in the nice corporeal order of our science.

In algebra and geometry, the ideas themselves being absolute, the terms or names also may be; but in mental science and religion, no such exactness is possible, because our apprehensions of truth are here only proximate and relative. I see not, therefore, how the subject matter of mental science and religion can ever be included under the fixed forms of dogma. Definitions cannot bring us over the difficulty; for definitions are, in fact, only changes of symbol, and, if we take them to be more, will infallibly lead us into error. In fact, no man is more certain to run himself into mischievous error, than he who places implicit confidence in definitions. After all, definitions will be words, and science will be words, and words, place them in whatever shapes we may, will be only shadows of truth.

Accordingly, it will ever be found, that in mental science, the investigators are, in fact, only trying to see if they can make up a true man out of some ten or twenty or forty words in the dictionary. The phrenologists claim to have done it, and even to show us the localities of these words in our heads, and how very man-like their word-elements will work when put together. All the systems are plausible—some, we are told, are infallible—the last and completed results of mental science! And yet there seem to be questions coming after. And probably it will be found, after all, that the only way to make up a real man is to put the whole dictionary into him; and then, most likely, some spaces will be found vacant, some members wanting. It will also be required, too, that the words be not packed together mechanically in the man, but that they all be alive in him—one living, plastic, organically perfect whole—acting, however, a little mysteriously sometimes, as the life-power even of an egg or a bean will presume to do; or what is more confusive to theory, acting diseasedly and contrarily, as if life had let in death, and a quarrel for possession were going on within. And then, if our complete dictionary man should be finally produced, alive, mysterious, acting diseasedly, in what shape would the now completed science be as likely to emerge, as in those forms of life which a Shakspeare, or some great universal poet of humanity might set before us? Poets, then, are the true metaphysicians, and if there be any complete science of man to come, they must bring it.

Is it to be otherwise in religion? Can there be produced, in human language, a complete and proper Christian theology; can the Christian truth be offered in the molds of any dogmatic statement? What is the Christian truth? Pre-eminently and principally, it is the expression of God—God coming into expression, through histories and rites, through an incarnation, and through language—in one syllable, by the WORD. The endeavor is, by means of expression, and under the laws of expression, to set forth God—His providence, and His government, and, what is more and higher than all, God's own feeling, His truth, love, justice, compassion. Well, if it be something for a poet to express man, it is doubtless somewhat more for a book to be constructed that will express God, and open His eternity to man. And if it would be somewhat difficult to put the poet of humanity into a few short formulas, that will communicate all he expresses, with his manifold, wondrous art, will it probably be easier to transfer the grand poem of salvation, that which expresses God, even the feeling of God, into a few dull propositions; which, when they are produced, we may call the sum total of the Christian truth? Let me freely confess that, when I see the human teacher elaborating a phrase of speech, or mere dialectic proposition, that is going to tell what God could only show me by the history of ages, and the mystic life and death of Jesus our Lord, I should be deeply shocked by his irreverence, if I were not rather occupied with pity for his infirmity.

It ought not to be necessary to remind any reader of the bible, that religion has a natural and profound alliance with poetry. Hence, a very large share of the bible is composed of poetic contributions. Another share, equally large, is that which comes to us in a form of history and fact; that is, of actual life, which is equally remote from all abstractions, and, in one view, equally poetic; for history is nothing but an evolution or expression of God and man in their own nature and character. The teachings of Christ are mere utterances of truth, not argumentations over it. He gives it forth in living symbols, without definition, without *proving* it, ever, as the logicians speak, well understanding that truth is that which shines in its own evidence that which *finds* us, to use an admirable expression of Coleridge, and thus enters into us.

But Paul,—was not Paul a dialectician? *the* dialectician, some say; for, confessedly, there is no other among all the scripture writers. Did Paul, then, it will be asked, set himself to an impossible task, when he undertook to reason out and frame into logical order, a scheme of Christian theology? To this, I answer, that I find no such Paul in the scripture, as this method of speaking supposes. Paul undertakes no theologic system, in any case. He only speaks to some actual want, to remove some error, rectify some hurtful mistake. There is nothing of the system-maker about him. Neither is he to be called a dogmatizer, or a dialectic writer, in any proper sense of the term. True, there is a form of reasoning, or argumentation about him, and he abounds in illatives; piling "For" upon "For" in constant succession. But, if he is narrowly watched, it will be seen that this is only a dialectic form that had settled on his language, under his old theologic discipline, previous to his conversion; for every man gets a language constructed early in life, which nothing can change afterwards. Notwithstanding his deductive manner, it will be plain to any one who reads him with a true insight, that, under the form of ratiocination, he is not so much theologizing, as flaming in the holy inspirations of truth; speaking not as a logician, but as a seer. Under so many illatives and deductive propositions, he is emitting fire, not formulas for the mere speculative understanding; rolling on, in the vehement power of a soul possessed with Christ, to declare the mystery that hath been hid for ages; conceiving nowhere that he is the first professor of Christian dogmatics; nowhere thinking, as a Christian Rabbi, to prepare a Targum on the Gospels.

Besides, it will be clear, on examination, that his illatives often miscarry, when taken as mere instruments, or terms of logic, while, if we conceive him rushing on through so many "Fors" and parentheses, which belong to his old Pharisaic culture, and serve as a continuous warp of connectives to his speech—now become the vehicle or channel, not for the modes of Rabbi Gamaliel, but for a stream of Christian fire—what before seemed to wear a look of inconsequence, assumes a port of amazing energy, and he becomes the fullest, heartiest, and most irresistible of all the inspired writers of the Christian scriptures. But, in order to this his true attitude, we must make him a seer, and not a system maker; we must read his epistle as a prophesying of the spirit, not as a Socratic lecture.

We find little, therefore, in the scriptures, to encourage the hope of a complete and sufficient Christian dogmatism, or of a satisfactory and truly adequate system of scientific theology. Language, under the laws of logic or speculation, does not seem to be adequate to any such use or purpose. The scriptures of God, in providing a clothing for religious truth, have little to do with mere dialectics, much to do with the freer creations of poetry; and that for reasons, evidently, which ought to waken a salutary scepticism in us, in regard to the possibility of that, which so many great minds have been attempting with so great confidence for so many hundreds of years. With due respect, also, I will venture to ask, whether the actual results of this immense engineering process, which we call dogmatic and polemic theology—as surely polemic as dogmatic—does not give some countenance to the doubt I am suggesting?

And, perhaps, the saying of Lord Bacon will turn out to have more of truth in it than he himself perceived: "Philosophy has three objects; God, nature, and man; as, also, three kinds of rays; for nature strikes the human intellect with a *direct* ray—God with a *refracted* ray, from the inequality of the medium betwixt the Creator and the creature—man, as exhibited to himself with a *reflected* ray." Now, language, as we have seen, has a literal character in regard to physical objects. It "writes," as Bacon also says it is the true aim of philosophy to do, "a revelation and real view of the stamps and signatures of the Creator upon the creatures." But, when we come to religion and mental science, our terms are only analogies, signs, shadows, so to speak, of the formless mysteries above us and within us. Here we see nothing, save in refracted or reflected rays; therefore, with but a limited capacity of mental understanding.

It accords, also, with this, that while natural science is advancing with so great rapidity and certainty of movement, the advances of mental science and theology are so irregular and obscure, and are wrought out by a process so conflicting and tortuous. They seem, in fact, to have no advance, save what may be called a cultivation of symbol, produced by the multifarious industry of debate and system-making. There is, however, one hope for mental and religious truth, and their final settlement, which I confess I see but dimly, and can but faintly express, or indicate. It is, that physical science, leading the way, setting outward things in their true proportions, opening up their true contents, revealing their genesis and final causes and laws, and weaving all into the unity of a real universe, will so perfect our knowledges and conceptions of them, that we can use them, in the second department of language, with more exactness. There is, we have also seen, in what we call nature, that is, in its objects, an outward grammar of relations, which constructs the grammar of language; or what is not far different, the logic of propositions. In the laws of nature, I suppose, there is, in like manner, an internal grammar, which is certain, as it is evolved, to pass into language, and be an internal grammar in that, systematizing and steadying its uses. And then language will be as much more full and intelligent, as it has more of God's intelligence, in the system of nature, imparted to its symbols. For, undoubtedly, the whole universe of nature is a perfect analogon of the whole universe of thought or spirit. Therefore, as nature becomes truly a universe only through science revealing its universal laws, the true universe of thought and spirit cannot sooner be conceived. It would be easy to show, in this connection, the immense force already exerted over the empire of spiritual truth, by astronomy, chemistry, geology, the revelations of light and electricity, and especially of the mysterious and plastic workings of life, in the animal and vegetable kingdoms. We are accustomed to say, that this is not the same world to live in that it was fifty years ago. Just as true is it, that it is not the same world to *think* in, that it then was,—of which, also, we shall, by and by, take notice.

If, then, it please any one to believe, notwithstanding the present incapacities of dogmatism, that when, through science, we are able to see things physical in their true force and relations, having, also, within us, inbreathed by the spirit of God, a comprehensive heart and feelings sufficiently cleared of prejudice, to behold, in the universal mirror of God, His universal truth,—if, I say, any one please to believe, that now the Christian world may arrive at some final and determinate apprehensions of Christian doctrine, I will not object. But, if they do, observe, it will only be that they have settled, at last, into a comprehensive reception of the universal symbolism, and not that they have invented a few propositions, so intensely significant and true, as to dispense with all besides.

14. It is important to notice, as connected with the subject of language, that dogmatical propositions, such as are commonly woven into creeds and catechisms of doctrine, have not the certainty they are commonly

supposed to have. They only give us the seeing of the authors, at the precise stand-point occupied by them, at the time, and they are true only as seen from that point,—not even there, save in a proximate sense. Passing on, descending the current of time, we will say, for two centuries, we are brought to a different point, as when we change positions in a landscape, and then we are doomed to see things in a different light, in spite of ourselves. It is not that the truth changes, but that we change. Our eye changes color, and then the color of our eye affects our seeing. We are different men, living as parts in a different system of things and thinkings, denyings, and affirmings; and, as our contents and our antagonisms are different, we cannot see the same truths in the same forms. It may even be necessary to change the forms, to hold us in the same truths.

I could name phrases that have been brought into the creeds of many of our New England churches, within the present half century, which are already waxing old, and are doomed, within the next half century, to ask a re-modification.

Besides, in the original formation of any creed, catechism, or system of divinity, there is always a latent element of figure, which, probably, the authors know not of, but without which, it is neither true to them, nor to anybody. But in a long course of repetition, the figure dies out, and the formula settles into a literality, and then, if the repetition goes on, it is really an assent to what is not true; for that which was true, at the beginning, has now become untrue—and that, however paradoxical it may seem, by being assented to. What I here speak of, might be easily illustrated by a reference to the dogmatic history of opinions, concerning sin and free will. The will is under no mechanical laws. Hence, in all the reasonings, affirmations, and denials relating to the will and its modes of responsible activity, language, being mostly derived from the mechanical world, must somehow be divorced, in the use, from all its mechanical laws, else it imports a falsity. But the difficulty is, to keep the language up to that self-active unmechanical sense in which, only, it was true in the original use; for a dull, unthinking repetition lets it down very soon under the old mechanical laws, and then the same, or closely similar, forms of reasoning and assertion are false. Hence, in part, the necessity, I suppose, that this particular class of subjects should be reinvestigated every fifty years. Considering the infirmities of language, therefore, all formulas of doctrine should be held in a certain spirit of accommodation. They cannot be pressed to the letter, for the very sufficient reason that the letter is never true. They can be regarded only as proximate representations, and should therefore be accepted not as laws over belief, or opinion, but more as badges of consent and good understanding. The moment we begin to speak of them as guards and tests of purity, we confess that we have lost the sense of purity, and, with about equal certainty, the virtue itself.

At the same time, it is remarkable with what ease a man, who is sensible of the fluxing nature and significance of words, may assent to almost any creed, and that, with a perfectly sincere doubt, whether he does not receive it in its most interior and real meaning; that is, whether going back to the men who made it, taking their stand point, and abating what belongs to the form of a truth, in distinction from the truth itself, he does not come into the real senses or interior beliefs they clothed in these forms. Perhaps it is on this account that I have never been able to sympathise, at all, with the abundant protesting of the New England Unitarians, against creeds. So far from suffering even the least consciousness of constraint, or oppression, under any creed, I have been readier to accept as great a number as fell in my way; for when they are subjected to the deepest chemistry of thought, that which descends to the point of relationship between the form of the truth and its interior formless nature, they become, thereupon, so elastic, and run so freely into each other, that one seldom need have any difficulty in accepting as many as are offered him. He may regard them as only a kind of battle-dooring of words, blow answering to blow, while the reality of the play, viz. *exercise*, is the same, whichever side of the room is taken, and whether the stroke is given by the right hand or the left.

The greatest objection that I know, to creeds,—that is, to creeds of a theoretic or dogmatic character,—is that they make so many appearances of division, where there really is none, till the appearances make it. They are likely, also, unless some debate or controversy sharpens the mind to them, and keeps them alive, to die out of meaning, and be assented to, at last, as a mere jingle of words. Thus we have, in many of our orthodox formulas of trinity, the phrase—"the same in substance," and yet, how many are there, even of our theologians, to whom it will now seem a heresy, to say this with a meaning. And the clause following, "equal in power and glory," will be scarcely less supportable, when a view of trinity is offered which gives the terms an earnest and real significance.

On these accounts, the best creed is that which stays by the concrete most faithfully, and carries its doctrine, as far as possible, in a vehicle of fact and of real life. This is the peculiar excellence and beauty of what is called the "Apostle's Creed." If, however, creeds of theory, or systematic dogma, must be retained, the next best arrangement would be to allow assent to a great number of such creeds at once; letting them qualify, assist, and mitigate each other. And a virtual allowance of this is, in fact, one of the best points in our Saybrook Platform, which accepts the acknowledgment, either of its own Articles, or of the "Doctrinal Articles of the Church of England," or of the "Westminster Confession," or of the "Confession agreed on at the Savoy;" and if it be indifferent which of the four is received, there can be no objection, certainly, if all are received. And it is in just this way that the scripture has its meaning filled out, qualified, fortified, secured against subsiding into falsity, or becoming a mere jingle of sounds. We have so many writers set before us, each in his own habit, and giving his own form of the truth; offering the truth, some at one pole, and some at the other, that, when we receive and entertain them all, making, in fact, a creed of them all, they act as complementary forces, and, by their joint effect, keep us ever in the fullest, liveliest, and most many-sided apprehension of the Christian truth.

15. I have said nothing of the manner in which the user of language imparts himself to it. Undoubtedly every human language has, in its words and forms, indelible marks of the personal character and habit of the men by whom it was originally produced. Nay, it may, even, be said that every language carries in its bosom some flavor of meaning or import, derived from all the past generations that have lived in it. Not more truly does it represent the forms of nature, than it does within, or under these forms, the contents, also, of history. And, therefore, what is called usage, has a certain importance, when we seek the import or right use of words. But not any such importance as the lexicographers, and the Blairizing critics, have given it. Usage is a guide to use, but never a limit upon use. We have our freedom, as our fathers had, and as good a right to use words with new meanings, certainly, as to have new thoughts.

And just here, it is, that we come upon a matter, which, if it be too mysterious to be investigated, is yet too important to be overlooked. In every writer, distinguished by mental life, words have a significance and power breathed into them, which is wholly peculiar—whether it be in the rhythm, the collocations, the cadences, or the internal ideas, it may be impossible to guess. But his language is his own, and there is some chemistry of life in it that belongs only to him, as does the vital chemistry of his body. This holds of every writer, who can properly be called a living soul. If he be a dead soul, or one that is coffined in mere logic and uses, then his language, being dead, will be like all other dead language; for death is always like itself. In what manner it is, that words, in common, ordinary use—words that have been staled in their significance, as raisins are preserved in their own sugar,—receive a new inbreathing of life and power, it is impossible, I have said, to explain. Pascal cites, for illustration, the different games that may be played with the same tennis balls, which, in fact, is only appealing to death and chance for the illustration of life. Better, is it, to conceive the spirit of the author, as living in his words, in the same manner as Coleridge conceives the spirit of his country living in its outward sceneries and objects :—

> "I had found
> That outward forms, the loftiest, still receive
> Their finer influence from the Life within."

Accordingly, it is the right of every author, who deserves attention at all, to claim a certain liberty, and even to have it for a merit that he cannot be judged exactly by old uses and formulas. Life is organic; and if there be life in his work, it will be found not in some noun or verb that he uses, but in the organic whole of his creations. Hence, it is clear that he must be apprehended in some sense, as a whole, before his full import can be received in paragraphs and sentences. Until then, he will, of necessity, appear to be obscure, enigmatical, extravagant, or even absurd. He cannot be tested by the jingle of his words, or by auscultation applied to the breathing of his sentences. No decree of condemnation must be passed upon him, because he does not make himself understood, sentence by sentence; for, if he infuses into words a life-power of his own, or does more than simply to recombine old impressions, he cannot make himself intelligible, fully, save through a kind of general acquaintance. It may, even, be to his praise, that he is not too easily understood. For, in this matter of understanding, two things are requisite; first, a matter which is understandable; and, second, a power that is capable of understanding; and if there be some things offered, hard to be understood, then there must be a power of digestion strong enough to master them; and if, in fault of that, some crude, and over-confident sophister dangerously wrests the words, the blame is with him. Nor is it enough, in such a case, that the reading man, or public, be of a naturally sound mind, or even that they bring to the subject, capacities of a very high order; for words, as we have seen, never carry, or transfer a thought; they only offer hints or symbols, to put others on generating the same thought, which, in many cases, they are not likely to do, unless they have been long enough practiced in the subject discussed, to know where it lies; and not even then, if the writer is at all out of the system of his day, without such a degree of exercise in his forms of thought as will beget a certain general insight of his method and symbol.

They cannot run to a dictionary, and draw out the shroud of an old meaning from that, by which to conceive, or in which to clothe words and phrases that have their vital force, in no small part, from the man himself; and which, therefore, can be fully understood only by reference to the total organism of which they are members. The reading man, therefore, before he thinks to judge the writing man, must first endeavor to generate the writing man. And this, without supposing any defect of capacity in himself, will sometimes be difficult. He may be too young, or too old; having too little breadth, or too little flexibility, to make a sufficient realization of the truth presented. It costs me no mortification, to confess that the most fructifying writer I ever read, was one in whom I was, at first, able only to see glimspes, or gleams of truth; one whom it required years of study and reflection, of patient suspension and laborious self-questioning, to be able fully to understand; and, indeed, whom I never since have read, at all, save in a chapter or two, which I glanced over, just to see how obvious and clear, what before was impossible, had now become.

Shall I dare to go further? Shall I say that of all the "clear" writers and speakers I have ever met with,—those, I mean, who are praised by the multitude for their transparency,—I have never yet found one that was able to send me forward an inch; or one that was really true, save in a certain superficial, or pedagogical sense, as being an accurate distributor of that which is known. The roots of the known are always in the unknown, and, if a man will never show the root of any thing, if he will treat of the known as *separate* from the unknown, and as having a complete knowledge of it, which he has not—pretending, still, to be an investigator, and to exert an obstetric force, when he is only handling over old knowledges and impressions—he may easily enough be clear. Nothing, in fact, is easier, if one is either able to be shallow, or willing to be false. He is clear, because he stands out *before* the infinite and the unknown ; separated, bounded off [de-finite] so that you see the whole compass of his head, just so many inches in diameter. But the writer, who is to help us on, by some real advance or higher revelation, will, for that reason, be less comprehensible, and offer more things hard to be understood. He will be, as it were, a face, setting *out from* a back ground of mystery ; a symbolism, through which the infinite and the unknown are looking out upon us, and by kind significances, tempting us to struggle into that holy, but dark profound, which they are opening. Of course, we are not to make a merit of obscurity ; for nothing is more to be admired than the wondrous art by which some men are able to propitiate and assist the generative understanding of others, so as to draw them readily into higher realizations of truth. But there is a limit, we must acknowledge, even to this highest power of genius ; it cannot quite create a soul under the ribs of death.

Whatever may be thought of these suggestions, for some, I suppose, will give them little weight, it is obvious that, since language is rather an instrument of suggestion, than of absolute conveyance for thought, since it acts suggestively, through symbols held up in the words, which symbols and words are never exact measures of any truth (always imputing somewhat of form to the truth which does not belong to it, always somewhat contrary to each other)—this being true, it is obvious that a very little of perverse effort expended on his words, can subject a writer to almost any degree of apparent absurdity. And, what is specially to be noticed, there is no other human work, in which so much of applause can be gotten at so cheap a rate, and with so small a modicum of talent. The work, indeed, is always half done beforehand. The words are ready to quarrel, as soon as any one will see them, and nothing is necessary, in fact, but to play off a little of constructive ingenuity on their forms, to set them at war with one another and the whole universe besides. And, when it is done, many will be sure to admire and praise what they call the profound and searching logic displayed. Now, the truth is, that no many-sided writer, no one who embraces all the complementary forces of truth, is ever able to stand in harmony before himself, (such is the nature of language,) save by an act of internal construction favorable to himself, and preservative of his mental unity. It follows, of necessity, that without this favorable act of construction extended to his words, no true teacher can be saved from contradiction and confusion,—no one, especially, who presents more than a half, or tenth part of a truth. Therefore, every writer, not manifestly actuated by a malignant or evil spirit, is entitled to this indulgence. The mind must be offered up to him, for the time, with a certain degree of sympathy. It must draw itself into the same position; take his constructions; feel out, so to speak, his meanings, and keep him, as far as may be, in a form of general consistency. Then, having endeavored thus, and for a sufficient length of time, to reproduce him or his thought, that is, to make a realization of him, some proper judgment may be formed in regard to the soundness of his doctrine.

I need not say how different is the method ordinarily pursued. The decision is an off-hand decision. No time is allowed to cross-question the writer's representations, and see how one symbol interprets, qualifies, and corrects another. First impressions are sufficient and infallible. It is found that a very little pressure against the harmony of words and phrases, produces woful discords and absurdities, which it will be a pleasant proof of superior acumen to exhibit. And then, as a vulture lighting upon a lamb, tears out some member, and bears it off, screaming over the prey, as if he were saying,—See how absurdly that lamb was put together!—so we are to see a member torn out here or there, separated from all the vital connections of reason, turned about in the screws of constructive logic, properly so called, and held up as a foolish thing, to pity or derision! May we not believe, that when the nature of language, as an instrument of thought, is properly understood, this vulture talent, which has so long violated the delicate integrity of opinions, and the sacred rights of truth, will be estimated according to its dignity?

It needs also to be remarked, in this connection, that a writer is not, of course, to be blamed because he is variriously interpreted by his readers, or because the public masses have a degree of difficulty in conceiving his pre cise meaning. It should be so, and will be, if he has any thing of real moment to say. There has always been most of controversy, for this reason, about the meaning of the greatest authors and teachers,—Plato, for example, and Aristotle; Bacon, Shakspeare, and Goethe; Job, Paul, John, and especially CHRIST HIMSELF. What, in fact, do we see, in the endless debate, kept up for these eighteen hundred years, over the words of Jesus, but an illustration of the truth, that infinitesimals, though there be many of them, are not the best judges of infinites. And something of the same principle pertains, in the judgment or inspection of merely human teachers. They may be obscure, not from weakness only, which, certainly, is most frequent, but quite as truly by reason of their exceeding breadth, and the piercing vigor of their insight. And when this latter is true, as it sometimes may be, then to invoke a sentence of popular condemnation, because the writer has not made himself perfectly intelligible, or clear to the whole public, is, in fact, to assist or instigate the multitude in practicing a fraud against themselves. And, what is worse, if possible, it encourages an ill-natured and really unchristian spirit in them, excusing their impatience with every form of teaching that requires an effort of candor, or an ingenuous spirit.

16. That I may not seem to be offering to the public, doctrines, the real import of which I have not considered myself, something must be said of the consequences likely to result to religion, from the admission of views such as I have here presented. Only, be it observed, that their truth depends, in no degree, on any expectations of good, or any vaticinations of evil, which the faith of one, or the panic of another may raise.

Unquestionably, the view of language here presented must produce, if received, a decided mitigation of our dogmatic tendencies in religion. It throws a heavy shade of discouragement on our efforts in this direction. It shows that language is, probably, incapable of any such definite and determinate use as we have supposed it to be in our theological speculations; that, for this reason, dogma has failed hitherto, and about as certainly will hereafter. Taking away, thus, the confidence of the speculative theologer, it will limit, proportionally, his eagerness. It will, also, reduce the very excessive eminence he has, at present, in the public estimation, requiring a re-adjustment of the scale that now pertains between this and the historical, literary, and practical departments of Christian study. Or, better still, showing that the advancement and the real amount of true theology depends, not on logical deductions and systematic solutions, but principally on the more cultivated and nicer apprehension of symbol, it may turn the industry of our teachers more in this direction, giving a more esthetic character to their studies and theories, and drawing them as much closer to the practical life of religion.

Without being at all aware of the fact, as it would seem, our theologic method in New England has been essentially rationalistic; though not exactly in the German sense. The possibility of reasoning out religion, though denied in words, has yet been tacitly assumed. Not allowing ourselves to be rationalists *over* the scriptures, we have yet been as active and confident rationalists *under* them, as it was possible to be—assuming, always, that they address their contents to the systematic, speculative reason of men, into which they are to be received, and by which they are to be digested into formulas—when they are ready for use. We have had a certain negative way of declaring against the competence of the natural man to understand spiritual things, but it has been done principally in that way only, and as a convenient method of cutting off speculative arguments that could not be speculatively answered. It has not been held, as a practical, positive, and earnest Christian truth, that there is a Perceptive Power in spiritual life, an unction of the Holy One, which is itself a kind of inspiration—an immediate, experimental knowledge of God, by virtue of which, and partly in the degree of which, Christian theology is possible. No real doubt has been held of the perfect sufficiency of formulas; or of natural logic, handled by the natural understanding, to settle them. The views of language, here offered, lead to a different method. The scriptures will be more studied than they have been, and in a different manner—not as a magazine of propositions and mere dialectic entities, but as inspirations and poetic forms of life; requiring, also, divine inbreathings and exaltations in us, that we may ascend into their meaning. Our opinions will be less catechetical and definite, using the word as our definers do, but they will be as much broader as they are more divine; as much truer, as they are more vital and closer to the plastic, undefinable mystery of spiritual life. We shall seem to understand less, and shall actually receive more. No false *pre-cision,* which the nature and conditions of spiritual truth forbid, will, by cutting up the body of truth into definite and dead morsels, throw us into states of excision and division, equally manifold. We shall receive the truth of God in a more entire, organic and organific, manner, as being itself an essentially vital power. It will not be our endeavor to pull the truth into analytic distinctions, as if theology were a kind of inorganic chemistry, and the last end of discovery an atomic theory; but we shall delight in truth, more as a concrete, vital nature, incarnated in all fact and symbol round us—a vast, mysterious, incomprehensible power, which best we know, when most we love.

Striving ever outward, towards the infinite, and not inward or downward, upon speculative minima or atoms, we shall be kept in a humbler, and far less positive state of mind. Our judgments of others will be less peremptory, and, as we are more modest, we shall be as much more patient and charitable. And our views of language, as an instrument wholly inadequate to the exact representation of thought, will operate, immediately, to favor the same result.

If any should be apprehensive that the views here offered may bring in an age of mysticism, and so of interminable confusion, they will greatly misconceive their import, and also the nature of mysticism itself. A mystic is one who finds a secret meaning, both in words and in things, back of their common or accepted meaning—some agency of LIFE, or LIVING THOUGHT, hid under the forms of words and institutions, and historical events. Hence, all religious writers and teachers, who dwell on the representative character of words and things, or hold the truths of religion, not in mechanical measures and relations, but as forms of life, are so far mystics. Thus Neander gives it, as a charac teristic of the apostle John,—"that a reference to communion with the Redeemer, in the inward life, and in the present, predominates over the reference to the future, and to outward facts; he dwells upon the elements of the inner life, the facts of Christian consciousness, and only slightly adverts to outward matters of fact and ecclesiastical arrangements. In accordance with this spirit, he exhibits all the particular incidents in the outward history of Christ, only as a manifestation of his indwelling glory, by which this may be brought home to the heart; he always avails himself of these narratives, to introduce what the Redeemer declared, respecting his relation to mankind, as the source of life. John is the representative of the truth which lies at the basis of that tendency of the Christian spirit, which sets itself in opposition to a one-sided intellectualism, and ecclesiastical formality—and is distinguished by the name of mysticism."

I make no disavowal, then, of the fact, that there is a mystic element, as there should be, in what I have represented as the source of meaning in language, and, also, in the views of Christian life and doctrine, that follow. Man is designed, in his very nature, to be a partially mystic being; the world to be looked upon as a mystic world. Christ himself revealed a decidedly mystic element in his teachings. There is something of a mystic quality in almost every writing of the New Testament. In John, it is a character. In "the dialectic" Paul, there are very many passages quite as mystical as any in John.

Now, the very cautious and salutary scepticism I have

maintained, concerning the insufficiency and the partially repugnant character of words, leaves as little room as possible to apprehend any danger of wildness, or confusion from the entrance of a mystic element, thus qualified and guarded. There is nothing, in fact, that we so much need, as an apostle John among our other apostles; and I fervently hope that God will sometime send us such a gift. The very last thing to be feared is, that our loss-and-gain style of religion, the stern, iron-limbed speculative logic of our New England theology, will receive some fatal damage from a trace of the mystic element. It will produce no overturnings, sap no foundations, dissolve no formulas, run to no license or extravagance. It will enter only as life came into the bones; which, though they rose up into a limbered and active state, and were hidden somewhat from the eye, by an envelop of muscle and skin, were yet as good bones as before; probably as much better and more systematic, as there was more of the life-order in them and about them.

The two principal results, then, which I suppose may follow, should these views of language be allowed to have their effect in our theology, are a more comprehensive, friendly, and fraternal state, than now exists between different families of Christians; and, as the confidence of dogma is mitigated, a more present, powerful, and universal conviction entering into the Christian body, that truth, in its highest and freest forms, is not of the natural understanding, but is, rather, as Christ himself declared—spirit and life. We shall have more of union, therefore, and more of true piety enlightened by the spirit of God —neither of which involves any harm or danger.

The 'Discourses' which follow, are already known to the public; for a somewhat evil notoriety appears to have gone before them. In their publication, however, I suffer no anxiety for the result. I can only wish that my readers may be candid enough to be just, and patient enough to withhold their judgment till they have become fully possessed of my meaning; or, if that be too much, till they have sufficiently ascertained that I have no intelligent meaning. Whatever sentence they may pass upon my views and arguments, they will look in vain, I am quite sure, for any such substantial aberrations in Christian doctrine as could properly excite the alarm, or provoke the sensitiveness, known to have been suffered by many on my account. Indeed, I think it will be more and more a mystery to them, how it came to pass that I was able, in so innocent a way, to awaken so much of painful concern—a mystery which, probably, they will have little success in solving, unless they remember that I dared to preach, on invitation, as I supposed my Master also would, before the Divinity School at Cambridge.

I suppose it is proper to say, that I did not prepare the occasions, on which these 'Discourses' were delivered, and seem scarcely to have chosen the subjects themselves. Indeed, I seem, too, as regards the views presented, to have had only about the same agency in forming them, that I have in preparing the blood I circulate, and the anatomic frame I occupy. They are not my choice, or invention, so much as a necessary growth, whose process I can hardly trace myself. And now, in giving them to the public, I seem only to have about the same kind of option left me that I have in the matter of appearing in corporal manifestation myself,—about the same anxiety, I will add, concerning the unfavorable judgments to be encountered; for though a man's opinions are of vastly greater moment than his looks, yet, if he is equally simple in them, as in his growth, and equally subject to his law, he is responsible only in the same degree, and ought not, in fact, to suffer any greater concern about their reception, than about the judgments passed upon his person.

I say this, not as disrespecting or undervaluing the good opinions of others; for it would be more agreeable, I confess, to have my thoughts received with favor, especially by wise and candid Christian men. I only speak in this manner, because of the very great happiness and repose it gives me to feel that, in everything pertaining to these 'Discourses,' I seem to have exerted so little choice for myself; to have been called for, to have had my themes appointed, to have spoken what was in me to say, and what alone I was able. If, in yielding thus to the lead of some higher necessity, I have really been yielding as to fate or destiny, it is not well; if, as to Providence, is it superstition to hope, that the Being, whose way it is to bring the highest things into combination, by the mediation of the humblest, who appoints that even the pith-ball, by its play, shall interpret the current of his thunders, may have some comprehensive design preparing, in reference to the sundered churches of New England, as an introductory to which, the peculiar combinations touched in these 'Discourses,' if not their spirit or doctrine, may have some fit relation.

The first two of the 'Discourses,' and, in a less immediate, but more fundamental sense, the third, also, relate to matters in issue between us and the Unitarians. I am not aware that I have surrendered any truth to them—that is, anything which is truth to me. If I have surrendered some other man's truth, he must reclaim it for himself. Notwithstanding the profound sympathy, and the real respect I have always felt for the Unitarians, a sympathy and respect grounded, I will add, in a participation of similar difficulties; though I do not, for the same reason, feel the extreme horror of their persons, sometimes manifested; I am, probably, as far from being in any mood of surrender to them, as could be desired by the stiffest champion of orthodoxy. It is my settled conviction, a conviction not the less firmly held because it is deliberately formed, that to escape certain scholastic and dogmatic forms of orthodoxy, they have so far renounced, or obscured many great Christian truths, pertaining to the trinity, the person of Christ, depravity, regeneration and the Spirit of God as a supernatural grace, that what I should call the tone or tonic energy of the gospel is lost. And, were it not for the ingenuous spirit of self-correction they so often manifest, and especially for the earnestness with which many are now applying themselves, to discover the errors and readjust the principles of their system, I should suppose they might be doomed to sink into a typhoid state, and, finally, to die. At first their movement could not reveal its inherent defects for both ministers and people, growing up under orthodoxy, with a high religious tone produced in their nature, by the resonant and somewhat brassy energies of Calvinism, were likely to suppose a degree of quality in their system, which it really had not. But, as a true Cremona cannot be made out of green wood, or any but some ancient timber curiously selected, and found to have been rightly moved by the rhythmic sweep of winds and storms, so they are likely at last to find, as they are withdrawn to receive more exclusively the proper consequences of their system, that it fails to impart to those who grow up under it from childhood, that deep vibratory sense of religion, which is needful to its volume and power. It may be found, that a third generation is more deficient than the second. Possibly it may, also, be found, as a general truth, on adverting to the past, that their most earnest and stirring preachers, those who have had the deepest convictions, and most of that sonorous quality which rings conviction into others, were persons who came out from orthodoxy, not those who had been trained up in the vernacular of Unitarianism.

I may be wrong in the estimate indicated by these suggestions; it is, nevertheless, such as my own inquiries and reflections have forced upon me. And as I speak in this manner not to judge them, but simply to indicate my own position, they will deem it no offence. Meantime, let us be ready to accept, in good nature, any counter convictions, by which they will expose, with equal frankness, their sense of errors and deficiencies existing in us; not objecting, if it should also be made to appear, that Unitarianism was raised up as a necessary antagonism and corrective to these precise errors and defects.

Actuated by views like these, it will be seen, clearly enough, that I am in no mood of surrender to Unitarianism. I suppose, indeed, observing the ordinary method of such changes, that I am really less likely to undergo the conversion I speak of, than nineteen twentieths of our orthodox teachers, including those, especially, who are most alarmed, and who suffer, just now, the deepest nervous horror on my account. It is proper, also, to say, that I have no thought, in the discussion that follows, or in the views maintained, of proposing any composition, or compromise, with the Unitarians. I have no confidence in any organic and combined effort of pacification between us. If we are ever re-united, it will be by a gradual and natural process, working in individual minds. We must think ourselves together, not as fixing our minds on some halfway place, where we may meet, but simply as striving after the divine verities of the gospel, and the unity of the spirit. This only is my aim, in the 'Discourses' that follow. Not one doctrine or sentiment, here offered, has been adjusted with a view to conciliation. Nothing is advanced, which I did not hold before the preparing of these 'Discourses;' nothing, in fact, which I had not held for substance, ever since my entrance into the ministry; except that, under the atonement, I had just been able to bring together into one view, elements which I had before held separately, and without perceiving the mode of their agreement. If

9*

I seem to be throwing doctrines into a shape that may accommodate their difficulties, I had done it before to accommodate my own. If I speak of them in terms of patience and sympathy, if I handle their views with candor, this may be my sin. When I discover it to be so, I hope I may have grace to repent of it.

There is an intimate, or interior connection, it will be seen, between all these 'Discourses,' and the views of language presented in this 'Preliminary Dissertation.' I must, therefore, be allowed to request, that this 'Dissertation' may receive a little more attention than is ordinarily given to Introductions. For, if these views of language have been historically introductory to me, it is hardly possible that others will enter fully into my positions, without any introduction at all.

I have given a view or solution of the Incarnation and the Trinity, which puts them on the same footing, in fact, with all language of thought or spirit. They offer God, not so much to the reason, or logical understanding, as to the imagination and the perceptive, or esthetic apprehension of faith. Then, also, their contrarious, or logically insoluble matter is to be handled in the same way, as that of all language, when applied to thought. And if I seem, in this, to assert the unreality of the incarnation and the trinity, or to make a mere shadow or figment of it, the reality of language, I answer, is not in the vocal names, or sounds, but in the solid things, or physical images they represent; and there, too, I ought to add, not in their material solidity, but in the significances which the Divine Word has insensed in them, or imparted to them. Accordingly, as the reality of the world is what it is to thought and the uses of the soul, not what it is to mere hammers and axes, the incarnation and the trinity are just as real and historical as the world is.

Similar objections have been offered to the representation I have given of the atonement. To some Unitarians, what I called the "objective view," seemed, I believe, to be only a fetch, to save the orthodoxy of my position. To some of my orthodox friends, on the other hand, it seemed equally unreal, because it only made a sacrifice, objectively, of that which, taken subjectively, is simply a truth and a power; neither party observing that the life and death of Christ become most thoroughly real, most truly powerful, only when they are offered to the mind in this Objective Form. Whereas, it is, if I am right, the very art and philosophy of God's redemptive plan, that He prepares a language and objective form for Christ, by a long historic process, instituted, in great part, for this very purpose. The grace of Christ being wholly supernatural, there were, of course, no sufficient bases of words in nature, to represent or adequately to convey it. Hence, it was necessary to prepare, by an artificial process, new types of words, that should serve this sacred use. This is done in and through the sacrificial system of the Old Testament. These sacrifices served as a ritual, or liturgic exercise for the time then present, and then, taken as *forms* wrought into the Jewish mind, and, indeed, into the mind of the whole world, they were ready for a higher use, in what I have called the second department of language—ready to be employed as bases of words, and vehicles, thus, of the spiritual truths of the

New Testament. It is not, as we all know perfectly well, that Christ was a physical sacrifice, offered by fire upon an altar, not that he was a lamb, not that his blood was sprinkled by any priest, not that there was any confession of sins upon his head, and yet all these terms, which are names of mere physical act and proceeding, are prepared with an art, none of us can perfectly fathom, to be the FORM of Christ and his truth. In him they are "fulfilled" as he himself represented. And, in that view, when presented to us in the forms of the altar, he is a more real sacrifice than the sacrifice, a more real lamb, than the lamb. Nor is anything more clear to me, than that any class of Christians, who undertake, as avoiding cant, or as being more philosophical, to get rid of the Altar Form, and present the Saviour's death in terms of mere natural language, will make full proof, in the end, that the foolishness of God is wiser than men.

In this matter of trinity and atonement, though I am as far as possible from all mere phantasm or allegory, adhering strictly to the historic verity of the scripture representations, I seem to encounter the same difficulty with poor Bunyan, when he consults his friends in regard to the publication of his 'Pilgrim.' Many prophesy that his book will not "stand when soundly tried"—(that is, I suppose, when tried by the dialectic methods of speculative theology)—they are specially scandalized by the light, imaginative air of his book, and tell him that his words "*want solidness*"—"metaphors make us blind." But he rallies courage to say, and his reply is even more to the point for me than for him:—

"But must I needs want solidness, because
By metaphors I speak? Were not God's laws,
His gospel laws, in olden time, held forth
By Shadows, Types, and Metaphors? Yet loth
Will any sober man be, to find fault
With them, lest he be found for to assault
The highest wisdom! No, he rather stoops
And seeks to find out by what 'Pins' and 'Loops,'
By 'Calves' and 'Sheep,' by 'Heifers' and by 'Rams,'
By 'Birds' and 'Herbs,' and by the blood of 'Lambs,'
God speaketh to him; and happy is he
THAT FINDS THE LIGHT AND GRACE THAT IN THEM BE."

The world, I need not add, has finally verified his judgment to the full. No man complains of this Pilgrim's Progress that it wants 'solidness.' By this wonderful book, it has been proved to the judgment of all Christian men, that right words and forms offered to the imagination, have really more of solidity and true moment than any which can be offered to the logical understanding. And if this be true of a mere Allegory, how much more of a History prepared with manifold greater skill, to set forth God and His love in forms of life and feeling before the imaginative sense of our race. Shall we judge that there is no proper reality in it, till we have put out the fire, cut short the freedom, brought down all the living forms to be handled and shaped into wooden dogmas by the hand of our constructive logic? Here, again, says Bunyan, giving us even a vaster truth than he himself supposed, and one that is worthy to be specially meditated by all abstractionists and system-mongers:

"All things solid in show, not solid be."

Nothing, in fact, is so unsolid, many times—no figment so vacant of meaning as that dead body of abstractions, or logical propositions, called theology; which, professing to give us the contents of God's truth, puts us off, too generally, with the mere exuviæ of reason; which extinguishes the living fires of truth to show us the figures it can draw in the ashes.

I speak in this manner, not as interposing a caveat against the speculative objections that may be raised against my 'Discourses.' I am perfectly well aware that my readers can run me into just what absurdity they please. Nothing is more easy. I suppose it might be almost as easy for me to do it as for them. Indeed, I seem to have the whole argument which a certain class of speculators must raise upon my 'Discourses,' in order to be characteristic, fully before me. I see the words footing it along to their conclusions. I see the terrible syllogisms wheeling out their infantry upon my fallacies and absurdities. Indeed, I have thought that I might possibly win some laurels by an anonymous attack of this kind upon myself.

I should take no notice, in such an attempt, of the representation that trinity and atonement belong to the sphere of expression, not to the sphere of logic. Though the declaration is that they are forms of truth which have their reality in and through the imaginative and morally æsthetic powers—truths of form and feeling, not of the logical understanding—I would silently change the venue, and bring on the trial before this latter tribunal somewhat as follows:—

"Dr. B. says that the trinity is involved in the process

of revelation—that the Absolute Being becomes Father Son, and Holy Ghost, in the way of communicating himself to knowledge. God, then, is really One, and apparently Three; that is, the trinity is a false appearance!

God, also, is an impassible being. Christ suffers. If, then, Christ is God, it follows that he suffers only in appearance; that is, that his suffering is a false appearance!

In the great work of redemption, the Father is the Son whom he sends—the Son, the Father who sent him. Being both Father and Son, he prays to himself, submits to his own will, offers an atonement to himself, and ascends, at last, to his own bosom, to gather in those whom he gave to himself, before the world began!

Meantime, as God cannot die, there is really no death in the case; it is all a vain show!

And, again, as Christ is not the Absolute God, save in a representative sense, God is really not in the transaction any where. It is a transaction of nobody, or rather between three nobodies!"

"A most legitimate answer! a most rigid and fatal refutation!" I suppose many will say, "of the whole doctrine of my 'Discourses.'" Very well, be it so. Then it is, at least, clear that I know how to reason correctly. Be it so, I say, but if only I can get my readers to go down with me into the real view of my 'Discourses,' and of this 'Preliminary Dissertation,' I am quite willing to risk their opinion of the puerility and shallowness of all such constructive sophistries.

Or, if still they seem to be true and legitimate arguments, I will simply ask it of my reader—(1.) To invent some method by which the Infinite and Absolute can appear in the finite, or the forms of the finite, without involving all the logical absurdities here perceived. (2.) To observe that all the terms of language, applied to matters of thought and spirit, involved originally the same contradictious results, and do so now to a very considerable extent, only in a more latent manner. (3.) To notice that there may be solid, living, really consistent truth in the views I have offered, considering the trinity and atonement as addressed to feeling and imagination, when, considered as addressed to logic, there is only absurdity and confusion in them. (4.) To notice that the more common orthodox views of trinity and atonement, if any one can settle what they are, involve all the contrarieties and absurdities just set forth, with the disadvantage, that being held as truths of dogma, the absurdities and contrarieties are real, and suffer no explication.

And here, exactly, is the field in which Unitarianism has luxuriated. It had everything made ready; it was called for, sent for, to come up from the vasty deep, or somewhere else, and clear away this dialectic rubbish and confusion.

It began by saying, what is quite intelligible—that one is one, and three are three. If, then, the Father, Son, and Holy Ghost are each God in himself, and all God together, then there must, of necessity, be two sorts of Gods; one sort, or grade, (of which there are three,) that consist of a single person each; another sort or grade (of which there is but one,) that consists of three persons—three Gods who are *Dei simplices*—one God who is *Deus triplex.* We have, then, two sorts of God, and four Gods—a real quaternity, instead of a trinity of persons!

It would seem, too, that if the Father sends the Son, hears the Son, raises the Son, and both dispense the Spirit, there is a very marked subordination of one God, in the first class, to another; that is, of one *Deus simplex* to another. And, if so, the four Gods are all very distinct Beings in nature, scope, and order—as distinct as Cæsar, Pompey, Crassus, and the Triumvirate!

But, instead of this, the actual supremacy of each and all is strenuously asserted as a radical test of orthodoxy. Then, as the Father sends the Son, God (the Supreme,) sends God (the Supreme,) and, in the same manner, God atones before God, God prays to God, God submits to God, God ascends to God. God also suffers, and God dies!

But, to escape these absurdities, the Son empties himself, it is said, of his proper majesty and glory. This can be understood if it only mean that he does an act of condescension. But if it be supposed to mean that he empties himself of his *real nature,* as the essentially Supreme Being, it follows that he is no longer God—we know not what he is. Where, meantime, is that part of his nature that he has put away; where, in what constellation or third heaven is this grand deposit of infinity and deity laid by!

It is also said, to escape the same difficulties, that the human nature only of Jesus suffers, prays, and dies. Then, in this matter of atonement, there is no real implication of deity at all; it is only appearance, and if more is pretended, false appearance! After all, the atonement is made only by the man Jesus! The man Jesus turns away from the God in whose very person he is, as if that person were not, to pray to the Father—prays to him out of the Son, as Jonah to the Lord his God, from the heart of the sea—appeals, in fact, from the God who has taken possession of his humanity, to a God who has not! So the man Jesus suffers and dies, and the suffering and death really touch not the Son. It is only so arranged that the Son is in *local* proximity, cohabiting in the same tenement, while, in reality, he has nothing more to do with the fortunes of the man Jesus, than if he were beyond the Pleiades—unless it be that he implicates the man in griefs and disasters which do not reach himself! To offer, therefore, what the man only suffers, as a proof or expression of his own compassion, is only to blind the world's perceptions under pretext of winning its love!

Now, by this kind of argumentation, which is perfectly legitimate, as against our common orthodoxy, because it is in the logical method of orthodoxy, but which, to me and as against me, has no substance or verity whatever—by this I say, it is that Unitarianism is ever at work to clear away what it calls the scholastic rubbish and absurdity of past ages, and reduce the Christian truth to some less offensive and more credible shape. Thus emerges a new liberal theology—very simple, perfectly comprehensible, never difficult, a last fruit of reason, a completed model of— inefficiency, perhaps time will say, and therefore I will not anticipate the verdict.

If, now, we wish to be clear of scripture, made into logical jargon on one side, and unmade or emptied of divinity and grandeur on the other, I know no better method than to accept these great truths of trinity and atonement as realities or verities addressed to faith: or, what is not far different, to feeling and imaginative reason—not any more as logical and metaphysical entities, for the natural understanding. If any one can show me a better way, I am quite willing to embrace it.

It has been customary, as all theologians know, to allow a wide range of liberty, under these doctrines of trinity and atonement. The essential matter seems to be that some trinity shall be held, such as will answer the practical uses of the life, and bring God into a lively, glowing, manifold power over the inner man—Father, Son, Holy Ghost, historically three, and also really one; —some scheme of atonement that upholds law, as eternal verity and sanctity; delivering still from bondage under it, and writing it as a law of liberty in the heart. I am not aware that I have transcended the limits of sufferance or pardon in regard to either of these doctrines, though I should not hesitate to do it if the truth required. As regards the latter, in reference to which I seem to have excited the most of apprehension, my only sin appears to be, that I have discovered so much *more* in the work of Christ than our common forensic theory of justification presents, that the real equivalent I have given for this latter is thrown into shade.

Thirteen or fourteen years ago, Professor Stuart translated and published, in the Biblical Repository, a translation of Schleiermacher's critique on Sabellius, adding copious remarks of his own. The general view of the trinity given in that article coincides, it will be discovered, with the view I have presented; though the reasonings are not, in all points, the same. I was greatly obliged to Professor S. for giving it to the public, and not the less because it confirmed me in results to which I had come by my own private struggles. That article, I believe, awakened no jealousy or uneasiness on account of his orthodoxy, although it was frankly intimated by the Professor that it had given him new light, and changed the complexion of his own views. He sought, indeed, to throw in a modification of Schleiermacher's view, which seemed to him to be important, viz: that while "the names, Father, Son, and Holy Ghost, seem to be given, principally in reference to the *revelation of God in these characters*," "there was, from eternity, such a distinction in the nature of the Godhead, as would certainly lead to the *development of it*, as Father, Son, and Holy Ghost."—*Bib. Rep.* vol. vi. p. 108.

Doubtless there is some reason or ground in the Godhead, or in God, for every thing developed out of Him in time, whether it be a stone or a fly. And if that is what the Professor means by the word "*distinction*," I certainly agree. But if the word means something more—if it means that the names, Father, Son, and Holy Ghost, are incidental to the process of "revelation," and yet referable to some equivalent distinction back of it, then Schleiermacher's opinion seems to be both accepted and rejected; for if, supposing the strict simplicity of God, it is still discovered that His revelation will involve a threefold impersonation, then to imagine that this latter indicates a threefold distinction in His nature, as its ground, is, in fact, to abandon, or, by an inverse proceeding, to overthrow the solution accepted. I have said what is a little different, but certainly not more remote from orthodoxy, viz: that Father, Son, and Holy Ghost, being incidental to the revelation of God, may be and probably are, from eternity and to eternity, inasmuch as God may have revealed Himself from eternity, and certainly will reveal Himself as long as there are minds to know Him. It may be, in fact, the nature of God to reveal Himself, as truly as it is of the sun to shine, or of living mind to think.

I am well aware that the exhibition I have made of the atonement is not apprehended with as great facility as could be desired, and I think we have some reason to admit that the exhibitions of Paul and of John are open to the same objection, if it be an objection; for how else have good men been obliged to spend so much of toil on their representations, with results so unequal and diverse? The difficulty, however, belongs rather to the greatness of the subject; drawing into view, as it does, all the relations of God on one part and man on the other; involving the deepest questions and profoundest mysteries of the moral government of God.

I suppose it may require a little effort on the part of those who are not versed in such forms of statement, to apprehend the precise import of the double view I have given—the subjective and objective view, one as equivalent to the other—but, when it is apprehended, I think it will be found to offer a comprehensive and satisfactory conception of the whole subject. In this confidence, I venture to ask it of the reader that he will exercise a little patience with me here, and be willing to turn himself about in such tentative efforts as may be necessary, till he comes into the stand-point I hold. Since this discourse was delivered, my attention has been called to Neander's volume on the "Planting and Training of the Church," where I find also a subjective and objective view maintained, as belonging to the true conception of the Pauline theology. I take pleasure in referring the reader to so high an authority. Indeed, I could wish that all who design to investigate these subjects, would make a study of the very able expositions he has here given of the character, stand-point and Christian doctrine of each of the apostles—the more so, that I am able so generally to concur with his views.

It was regarded by some, I believe, as a defect of my 'Discourse,' at Andover, that I did not make the distinction between "spirit" and "dogma" more clear. I have endeavored to do so. But I submit whether it is exactly reasonable to require of me that I shall clear the apostle Paul in the very deliberate statements he has given of this distinction, in both his epistles to the Corinthians. Is it more reasonable to require of me that I shall perfectly settle a distinction which no intelligent Christian has doubted since the relations of Faith and Knowledge [*Pistis* and *Gnosis*] began to be discussed, but which no one before me has been able to state so exactly as to exclude ambiguity?

It has been intimated to me, that what I said in reference to the Apostles' Creed, is grounded in a false assumption; the German critics having shown that this creed was really produced subsequently to the Nicene. But what have not the German critics shown? I have not investigated this question, farther than simply to refer to the authorities at hand in my own library; for this is one of those questions where the evidence of inspection suffices, and without any other and against all other, I am quite willing to risk the affirmation, that the Apostles' Creed is not of a date subsequent to the Nicene. It is not, for the very sufficient reason that it could not be. The phrase "descended into hell" is known to have been added at a later date;—it wears, in fact, a post-Nicene look—but the other parts of the document appear to have been gradually collected in the first and second centuries.

It is proper to add that I have taken the liberty to re-cast this latter 'Discourse,' which had been somewhat hastily prepared, and that I have so far modified its form as even to vary a little the import of the subject.

Some persons anticipate, I perceive, in the publication of these 'Discourses,' the opening of another great religious controversy. There may be such a controversy, but I really do not see whence it is to come; for, as regards myself, I am quite resolved that I will be drawn to no reply, unless there is produced against me some argument of so great force that I feel myself required, out of simple duty to the truth, either to surrender, or to make important modifications in the views I have advanced.

I anticipate, of course, no such necessity, though I do anticipate that arguments and reviews, very much in the character of that which I just now gave myself, will be advanced—such as will show off my absurdities in a very glaring light, and such as many persons of acknowledged character will accept with applause, as conclusive, or even explosive refutations. Therefore, I advertise it beforehand, to prevent a misconstruction of my silence, that I am silenced now, on the publication of my volume. It has been a question whether my duty to the truth would suffer the taking of this ground; but I have come to the opinion that replications are generally of little use, and that, though the truth may be somewhat hindered or retarded by adverse criticism, it will yet break through at last, unassisted, and have its triumph. Furthermore, the truths here uttered are not mine. They live in their own majesty. Ought I not, therefore, to believe that going forth in silence, having time on their side, and God in company, they will open their way, even the more securely, the less of human bustle and tumult is made in their behalf.

This it is my happiness to think. Therefore I drop them into the world, leaving them to care for themselves, and assert their own power. If they create disturbance, I hope it may be a salutary disturbance. If they are received, and find advocates ready to assert them, as I do myself, out of simple reverence to the truth, I shall rejoice. If they are rejected universally, then I leave them to time, as the body of Christ was left, believing that after three days they will rise again. For there is most assuredly to be a time, when the apostolic spirit of religion will be restored, and resume its sway in the world; when our narrow and restrictive dogmas, our forms of opinion elevated into measures of piety, our low views of faith, and our legal, uninspired charities—in a word, the huge piles of wood, hay, and stubble, we have accumulated, will be burned up in the original fires of the apostolic age, re-kindled in the church. And in the restored simplicity, the enlarged union, the quickened and quickening life of that day, which I hope may not be distant, it may possibly be found that views, such I have here offered, have more of the Christian spirit and power, than many are now able to believe.

CONCIO AD CLERUM:

A

DISCOURSE

ON THE

DIVINITY OF CHRIST;

DELIVERED AT THE

ANNUAL COMMENCEMENT OF YALE COLLEGE.

AUGUST 15, 1848.

THE DIVINITY OF CHRIST.

It is laid upon me, by the General Association of Connecticut, to discuss before you, this evening, the Divinity of Christ—a duty which I most willingly undertake, because I think the time has now come when a re-investigation of the subject will be more likely than at any former period, to issue in a practical settlement, or approach to settlement, of the questions involved. It will be understood, in this discussion, that I speak *ad clerum,* and not *ad populum.* I am not of course responsible for the difficulty of the subject, as I am not for the subject itself. I am only responsible for the thoroughness of the argument; a responsibility which I must endeavor to meet as best I am able. And if the reasonings necessary to a sufficient exhibition of the subject are sometimes remote or distant from the range of popular thought, I must not therefore withhold. On the contrary, I must yield to the high necessities of the subject, and regard nothing else; least of all, any desire I might feel to accommodate the ease and patience of my audience. However, I will endeavor to make the argument as simple and clear as I am able—only reminding you that the subject we investigate is God's own nature; which, to say nothing of ease or the entertainment of a leisure hour, it were the greatest presumption in me, and the greatest levity in you, to suppose it possible, by any human argument, to render even comprehensible. God exceeds our measure, and must, until either He becomes less than infinite or we more than finite. If we can apprehend Him so as to be clear of distraction, and of terms that are absolutely cross to faith itself, it is all that can be hoped.

The text that I have chosen for my theme, is :—

1 John i. 2.—"*For the Life was manifested, and we have seen it, and bear witness, and shew unto you that Eternal Life which was with the Father, and was manifested unto us.*"

If we raise the question whether Christ is divine, or only a mere human person appearing in his proper humanity, this passage of scripture furnishes the simplest and most beautiful answer that can be given in words It declares that Christ was a manifestation of the Life of God, that Eternal Life that was with the Father before the manifestation. Accordingly, we are to see, in the language, not merely that the reality of Christ is God, but we have an indication in the term *was manifested* of that which is the real end of his mission, and the proper solvent of whatever inquiries may be started by his person as appearing in the flesh, or under the historic conditions of humanity. In this view, my whole discourse will only be a development of the text, and therefore I need not stay upon it longer.

By the *divinity* of Christ, I do not understand simply

that Christ differs from other men, in the sense that he is better, more inspired, and so a more complete vehicle of God to the world than others have been. He differs from us, not in degree, but in kind; as the half divine parentage under which he enters the world most certainly indicates. He is in such a sense God, or God manifested, that the unknown term of his nature, that which we are most in doubt of, and about which we are least capable of any positive affirmation, is the human. No person, I think, would ever doubt for a moment, the superhuman quality of Jesus, if it were not for the speculative difficulties encountered by an acknowledgment of his superhuman quality. Instead, therefore, of placing the main stress of my discourse on the direct argument for Christ's divinity, I shall barely name or catalogue a few of the proofs, and then proceed to the difficulties raised by such a view of his person. I allege,—

1. What is said of his pre-existence. "I came out from God." "I came forth from the Father, and am come into the world." "I came down from heaven." "Ye are from beneath, I am from above." "The glory which I had with thee before the world was." If these passages do not affirm the pre-existence of Christ in the plainest manner conceivable, I mistake their import. And, in this view, they are totally repugnant to the idea of Christ's simple humanity.

2. The miraculous birth of Christ is either a fable, or else it denotes the entrance into humanity of something that is distinct from it. This argument holds only with those who admit the truth of the history—a question which cannot be argued here. I will only say that this

event of history, so flippantly rejected by some, has, to me, the profoundest air of verity; setting forth, as it does, in the most artless form, that which corresponds philosophically with the doctrine of a divine incarnation elsewhere advanced. If God were ever to be incarnate in the world, in what other manner, so natural, beautiful, and real, could He enter into the life of the race?

3. The incarnation itself plainly asserted. "The Word was made flesh." "That which we have seen with our eyes, which we have looked upon, which our hands have handled of the word of Life." "He that was in the form of God, and was made in fashion as a man." Who can imagine, without great violence, that language of this nature is applicable to any mere man? To make it even supportable, the man, so called, must be different from all other men, to such a degree that you may far more easily doubt his humanity than his divinity.

4. What is said of the import, or the contents of his person, in passages like these: "In whom dwelt all the fullness of the Godhead bodily." "The church which is his body, the fullness of Him that is all in all." "The express image of His person." "The image of the invisible God." "Complete in Him which is the Head of all principality and power." How expressions of this nature, transcending so manifestly all human measures, can yet be interpreted so as to consist with the simple humanity of Jesus, I willingly confess my inability to conceive.

5. What Christ himself declares concerning his relations to the Father. "I and the Father that sent me." "Ye neither know me nor my Father." "That which I

have seen with my Father." "The Father is in me and I in him." "He that hath seen me hath seen the Father." How can we imagine any mere man of our race daring to use language like this concerning himself and God? Nay, he even goes beyond any one of the expressions here cited. He has the audacity (for what else can we call it, regarding him simply as a man?) to promise that he and the Father—they two—will come to men together, and be spiritually manifest in them—"WE will come unto him and make OUR abode with him."

6. The negatives he uses concerning himself, as related to the Father, are even more convincing still, if possible. Thus, when he says—"my Father is greater than I,"—how preposterous for any mere human being of our race to be gravely telling the world that God is greater than he is! So, also, it is often argued from those numerous expressions of Christ, in which he calls himself the "Son of Man," that he there concedes his humanity. Undoubtedly he does, (for he does not appear to use the language in the lighter significance of the old prophets,) but what kind of being is this who is *conceding* his humanity? Could there be displayed, by any human creature, a bolder stretch of presumption than to declare that God is superior to him, or to call himself "the Son of Man" by condescension?

7. Christ assumes a relation to the world which is most offensive, on the supposition that he is a merely human being. Nor does it mitigate, in the least, the egregious want of modesty displayed in his attitude, to say that he was specially inspired; for, in all other cases, the inspiration of the man has made him humbler in spirit than he

was before—made him even to sigh before the purity of God—"Woe is me, for I am a man of unclean lips!" Imagine, now, a human being, one of ourselves, coming forth and declaring to the race—"I am the light of the world." "I am the way, the truth, and the life." "I am the living bread that came down from heaven." "No man cometh unto the Father but by me." What greater effrontery could be conceived?

8. Christ assumes his own sinlessness, saying—"which of you convinceth me of sin?"—never confessing a fault, never asking pardon for any transgression. His sinlessness, too, is generally conceded by those who hold his simple humanity. But what is it to be human, but to have a tentative nature—one that learns the import of things, and especially of good and evil by experiment? Accordingly, if the man Jesus never makes the experiment of sin, it must be because the divine is so far uppermost in him as to suspend the proper manhood of his person. He does not any longer act the man; practically speaking, the man sleeps in him. It is as if the man were not there, and, judging only from the sinlessness of his life, we should make no account of the human element in his nature. He acts the divine, not the human, and the only true reality in him, as far as moral conduct is concerned, is the divine. Set in connection with this conclusion, the universal unqualified determination of the race never to believe in a perfect man—always to assume the fallibility and imperfection of every human being—and the sinlessness of Jesus becomes, itself, a stubborn evidence of his superhuman character.

9. We want Jesus as divine, not as human; least of

all, do we want Him as the human, still out of humanity and above it, as held by many Unitarians. It is God that we want, to know Him, to be near Him, to have His feeling unbosomed to us. As to the real human, we have enough of that. And, as to the unreal, superhuman human, that is, the human acted wholly by the divine, so as to have no action of its own, save in pretence, what is it to us but a mockery? What can we learn from it? True, we may draw from it the ideal of a beautiful and sinless life, and, in that, there may be a certain power. Still, it is an ideal, presented or conceived only to be despaired of. For this beautiful life, being sinless, is really not human, after all; and *we* cannot have it, unless our nature is overborne and acted wholly by God in the same manner which, alas! is no longer possible, for we are deep in sin already. No! let us have the divine, the deific itself—the very feeling of God, God's own beauty, truth, and love. Then we shall have both the pure ideal of a life, and a power flowing out from God to ingenerate that life in us. God; God is what we want, not a man; God, revealed through man, that we may see His Heart, and hide our guilty nature in the bosom of His love: God so identified with our race, as to signify the possible union and eternal identification of our nature with His.

10. As a last evidence on this subject, and one that, in my view, winds up all debate, I add, the holy formula of baptism—"into the name of the Father, Son, and Holy Ghost." That the Father is God, is conceded, so, also, that the Spirit is God, and then, between these terms on either hand, we have, dropped in, "*the Son*,"—a

man, we are told, a mere human creature, who is one of ourselves! This, too, in a solemn formula that is appointed for the consecration of a believing soul to God. I am well aware that one or two passages are cited to countenance this very harsh construction, but they are not parallel. If we read, for example—" to the general assembly and church of the first born, and to God the judge of all, and to the spirits of just men made perfect, and to Jesus, the mediator of the new covenant,"—this is only a case of mixed rhetoric, produced, in part, by the order of ideas. But, in this baptismal formula, we have nothing but a mere collocation of names, and one that suffers no dignified, or endurable construction, unless each term is taken to import the real divinity of the subject. It appears evident to me, that our Unitarian brethren impose upon themselves, in the construction they give to this formula, by collecting about the person of Christ associations that do not belong to his proper humanity—associations which really belong to our view of his person, not to theirs. Were they to read—" in the name of the Father, A. B. the carpenter, and the Holy Ghost," they would be sensible, I think, of some very great violence done to the words by any construction which holds the strict humanity of Christ.

Indeed, it has always seemed to me that any attempt to get away from the proper divinity of Christ, as held in this formula, must be taken to proceed from a most disingenuous spirit; were it not that the practical difficulties thrown upon the souls of men, the bewilderment they have suffered, the confusion that has enveloped their religious nature, under our supposed orthodox views of the trinity, may have created such a necessity as must be allowed to excuse almost any kind of violence. And, were it not for this, I do not believe that any reader of the New Testament, least of all, any true believer in it, would ever have questioned, for a moment, the real divinity of Christ. In fact, it never was seriously questioned until after the easy and free representations of the scripture and of the apostolic fathers had been hardened into dogma, or converted by the Nicene theologues and those of the subsequent ages, into a doctrine of the mere human understanding; an assertion of three metaphysical persons in the divine nature. I do not say that such a mistake must not have been committed. And then, when a trinity of this kind was once inaugurated, it was equally necessary that speculation should rise up, sometime or other, to clear away the rubbish that speculation had accumulated. A metaphysical trinity must be assaulted by a metaphysical unity. And then, coming after both, and taking up the suspicion that, possibly, dogma is not the whole wisdom of man; seeing, in fact, that it is wholly incompetent to represent the living truths of Christianity, we may be induced to let go a trinity that mocks our reason, and a unity that freezes our hearts, and return to the simple Father, Son, and Holy Ghost of the scriptures and the Apostolic Fathers; there to rest in the living and life-giving forms of the spirit. To this, it is my design, if possible, to bring you; for, in maintaining the essential divinity of Christ, there is no difficulty whatever, till we begin to speculate or dogmatize about the humanity, or find ourselves in contact with the more commonly accepted doctrine of trinity.

I speak of the more commonly accepted doctrine. What that doctrine is, I am well aware it would be exceedingly difficult to state. Let us pause here, a moment, and see if we can find our way to any proximate conception of it.

It seems to be agreed by the orthodox, that there are three persons, Father, Son, and Holy Ghost, in the divine nature. These three persons, too, are generally regarded as belonging, not to the *machina Dei,* by which God is revealed, but to the very *esse,* the substantial being of God, or the interior contents of His being. They are declared to be equal; all to be infinite; all to be the same in substance; all to be one. But, as soon as the question is raised, what are we to intend by the word *person,* the appearance of agreement, and often of self-understanding, vanishes.

A very large portion of the Christian teachers, together with the general mass of disciples, undoubtedly hold three real living persons in the interior nature of God; that is, three consciousnesses, wills, hearts, understandings. Certain passages of scripture supposed to represent the three persons as covenanting, co-operating, and co-presiding, are taken, accordingly, so to affirm, in the most literal and dogmatic sense. And some very distinguished living teachers are frank enough to acknowledge, that any intermediate doctrine, between the absolute unity of God and a social unity, is impossible and incredible; therefore, that they take the latter. Accordingly, Father,

Son, and Holy Ghost, are, in their view, socially united only, and preside in that way, as a kind of celestial tritheocracy over the world. They are one God simply in the sense that the three will always act together, with a perfect consent, or coincidence. This view has the merit that it takes consequences fairly, states them frankly, and boldly renounces orthodoxy, at the point opposite to Unitarianism, to escape the same difficulties. It denies that the three persons are "the *same* in substance," and asserts instead, three substances; and yet, because of its clear opposition to Unitarianism, it is counted safe, and never treated as a heresy. However, when it is applied to Christ and his work, then it breaks down into the same confusion as the more common view, reducing the Son to a really subordinate and subject position, in which the proper attributes of deity are no longer visible or supposable.

But our properly orthodox teachers and churches, while professing three persons, also retain the verbal profession of one person. They suppose themselves really to hold that God is one person. And yet they most certainly do not; they only confuse their understanding, and call their confusion faith. This, I affirm, not as speaking reproachfully, but, as I suppose, on the ground of sufficient evidence—partly because it cannot be otherwise, and partly because it visibly is not.

No man can assert three persons, meaning three consciousnesses, wills, and understandings, and still have any intelligent meaning in his mind, when he asserts that they are yet one person. For, as he now uses the term, the very idea of a person is that of an essential, incommunicable monad, bounded by consciousness, and vitalized by self-active will, which being true, he might as wel. profess to hold that three units are yet one unit. When he does it, his words will, of necessity, be only substitutes for sense.

At the same time, there are too many signs of the mental confusion I speak of, not to believe that it exists. Thus, if the class I speak of were to hear a discourse insisting on the proper personal unity of God, it would awaken suspicion in their minds; while a discourse insisting on the existence of three persons, would be only a certain proof of orthodoxy; showing that they profess three persons, meaning what they profess, and one person, really not meaning it.

Methods are also resorted to, in the way of explaining God's oneness in consistency with His existence in three persons, which show that His real oneness, as a spirit, is virtually lost. Thus it will sometimes be represented, that the three persons are three sets of attributes inhering in a common substance; in which method, the three intelligences come to their unity in a virtually inorganic ground; for if the substance supposed, be itself of a vital quality, a Life, then we have only more difficulties on hand, and not fewer; viz., to conceive a Living Person having in Himself, first, the attributes of a person, and secondly, three more persons who are attributes, in the second degree,—that is, attributes of attributes. It can hardly be supposed that any such monster is intended, in the way of bringing the three persons into unity; therefore, taking the "substance" as inorganic, we have three vital personal Gods, and back of them, or under them as their ground of unity, an Inorganic Deity. I make no objection here to the supposition, that the persons are mere attributes of a substance not themselves; I ask not how attributes can be real enough to make persons, and not real enough to make substances; I urge it not as an objection, that our very idea of person, as the word is here used, is that of a living substance manifested through attributes—itself the most real and substantial thing to thought in the universe of God—I only call attention to the fact that this theory of divine unity, making it essentially inorganic, indicates such a holding of the three persons as virtually leaves no unity at all, which is more distinct than a profession of mental confusion on the subject.

But, while the unity is thus confused and lost in the threeness, perhaps I should also admit that the threeness sometimes appears to be clouded or obscured by the unity. Thus, it is sometimes protested that, in the word *person*, nothing is meant beyond a "threefold distinction;" though it will always be observed that, nothing is really meant by the protestation—that the protester goes on to speak and reason of the three, not as being only somewhats, or distinctions, but as metaphysical and real persons. Or, the three are sometimes compared, in their union, to the soul, the life principle and the body united in one person called a man—an illustration, which, if it has any point or appositeness, at all, shows how God may be one and not three; for the life and the body are not persons. Or, if the soul be itself the life, and the body its external development, which is possible, then, in a yet stricter sense, there is but one person in them all.

12

Probably there is a degree of alternation, or inclining from one side to the other, in this view of trinity, as the mind struggles, now to embrace one, and now the other of two incompatible notions. Some persons are more habitually inclined to hold the three; a very much smaller number to hold the one. Meantime, and especially in the former class of those who range themselves under this view of metaphysical tripersonality, mournful evidence will be found that a confused and painfully bewildered state is often produced by it. They are practically at work, in their thoughts, to choose between the three; sometimes actually and decidedly preferring one to another; doubting how to adjust their mind in worship; uncertain, often, which of the three to obey; turning away, possibly, from one in a feeling of dread that might well be called aversion; devoting themselves to another, as the Romanist to his patron saint. This, in fact, is polytheism, and not the clear, simple love of God. There is true love in it, doubtless, but the comfort of love is not here. The mind is involved in a dismal confusion, which we cannot think of without the sincerest pity. No soul can truly rest in God, when God is two or three, and these in such a sense that a choice between them must be continually suggested.

Besides, it is another source of mental confusion, connected with this view of three metaphysical persons, that, though they are all declared to be infinite and equal, they really are not so. The proper deity of Christ is not held in this view. He is begotten, sent, supported, directed, by the Father, in such a sense as really annihilates his deity. This has been shown in a truly searching and convincing manner by Schleiermacher, in his historical essay on the trinity. And, indeed, you will see, at a glance, that this view of a metaphysical trinity of persons, breaks down in the very point which is commonly regarded as its excellence—its assertion of the proper deity of Christ.

Indeed, it is a somewhat curious fact in theology, that the class of teachers who protest over the word *person,* declaring that they mean only a *threefold distinction,* cannot show that there is really a hair's-breadth of difference between their doctrine and the doctrine asserted by many of the later Unitarians. They may teach or preach in a very different manner,—they probably do, but the theoretic contents of their opinion cannot be distinguished. Thus, they say that there is a certain divine person in the man Christ Jesus, but that when they use the term *person,* they mean not a person, but a certain indefinite and indefinable distinction. The later Unitarians, meantime, are found asserting that God is present in Christ, in a mysterious and peculiar communication of His being, so that he is the living embodiment and express image of God. If, now, the question be raised, wherein does the indefinable *distinction* of one, differ from the mysterious and peculiar *communication* of the other, or how does it appear that there is any difference, there is no living man, I am quite sure, who can invent an answer.

Such is the confusion produced by attempting to assert a real and metaphysical trinity of persons in the divine nature. Whether the word is taken at its full import, or diminished away to a mere something called a distinction, there is produced only contrariety, confusion, practical negation, not light.

And now the question comes upon us—how shall we resolve the divinity or deity of Christ, already proved, so as to make it consist with the proper unity of God? To state the question as boldly and definitely as possible, we have two terms before us. First, we have the essential unity and supremacy of God. This we are to assume. I am willing to assume it without argument. Indeed, there is no place for argument; for if any one will say that he believes in three metaphysical or essential persons in the being of God, there is no argument that can set him in a more unsatisfactory position, whether intellectually or practically, than he takes himself. Or if any one endeavors to relieve his position, by declaring that he only means distinctions by the word *persons*, he then flies into darkness and negation for his comfort, and there he may safely be left. We take, then, as a first point, to be held immovably, the strict personal unity of God—one mind, will, consciousness. Then, secondly, we have, as a term to be reconciled with this, the three of scripture, and the living person walking the earth, in the human form, called Jesus Christ—a subject, suffering being, whose highest and truest reality is that he is God. Such is the work we have on hand, and it must be performed so as to justify the language of scripture, and be clear of any real absurdity.

To indicate, beforehand, the general tenor of my argument, which may assist you to apprehend the matter of it more easily, I here suggest that the trinity we seek will be a trinity that results of necessity from the *revelation* of God to man. I do not undertake to fathom the interior being of God, and tell how it is composed. That is a matter too high for me, and, I think, for us all. I only insist that, assuming the strictest unity and even simplicity of God's nature, He could not be efficiently or sufficiently revealed to us, without evolving a trinity of persons, such as we meet in the scriptures. These persons or personalities are the *dramatis personæ* of revelation, and their reality is measured by what of the infinite they convey in these finite forms. As such, they bear, on the one hand, a relation to God, who is to be conveyed or imported into knowledge; on the other, they are related to our human capacities and wants, being that presentation of God which is necessary to make Him a subject of thought, or bring Him within the discourse of reason; that also which is necessary to produce mutuality, or terms of conversableness, between us and Him, and pour His love most effectually into our feeling.

To bring the whole subject fully before us, let us endeavor, first of all, to form the distinctest notion possible of God, as existing in Himself, and unrevealed. Then we shall understand, the better, what is necessary to reveal Him. Of course we mean, when we speak of God as unrevealed, to speak of Him anterior to His act of creation; for the worlds created are all outgoings from Himself, and in that view, revealments of Him. God unrevealed is God simply existing, as spirit, in Himself.

Who, now, is God thus existing in Himself? Has He any external form, by which He may be figured or conceived? No. Is He a point without space—is He space without limit? Neither. Is His activity connected with any sort of motion? Certainly not; motion belongs to a finite creature ranging in the infinite. Is there any color, sound, sign, measure, by which He may be known? No. He dwells in eternal silence, without parts, above time. If, then, we can apprehend Him by nothing outward, let us consider, as we may without irreverence, things of a more interior quality in His being. Does He, then, act under the law of action and reaction, as we do? Never. This, in fact, is the very notion of absolute being and power, that it acts without reaction, requiring no supports, living between no contrasts or antagonisms. He simply IS, which contains everything. Does He, then, reason? No; for to reason in the active sense, as deducing one thing from another, implies a want of knowledge. Does He, then, deliberate? No; for He sees all conclusions without deliberation, intuitively. Does He inquire? No; for He knows all things already. Does He remember? Never; for to remember is to call up what was out of mind, and nothing is out of mind. Does He believe? No; the virtue that He exercises is a virtue without faith, and radically distinct, in that view, from anything called virtue in us. Where, then, is God? by what searching shall we find Him out? by what sign is He to be known or conceived? Does He think? No, never, in any human sense of the term; for thought, with us, is only a finite activity under the law of succession and time; and besides this, we have no other conception of it. Has He new emotions rising up, which, if we could see them rise, would show us that He is? No; emotion, according to our human sense, is a mere jet of feeling—one feeling moving out just now into the foreground before others; and this can be true only of a finite nature. God, in such a sense, certainly, has no emotions.

What, then, shall we say; what conception form of God as simply existing in Himself, and as yet unrevealed? Only that He is the Absolute Being—the Infinite—the I Am that I am, giving no sign that He is, other than that He is.

"A very unsatisfactory, unpleasant, unsignificant, and practically untrue representation of God," you will say. Exactly so! that is the point I wish to be discovered. And without a trinity, and incarnation, and other like devices of revelation, we should never have a better.

Having now come down hither, as it were, upon the shore of the Absolute—that Absolute which has no shore—let us pause just here, a moment, and take note, distinctly, of two or three matters that will assist us to open what remains of our subject with a better intelligence. And

1. Observe that, when God is revealed, it cannot be as the One, as the Infinite, or Absolute, but only as through media. And as there are no infinite media, no signs that express the infinite, no minds, in fact, that can apprehend the infinite by direct inspection, the One must appear in the manifold; the Absolute in the conditional; Spirit in form; the Motionless in motion; the Infinite in the

finite. He must distribute Himself, He must let forth His nature in sounds, colors, forms, works, definite objects and signs. It must be to us as if Brama were waking up; as if Jehovah, the Infinite I am, the Absolute, were dividing off Himself into innumerable activities that shall dramatize His immensity, and bring Him within the molds of language and discursive thought. And in whatever thing He appears, or is revealed, there will be something that misrepresents, as well as something that represents Him. The revealing process, that which makes Him appear, will envelop itself in clouds of formal contradiction—that is, of diction which is contrary, in some way, to the truth, and which, taken simply as diction, is continually setting forms against each other.

Thus, the God revealed, in distinction from the God Absolute, will have parts, forms, colors, utterances, motions, activities, assigned Him. He will think, deliberate, reason, remember, have emotions. Then, taking up all these manifold representations, casting out the matter in which they are cross to each other, and repugnant to the very idea of the God they represent, we shall settle into the true knowledge of God, and receive, as far as the finite can receive the Infinite, the contents of the divine nature.

2. To make this same view yet more evident, observe that we ourselves being finite, under time and succession, reasoning, deliberating, thinking, remembering, having emotions, can never come into the knowledge of God, save as God is brought within our finite molds of action. There are certain absolute verities which belong to our

own nature, and which, therefore, we can know as absolute, or which, I should rather say, we must know. They are such as the ideas of space, cause, truth, right, and the axioms of mathematical science. But these are simple ideas, and have their reality in us. God is a Being out of us, a Being in whom the possibilities and even facts of all other being have their spring. Taken in this view, as the absolute, all-comprehensive being, we can know Him only *as* being; that is, by a revelation, or rather by revelations, giving out one after another, and in one way or another, but always in finite forms, something that belongs to the knowledge of God. And then we know God only as we bring all our knowledges together. Thus we approach the knowledge of the Absolute Being, and there is no other way possible, or even conceivable.

Or, let me give the same truth under yet another form. God, as the Absolute Being, is not under the law of action and reaction, as I have said. He does not compare, try contrasts, raise definitions, in order to know Himself. He has all the poles of self-knowledge in His consciousness, and knows Himself by an absolute, eternal, infinite, self-intuition. We, on the other hand, exist under the law of action and reaction, and our minds are worked under this law, as truly as our bodies. The only absolute knowledge we have, relates to the few necessary ideas just alluded to. As regards all matters of opinion, fact, being, we are obliged to get our knowledge under the law of action and reaction—through finites that are relative to each other, through antagonisms, contrasts, comparisons, interactions, counteractions. And yet in God, considered as Absolute, there are none of these. Therefore, to set our minds in action, or to generate in us a knowledge of Himself, He must produce Himself in finite forms; under the relations of space, as above and below, on this side and on that; by motion towards, involving motion from. For instance, the Saviour, in his exaltation, goes up, by a visible ascent, into the heavens. That is, motion from and motion towards indicate his divine exaltation. And yet, if he had parted from his disciples on the other side of the world, he would have moved in exactly the contrary direction. Now, the reality of the ascension, as we call it, is not the motion, but what the motion signifies, viz., the change of state. So, when we pray for the Holy Spirit, it is for the descent of the Holy Spirit—not that there is any descent or motion in the case; we only work our thought under the great law of action and reaction, which belongs to the finite quality of our nature.

It was under this principle, and no other, that the special economy of the Jewish state was appointed. The whole universe of God is a real and proper theocracy, but here a special theocracy is organized for the purpose of raising contrasts, and by that means revealing God, or making His sway apparent. God was the God of Egypt, Babylon and Philistia, as truly as of Israel. But in a uniform handling of these nations, dark and brutish as their minds at that time were, all would miss of perceiving Him,—He would be only a lost idea. Hence, for the benefit of all, that is, to make His sway apparent to all, He selects one people of the four, to receive a special discipline and have a special outward future dispensed to them. He is to be called their God, and they His people; and it is to be seen, by the victories He gives, and the wondrous deliverances He vouchsafes, how superior He is to the other gods of the nations. And so He will be known, at length, as the Great God and King above all gods. In one view, this special theocracy has a fictitious and even absurd look; for, when we scan the matter more deeply, we find that God reigns in Philistia as truly as in Israel, and the contrast raised is only God contrasted with Himself. Still the truth communicated through the contrast—viz., God, is the fundamental verity of the transaction, and the Jewish polity is only the means He appointed to make His power known, and disclose, to all, that broader and more comprehensive theocracy, which is the shelter, blessing, and joy of all.

The scripture writers, too, are continually working this figure of contrast, even setting God, if we compare their representations, in a kind of antagonism with Himself. Here, for example, is the great and broad sea—full of His goodness. Here it is a raging monster, whose proud and turbulent waves it is the glory of His majesty to hold in check. In one case, the sea represents Him. In the other, He is seen triumphing over His representative. Just so in the heavens, which, at one time, are His very garment; while at another, it is half His grandeur, that He sits upon the great circle above them, to mold and sway their motions.

Now it is in this manner only, through relations, contrasts, actions and reactions, that we come into the knowledge of God. As Absolute Being, we know Him not. But our mind, acted under the law of action and reaction, is carried up to Him, or thrown back upon Him, to apprehend Him more and more perfectly. Nothing that we see, or can see, represents Him fully, or can represent Him truly; for the finite cannot show us the Infinite. But between various finites, acting so as to correct each other, and be supplements to each other, we get a true knowledge. Our method may be compared to that of resultant motions in philosophy. No one finite thing represents the Absolute Being; but between two or more finite forces acting obliquely on our mind, it is driven out, in a resultant motion, towards the Infinite. Meantime, a part of the two finite forces, being oblique or false, is destroyed by the mutual counteraction of forces.

Under this same law, I suggest that we look for a solution of the trinity, and of the person of Jesus Christ. They are relatives, to conduct us up to the Absolute.

3. Observe that, when God is revealed, He will not, if He is truly and efficiently revealed, be cleared of obscurity and mystery. He will not be a bald, philosophic unity, perfectly comprehended and measured by us. We shall not have His boundaries, He will not be simple to us as a man is. When we have reduced Him to that, and call it our reason or philosophy, we have only gotten up a somewhat larger man than ourselves, and set this larger man in the place of the Absolute Being. And if we perfectly understand Him, if we have no questions about Him, the colder, and in real truth the more unknown He is—the Infinite revealed away, not revealed. No; if He is revealed at all, it will be through infinite

repugnances and contrarieties; through forms, colors, motions, words, persons, or personalities; all presenting themselves to our sense and feeling, to pour in something of the divine into our nature. And a vast circle of mystery will be the back ground of all other representations, on which they will play and glitter in living threads of motion, as lightning on a cloud; and what they themselves do not reveal of God, the mystery will—a Being infinite, undiscovered, undiscoverable, therefore true. But if we could see the last boundaries of God, and hold Him clear of a question within the molds of logic and cognition, then He is not God any longer, we have lost the conception of God.

Having noted these points, we shall be able, I trust, to advance more securely and with a clearer intelligence, in the development of our subject. We go back, now, to the Absolute Being, to consider by what process He will be revealed, and to see that revelation unfolded. And here I must bring to view a singular and eminent distinction of the Divine nature, without which He could never be revealed.

There is in God, taken as the Absolute Being, a capacity of self-expression, so to speak, which is peculiar—a generative power of form, a creative imagination, in which, or by aid of which, He can produce Himself outwardly, or represent Himself in the finite. In this respect, God is wholly unlike to us. Our imagination is passive, stored with forms, colors and types of words from without, borrowed from the world we live in. But all such forms, God has in Himself, and this is the Logos, the Word, elsewhere called the Form of God. Now, this

Word. this Form of God, in which He sees Himself, is with God, as John says, from the beginning. It is God mirrored before His own understanding, and to be mirrored, as in fragments of the mirror, before us. Conceive Him now as creating the worlds, or creating worlds, if you please, from eternity. In so doing, He only represents, expresses, or outwardly produces Himself. He bodies out His own thoughts. What we call the creation, is, in another view, a revelation only of God, His first revelation.

And it is in this view that the Word, or Logos, elsewhere called Christ, or the Son of God, is represented as he Creator of the worlds. Or it is said, which is only another form of the same truth, that the worlds were made by or through him, and the apostle John adds, that without Him, is not anything made that was made. Now, as John also declares, there was light, the first revelation was made, God was expressed in the forms and relations of the finite. But the light shined in darkness, and the darkness comprehended it not. The divine Word was here; he had come to his own, but his own received him not. One thing more is possible that will yield a still more effulgent light, viz: that, as God has produced Himself in all the other finite forms oi being, so now he should appear in the human.

Indeed, He has appeared in the human before, in the same way as He has in all the created objects of the world. The human person, taken as a mere structure, adapted to the high uses of intelligence and moral action, is itself a noble illustration of His wisdom, and a token also of the exalted and good purposes cherished in our existence. But there was yet more of God to be exhibited in the Human Form of our race. As the spirit of man is made in the image of God, and his bodily form is prepared to be the fit vehicle and outward representative of his spirit, it follows that his bodily form has also some inherent, *a priori* relation to God's own nature; such probably as makes it the truest, most expressive finite type of Him. Continuing, therefore, in a pure upright character, our whole race would have been a visible revelation of the truth and beauty of God. But having not thus continued, having come under the power of evil, that which was to be the expression, or reflection of God, became appropriated to the expression of evil. Truth has no longer any living unblemished manifestation in the world; the beauty of goodness lives and smiles no more. Sin, prejudice, passion,—stains of every color—so deface and mar the race, that the face of God, the real glory of the Divine, is visible no longer. Now, therefore, God will reclaim this last type of Himself, possess it with His own life and feeling, and through that, live Himself into the acquaintance and biographic history of the world. "And the word was made flesh, and dwelt among us; and we beheld his glory as of the only begotten of the Father, full of grace and truth." "The only begotten Son, which is in the bosom of the Father, he hath declared Him." This is Christ whose proper deity or divinity we have proved.

Prior to this moment, there has been no appearance of trinity in the revelations God has made of His being; but just here, whether as resulting from the incarnation or as implied in it, we are not informed, a three-fold personality or impersonation of God begins to offer itself to view. Just here, accordingly, as the revelation culminates or completes the fullness of its form, many are staggered and confused by difficulties which they say are contrary to reason—impossible therefore to faith. I think otherwise. In these three persons or impersonations I only see a revelation of the Absolute Being, under just such relatives as by their mutual play, in and before our imaginative sense, will produce in us the truest knowledge of God—render Him most conversable, bring Him closest to feeling, give Him the freest, least obstructed access, as a quickening power, to our hearts.

To verify this view of Christ, which is now my object, I must apply it as a solvent to the two classes of difficulties created by the incarnation:

I. To the difficulties created by the supposed relations of the divine to the human, in the person of Jesus.

II. To those which spring of the supposed relations of His divine person to the other divine persons, or impersonations developed in the process of revelation. Under the

I. The relations of the divine to the human, we meet the objection, first of all, that here is an incarnation asserted of the divine nature; that God, the infinite God, is represented as dwelling in a finite human person, subject to its limitations and even to its evils; and this is incredible—an insult to reason. It may be so, and if it is, we must reject the doctrine. But we notice, while revolving this objection, that several other religions have believed or expected an incarnation of their deity, or the divine principle of their worship; and that these have been the most speculative and cultivated forms of false religion. If, then, whole nations of mankind, comprising thinkers, scholars and philosophers, have been ready to expect, or have actually believed in the incarnation of their god or highest divinity, it would not seem to be wholly cross to natural reason to believe in such an event. On the contrary, we are rather to suspect that some true instinct or conscious want of the race is here divining, so to speak, that blessed visitation, by which God shall sometime vouchsafe to give Himself to the world.

Then, again, it was just now made to appear that the human person was originally and specially related to the expression of God, specially fitted to be the organ of the Divine feeling and character. It is also clear that if God were to inhabit such a vehicle, one so fellow to ourselves, and live Himself as a perfect character into the biographic history of the world, a result would follow of as great magnificence as the creation of the world itself, viz: the Incorporation of the Divine in the history of the world—so a renovation, at last, of the moral and religious life of the world. If, now, the human person will express more of God than the whole created universe beside, (and it certainly will more of God's feeling and character,) and if a motive possessing as great consequence as the creation of the world invites Him to do it, is it any more extravagant to believe that the Word will become flesh, than that the Word has become, or produced in time, a material universe? If so, I cannot see in what manner. Many persons, I know, do not believe that the world has been produced in time; and of course, the argument I state is not for them. But I am speaking, mostly, to such as have faith to believe that the worlds were made, and find no difficulty in believing in God as a Creator. And, if a miracle, a putting forth of God in time, so vast as this, is credible, why not a miracle also that has a necessity as deep, involves consequences of as great moment, and makes an expression of God as much lovelier and holier as it exhibits more of His moral excellence and grandeur—His condescension, patience, gentleness, forgiveness, in one word, His love?

I am speaking, also, to such as believe the scriptures; and, therefore, it should be something to notice that they often represent the Saviour in ways that indicate the same view of his person: He is Emanuel, God with us—the Word made flesh—God manifest in the flesh—the express image of his person—the Life that was manifested—the glass in which we look to behold the glory of the Lord—the fullness of God revealed bodily—the power of God—the light of the knowledge of the glory of God in the face of Jesus Christ—the image of the invisible God. In all these, and in a very great number of similar instances, language is used in reference to Christ, which indicates an opinion that his advent is the appearing of God; his deepest reality, that he expresses the fullness of the Life of God. Nor does it satisfy this language at all, to conceive that Christ is a good man, or a perfect man, and that so he is an illustration, or image of God. Such a construction might be given to a single expression of the kind; for we use occasionally an almost violent figure. But this is cool, ordinary, undeclamatory language, and the same idea is turned round and round, appears and reappears in different shapes, and becomes, in fact, the hinge of the gospel—the central light of the glorious gospel of Christ, who is the image of God, shining unto men. It should also be added that, probably, a very great share of the difficulties that compass this subject, were originally created by overlooking, or making no sufficient account of, the very class of representations here referred to; for we throw away all the solvents of the incarnation and the trinity that are given us, and then complain of our difficulties.

But the human person, it will be said, is limited, and God is not. Very true. But you have the same objection in reference to the first revelation, the Word in the world. This also is limited—at least what you have known of it is limited; besides, you have a special delight in seeing God in the smallest things, the minutest specks of being. If, then, it be incredible that God should take the human to express Himself, because the human is finite, can the finite in the world, or in a living atom, express Him more worthily, or do it more accordantly with reason?

But Christ, you will say, perhaps, is a living intelligent person. Taking him, therefore, as a person, I must view him under the measures and limitations of a person. Very true, if you have a right to measure the contents of his person by his body; which, possibly, you have no more right to do than you have to measure God, as revealed in any object, by the object that reveals Him. For it no more follows that a human body measures God, when revealed through it, than that a star, a tree, or an insect measures Him, when He is revealed through that. As regards the interior nature of Christ, or the composition of his person, we perhaps know nothing; and if his outward nature represents an unknown quantity, it may, for aught that appears, represent an infinite quantity. A finite outward person, too, may as well be an organ or type of the Infinite as a finite thing or object; and God may act a human personality, without being measured by it, as well as to shine through a finite thing or a world, without being measured by that.

But this divine person, the Christ, grows, I shall be reminded, or is said to grow in wisdom and knowledge. There must, therefore, be some kind of intelligence in him, call it human or divine, which is under a law of development, and therefore of limitation. To this I answer (1.) that the language may well enough be taken as language of external description merely, or as only setting forth appearance as appearance; or (2.) it may be said, which is far more satisfactory, and leaves the question where it should be, that the body of Christ evidently grew up from infancy; and that all his actings grew out, so to speak, with it; and if the divine was manifested in the ways of a child, it creates no difficulty which does not exist when it is manifested in the ways of a man or a world. The whole question is, whether it is possible for the divine nature to be manifested in humanity, and, as it belongs to humanity to grow, I see nothing in that to create a difficulty, more than when it is considered to be the part of humanity to inquire, reason, remember, have emotions, and move about in space; for none of these belong to the true Absolute Deity. Even to say that Christ reasons and thinks, using the words in their human sense, is quite as repugnant to his proper Deity, as to say that he learns or grows in knowledge, after the manner of a child; for to reason and to think, are, in fact, the same as to learn.

But the history of Christ, it will be said, compels us to go farther. We cannot look at the external person of Christ on the one hand, and the Absolute Jehovah on the other, and regard the former simply as a representative or expression of the other. Christ, says the Unitarian, obeys, worships, suffers, and in that manner shows most plainly that his internal nature is under a limitation; therefore he is human only. Then the common Trinitarian replies, your argument is good; therefore we assert a human soul in the person of Jesus, which comes under these limitations, while the divine soul escapes; and so we save the divinity unharmed and unabridged.

Answering the latter first, I reply that, in holding such a theory of Christ's obedience and sufferings, he does an affront to the plain language of scripture. For the scripture does not say that a certain human soul called Jesus, born as such of Mary, obeyed and suffered; but it says in the boldest manner, that he who was in the form of God, humbled himself and became obedient unto death, even the death of the cross. A declaration, the very point of which is, not that the man Jesus was a being under human limitations, but that he who was in the Form of God, the real divinity, came into the finite, and was subject to human conditions. Then, again, Christ himself declared, not that a human soul, hid in his person, was placed under limitations, but more—that the Son, that is, the divine person—for the word *Son* is used as relative to the Father—the Son can do nothing of himself but what he seeth the Father do; for the Father loveth the Son and sheweth him all things that himself doeth. He also prays—"O Father, glorify thou me with thine own self, with the glory that I had with thee before the world was,"—a prayer which cannot be referred to the human soul, even if there was a human soul hid in his person; for that soul could speak of no glory it once had with the Father. Hence the supposition of a human soul existing distinctly, and acting by itself, clears no difficulty; for the Son, the divine part, or I should rather say, the whole Christ, is still represented as humbled, as weak, as divested of glory, and existing under limitations or conditions that do not belong to Deity.

Besides, this theory of two distinct subsistences, still maintaining their several kinds of action in Christ,—one growing, learning, obeying, suffering; the other infinite and impassible—only creates difficulties a hundred fold greater than any that it solves. It virtually denies any real unity between the human and the divine, and substitutes collocation or copartnership for unity. If the divine part were residing in Saturn, he would be as truly united with the human race as now. Instead of a person whose nature is the real unity of the divine and the human, we have two distinct persons, between whom our thoughts are continually alternating; referring this to one, that to the other, and imagining, all the while, not a union of the two, in which our possible union with God is signified and sealed forever, but a practical, historical assertion rather of his incommunicableness, thrust upon our notice, in a form more oppressive and chilling than it has to abstract thought. Meantime the whole work of Christ, as a subject, suffering Redeemer, is thrown upon the human side of his nature, and the divine side standing thus aloof, incommunicably distant, has nothing in fact to do with the transaction, other than to be a spectator of it. And then, while we are moved to ask of what so great consequence to us, or to the government of God, can be the obedience and suffering of this particular man Jesus, more than of any other, it is also represented, as part of the same general scheme, that he is, after all, scarcely more than a mere nominal man—that he is so removed from the fortunes and the proper trial of a man, by the proximity of the divine, as not even to unfold a human character! And thus, while the redemption even of the world is hung upon his human passibilities, he is shown, as a man, to have probably less of human significance than any other; to be a man whose character is not in himself, but in the custody that keeps him from being himself!

There is, then, I conclude, no solid foundation for the common trinitarian theory of two distinct or distinctly active subsistences in the person of Christ. It is not scriptural. It accounts for nothing. It only creates even greater difficulties. Indeed, it is a virtual denial, we should say, of that which is, in one view, the summi or highest glory of the incarnation, viz., the union signified, and historically begun between God and man.

Replying, now, both to the Unitarian and the common Trinitarian together, I deny that the obedience, worship, suffering, and other subject conditions of Christ, do, of necessity, create the difficulties supposed. To name God, or even to speak of Him, is, in one view, to raise a difficulty; for, in so doing, we are always seeking to represent the infinite by the finite; that is, by terms whose symbols and significances are relative only—subject to finite conditions and measures. But we are never troubled by any sense of absurdity or incompatibility, when we thus speak of God; for we know that our words have their truth or falsity in what they express, what they put others on thinking of God, not in their measures or boundaries, under the laws of space and time. Their reality is in what they signify, not in what they are.

And, precisely so, the reality of Christ is what he expresses of God, not what he is in his physical conditions, or under his human limitations. He is here to express the Absolute Being, especially His feeling, His love to man, His placableness, conversableness, and His real union to the race; in a word, to communicate His own Life to the race, and graft Himself historically into it. Therefore, when we see him thus under the conditions of increase, obedience, worship, suffering, we have nothing to do but to ask what is here expressed, and, as long as we do that, we shall have no difficulty. But if we insist on being more curious, viz., on understanding the composition of the person of Jesus, and the relations of the infinite to the finite in his person, we can create as much of difficulty as we please; though scarcely more than we could, if we pleased to investigate, in the same manner, the interior relations of words or the types of words to thoughts; for we can as easily perceive how Jesus is constructed for the expression of God, as how a straight line (*rectus, right,*) becomes the symbol of virtue. There is a point of mystery and even of contradiction in both —a something transcendent, which no investigation will ever reach.

Therefore, to insist on going beyond expression, investigating the mystery of the person of Jesus, when it is given us only to communicate God and His love, is in fact to puzzle ourselves with the vehicle, and rob ourselves of the grace it brings. It is killing the animal, that we may find where the life is hid in him, and detect the mode of its union with his body. It is taking the medicine that would cure us, and using it, not as a cure, but as a subject of investigation. God certainly is able to assume the human, to become incarnate in it so far as to express His union to it, and set Himself as Eternal Life in historic and real connection with it. He tells us plainly that He has done it. That we may know by what law to receive and interpret His proceeding, His object is declared; viz., to express or manifest Himself in the world, and thus to redeem the world.

We see at once, if it be so, that here is a matter presented, which is not psychologically or physiologically investigable, because it does not lie within the categories of ordinary, natural humanity. And yet, instead of turning to receive simply what is expressed of the divine, we immediately begin to try our science on the interior person of Jesus, to ascertain its contents or elements, and the mode of its composition! Nay, we must know who suffers, what worships, and all the hidden chemistries of the person must be understood! Then as to what is expressed, why, that is a matter of so little moment that many overlook it wholly.

It is as if Abraham, after he had entertained as a guest the Jehovah angel, or angel of the Lord, instead of receiving his message, had fallen to inquiring into the digestive process of the angel; or, since he came in human form and spoke with a human voice, whether he had a human soul or not; and, if so, how the two natures were put together! Let alone thy folly and thy shallow curiosity, O Abraham! we should say, hear the Lord speak to thee; what he commands thee, do, what he promises, believe! Suspend thy raw guesses at His nature, and take His message!

Or, it is as if Moses, when he saw the burning bush, had fallen at once to speculating about the fire: Is this real fire? No, if it was it would burn the wood. Well, if it is not fire, then there is nothing very wonderful in it; for it is nothing wonderful that that which is not fire should not burn! Nay, is it not a very dishonest fire? he might have said; for it is not what it pretends to be—it is no real fire at all. And yet it was better, methinks, to take the bush as it was meant, to see God in it, and let the chemists look after the fire!

It is very difficult, I know, for a certain class of men, whose nature it is to live in their logic and not in simple insight, to stay content with anything which has not been verified by some word-process. Instead of putting off their shoes before the burning bush, they would put out the fire rather—by such kind of constructive wisdom as I have just now given. A poem is ill to such, if it does not stand well in the predicaments. Receiving nothing by their imagination or by their heart, the verities they embrace are all dead verities. And as dead verities cannot impregnate, they live as being dead themselves—a sterile class of souls, whom not even the life-giving mysteries of the incarnation are able to fructify. See, they say, Christ obeys and suffers, how can the subject be the supreme; the suffering man, the impassible God! Probably they toss off their discovery with an air of superior sagacity, as if by some peculiar depth of argument they had reached a conclusion so profound. They cannot imagine that even the babes of true knowledge, the simple children of Christian faith, who open their hearts to the reconciling grace of God in Christ Jesus, are really wiser and deeper than they. As if it were some special wisdom to judge that the Lord Jesus came into the world, not simply to express God, and offer Him to the embrace of our love, but to submit a new riddle to the speculative chemistry and constructive logic of the race! Indeed, you may figure this whole tribe of sophisters as a man standing before that most beautiful and wondrous work of art, the 'Beatified Spirit' of Guido, and there commencing a quarrel with the artist, that he should be so absurd as to think of making a beatified spirit out of mere linseed, ochres, and oxides! Would it not be more dignified to let the pigments go and take the expression of the canvas? Just so are the human personality, the obedient, subject, suffering state of Jesus, all to be taken as colors of the Divine, and we are not to fool ourselves in practicing our logic on the colors, but to seize, at once, upon the divine import and significance thereof; ascending thus to the heart of God, there to rest, in the vision of His beatific glory.

I am well aware that we are never to believe, never can believe anything that is really absurd or contradictory; but we are to believe, constantly, things that, taken in their form, are contrary one to the other—contrary in diction. The highest and divinest truths are often to be expressed, or communicated only in this manner. I could name a poem of fifty lines, in which as many as four plain formal contradictions occur, all evolving truths of feeling, otherwise not in the power of any language to express. And so, the gospel of John is the most contradictory book in the world, one of which logic can make just what havoc it will—and this, because it is a book that embodies more of the highest and holiest forms of truth than any other. Accordingly, the only way to read this book is, first, to get the divine aim of Christ's mission before us, viz., to express God, then to let all the repugnant terms pour their contents into our thought and feeling, suffering whatever of repugnance there is in the vehicles to fall off and be forgotten—just as in the viewing of a picture, the colors that are used to make shades, and thus to develop the forms, are disregarded and rejected when you consider the matter of complexion; or just as the flatness of the canvas is not insisted on as contrary to the roundness of the forms; or just as you disregard everything else, when you come to the moral expression, and offer your simple feeling to that, as the living truth of all.

So in the matter of Christ's obedience, you are not so much to consider the obedience, as what the obedience expresses, or signifies. Man obeys for what obedience is, but the subject obedient state of Christ is accepted for what it conveys, or expresses. Ask, then, what his obedience signifies, in the light and shade of his own peculiar history. Possibly it signifies what is only a highest and first truth in the character of God; viz., that He Himself obeys and enthrones forever the right, honors it, enjoys it, as His own Pure Law; and so, or by the expression of this most powerful and divinest truth, it may be that Christ sanctifies the law that we have broken, erecting it again, in its original sacredness and majesty, before all mankind. Or, if we speak of the worship paid by Christ, can anything be more clear than that Christ, in expressing what is perfect in God through the human, must use the human type according to its nature, and the conditions to which it is subject? God does not weep, but it will be no absurd thing for Jesus to weep, and that, too, in the way even of revealing or expressing God. So if he renders worship, it creates no difficulty which does not belong to his simple identification with the human, as truly as to his worship. He is only absurd when he acts the heathen, and refuses to worship in the way of expressing God. To do this effectively, he must act the human perfectly—that is, he must worship.

I do not pretend, however, to solve this matter of wor ship. The mystery of the divine-human must remain a mystery. I cannot fathom it. Reason itself will jus tify me in no such attempt. And when we come to speak of the sufferings and death, I would withhold, in like manner, and require myself to look only at what the sufferings and death express. It is commonly held that God is impassible, though we never hesitate to affirm that He is displeased thus or thus, and this displeased state is, so far, of course, an un-pleased or painful state. But, even if it were otherwise, if God, in His own nature, were as unsusceptible as a rock, that fact would justify no inference concerning the person of Christ. The only question is, whether God, by a mysterious union with the human, can so far employ the element of suffering as to make it a vehicle for the expression of His own Grace and Tenderness —whether, indeed, God can be allowed, in any way, to exhibit those Passive Virtues which are really the most active and sublimest of all virtues ; because they are most irresistible, and require the truest greatness of spirit. Therefore, when we come to the agony of the garden, and the passion of the cross, we are not, with the speculative Unitarian, to set up as a dogma, beforehand, and as something that we perfectly know, that God can set Himself in no possible terms of connection with suffering; nor believing with the common Trinitarian, that there are two distinct natures in Christ, are we to conclude that no sort of pang can touch the divine nature, and that only his human part can suffer. We cannot thus intrude into the interior of God's mysteries. We are only to see the eternal Life approach our race—Divine Love manifested and sealed ; the Law sanctified by obedience unto death ; pardon certified by the 'Father Forgive ;' peace established and testified by the resurrection from the dead.

And then, if we desire more, if we must practice our physiology—why it is better to try a human subject.

Perhaps it may be imagined that I intend, in holding this view of the incarnation, or the person of Christ, to deny that he had a human soul, or anything human but a human body. I only deny that his human soul, or nature, is to be spoken of, or looked upon, as having a *distinct* subsistence, so as to live, think, learn, worship, suffer, by itself. Disclaiming all thought of denying, or affirming anything as regards the interior composition or construction of his person, I insist that he stands before us in simple unity, one person, the divine-human, representing the qualities of his double parentage as the Son of God, and the son of Mary. I do not say that he is composed of three elements, a divine person, a human soul and a human body; nor of these that they are distinctly three, or absolutely one. I look upon him only in the external way; for he comes to be viewed externally in what may be expressed through him, and not in any other way. As to any metaphysical or speculative difficulties involved in the union of the divine and the human, I dismiss them all, by observing that Christ is not here for the sake of something accomplished in his metaphysical or psychological interior, but for that which appears and is outwardly signified in his life. And it is certainly competent for God to work out the expression of His own feeling, and His union to the race in what way most approves itself to Him. Regarding Christ in this exterior, and, as it were, esthetic way, he is that Holy Thing in which my God is brought to me,—brought even down to a fellow relation with me. I shall not call him two. I shall not decompose him and label off his doings, one to the credit of his divinity, and another to the credit of his humanity. I shall receive him, in the simplicity of faith, as my one Lord and Saviour, nor any the less so that he is my brother.

I am well advised of the fact, that very few persons have their minds so far moderated by philosophy or reason as to be able to set any boundaries to their questions. Those who can do it, those who can think it even unreasonable to investigate the interior of this divine mystery, when it is framed only for its external significance, will find the view here given, simple, intelligent, and full of comfort. But those who cannot, must, of course, take the penalty. If they must still investigate what was not given to be investigated; if they must speculate still about this divine-human, its modes, its interior possibility or impossibility, refusing the spiritual brotherhood of God, till they can satisfy their questions about the rhetoric He uses to express it; in a word, if their most irrational reason must sow to the wind, in its questions, it can hope to reap nothing better than emptiness and whirlwind for its answers. Enough that I have shown them a better way.

Adhering, thus, immovably to the simple historic unity of Christ's person, it will be seen that, in the reference just now made to those remarkable divine exhibitions, or presentations made to Abraham and Moses, it was not my design to assert a general parallelism between them and the person of Christ. They were cited only as illustrations of the particular matter there in question These were mere theophanies—apparitions, if I may so speak, of God. In one view, they were not historical at all; for they do not rise out of historical elements. Christ is no such theophany, no such casual, unhistorical being as the Jehovah angel who visited Abraham. He is in and of the race, born of a woman, living in the line of humanity, subject to human conditions, an integral part, in one view, of the world's history; only bringing into it, and setting in organific union with it, the Eternal Life.

The most plausible objection that can be made to the view I am giving of Christ's person is, that he is too exclusively divine to make an effectual approach to our human sympathies. But it is only plausible. Obviously, nothing is gained in this respect, by holding three metaphysical persons in the divine nature; for if still the real deity of the Son is maintained, (which I fear many do unwittingly disallow, when verbally asserting it,) they have precisely the same remoteness, the same too excessive divineness to contend with. Nor do we gain anything as regards this matter of sympathy, by supposing a distinct human soul in the person of Christ, connecting itself with what may be called the humanities of Christ. Of what so great consequence to us are the humanities of a mere human soul? The very thing we want, is to find that God is moved by such humanities—touched with a feeling of our infirmities. And what can bring God closer to our human sympathies than to behold—if only we can believe so high a mystery—God manifest in the flesh, and historically united with our race? Therefore, if you find that Christ really comes down to your sphere only when a half-tint is thrown over his deity, by some confusion practiced on his person, I may reasonably ask, whether it were not better to add more faith in yourself, and subtract less of the divine from him—thus to make him, indeed and in truth, the express image of God ?

I have thus endeavored to verify the incarnation. I am well aware that one who discredits everything supernatural, will require something farther. But I can only intimate, here, a settled conviction that, if this great question of supernaturalism were once put upon a right basis, such as a competent investigator might lay for it, the incarnation, which now appears to be a prodigy too violent or stupendous for belief, would be seen to emerge as the crowning result of a grand, systematic, orderly work, which God has been forwarding in the history and heart of the race, ever since the world began—that the world, in fact, would be as chaotic and as wide of the true unity of reason without an incarnation, as without a sun. Happily, most of the later Unitarians maintain the credibility of that which is supernatural—indeed, they even hold that Christ is, in some very special and supernatural sense, a manifestation of God ; that the divine is, in fact, so far supreme in him, as to prevent the development of a properly human, thus to produce a really sinless character—and this differs, in reality, from the view I have presented, only as a *sub*-carnation, from an *in*-carnation. God is here, behind the man, or under the man, in such a way, that the man does not act himself. We have a man without a man—a perfect human character which is not unfolded by the human. And thus we have as much of mystery and contradiction, with the disadvantage that we have no countenance from the scripture, and a doctrine, withal, that has too little body and shape to have any important resulting use.

Having thus disposed of the difficulties growing out of the relations of the divine to the human, in the person of Christ received as an incarnation, I now turn,—

II. To those which are involved in the relations of his person to the Father and the Holy Spirit; and, of all, to the Absolute Being.

It is a fatal objection to the Unitarian theories of this subject, as viewed under the teaching of the scriptures, that God is nowhere represented, or named, as the Father, till after the appearing of Christ. It is also an objection equally fatal to the Sabellian theory, which, as commonly understood, represents that God is the Father, in virtue of His creation and government of the world. For if He is the Father simply as the one God, by what accident does it happen that He never gets the appellation till after the coming of Christ? Or, if He gets it as the Creator and Governor of the world, the world was created and governed long before that day—why, then, is He still unknown as the Father? True, He is called *a* Father, just as He is called a rock, or a tower, but never *the* Father, as in the baptismal formula, and by Christ ordinarily. There is, in fact, no real and proper development of the Father, which is older than Christianity, and here the designation is developed in connection with the Son and Holy Spirit as a threefold denomination of God. And this threefold denomination, again, (as I think must be evident,) is itself incidental to, and produced by the central fact, or mystery of the incarnation, as an imper sonation of God developed in time.

Thus, the Divine Word, or Logos, who is from eternity the Form or in the Form of God, after having first bodied Him forth in the creation and the government of the world, now makes another outgoing from the Absolute into the human, to reside in the human as being of it; thus to communicate God to the world, and thus to ingenerate in the world Goodness and Life as from Him. To make His approach to man as close, to identify Himself as perfectly as possible with man, he appears, or makes His advent through a human birth—Son of man, and Son, also, of God. Regarding him now in this light as set out before the Absolute Being, (who he representatively is,) existing under the conditions of the finite and the relative, we see at once that, for our sakes, if not for his own, he must have set over against him, in the finite, his appropriate relative term, or impersonation. A solitary finite thing, or person, that is, one that has no relative in the finite, is even absurd,—much more if the design be that we shall ascend, through it, to the Absolute; for we can do this only under the great mental law of action and reaction, which requires relative terms and forces, between which it may be maintained. Besides, there may have been some subjective, or internal necessity, in Christ himself, (for we know nothing of his interior structure and wants,) requiring that, in order to the proper support of his attitude, he should have in conception some finite relative impersonation. For one, or both these reasons, when he appears in the human state, bringing the divine into the human, there results, at one and the same time, a double impersonation, that of the Father and that of the Son,—one because of the other, and both as correspondent or relative terms. As Christ himself appears in the finite, he calls out into the finite with him, if I may so speak, another representative of the Absolute, one that is conceived to reside in the heavens, as he himself is seen to walk upon the earth. This he does to comfort his attitude, or more probably, to make it intelligible; for if he were to say, "Look unto me, and behold your God," then his mere human person would be taken as a proof that he is only a flagrant and impious impostor; or else, being accepted as God by those who are more credulous, they would, in fact, receive a God by apotheosis, and under human boundaries. Therefore, he calls out into thought, as residing in heaven, and possessing celestial exaltation, the Father, who is, in fact, the Absolute Being brought into a lively, conversible, definite (therefore finite) form of personal conception, and sets himself on terms of relationship with him at the other pole; so that, while he signifies, or reveals the light and love of God, in and through the human or subject life, he is able to exalt and deify what he reveals, by referring his mission to one that is greater and higher in state than himself, viz., the Father in heaven. And, in this way, double advantage is taken both of proximity and distance, in the process of revealing or expressing God. He does not say, I came forth from the One, the Absolute; from Him that dwells above time, silent, never moving, without parts, or emotions, but he gives us, above, the conception of an active, choosing, feeling Spirit, and says, "I came forth from the Father."

Now there is open to view, a relationship between heaven and earth. To keep us from subsiding into a regard of his simple person, as limited by human boundaries, and referring all his works to a being thus limited, he intimates a connection with one who has no such boundaries, saying, "My Father is greater than I." And then, again, that what he expresses may be referred to that essentially divine nature represented in his person, he exalts his attitude, saying, "I and my Father are one." Now he says, "the Father loves me, " and now, "he that hath seen me, hath seen the Father." And then, again, determined to keep himself and the whole process under a cloud of mystery, so that no one shall ever feel that he has gotten the measure, either of the Father or of himself, and that all may be wading ever outward through mystery, in both, towards the infinite, he says, "No man knoweth the Son but the Father, neither knoweth any man the Father, save the Son, and he to whomsoever the Son will reveal him." It is a revealing process, but yet enveloped in mystery—revealing even the more, by means of the mystery.

Meantime, it is by setting ourselves before this personal history of the Father in heaven, and the Son on earth, both as representatives standing out befoıe the Absolute Being, watching the relative history they unfold in finite forms, their acting and interacting, and discovering what is expressed thereby,—cleared of all the repugnant and contradictory matter that is attributable to the vehicle, in distinction from the truth—it is thus that we are to ascend, as by a resultant of the two forces, into a lively realization, and a free, spiritual embrace of God, as our Friend, Redeemer, Peace, and Portion. A mere philosophic unity, it will be seen at a glance, is cold and dead, in comparison—altogether insufficient to support the Christian uses of the soul.

But, in order to the full and complete apprehension of God, a third personality, the Holy Spirit, needs to appear. By the Logos, in the creation, and then by the Logos in the incarnation, assisted or set off by the Father as a relative personality, God's character, feeling, and truth, are now expressed. He has even brought down the mercies of His Heart to meet us on our human level. So far, the expression made, is moral; but there is yet needed, to complete our sense of God, the Absolute, another kind of expression, which will require the introduction or appearance of yet another and distinct kind of impersonation. We not only want a conception of God in His character and feeling towards us, but we want, also, to conceive Him as in *act* within us, working in us, under the conditions of time and progression, spiritual results of quickening, deliverance, and purification from evil. Now, action of any kind is representable to us only under the conditions of movement in time and space, which, as we have seen, is not predicable of the Absolute Being abstractly contemplated. God, in act, therefore, will be given us by another finite, relative impersonation.

Accordingly, the natural image, *spirit*, that is, breath, is taken up and clothed with a personal activity. The word signifies air in motion, and as air is invisible, it becomes the symbol or type of unseen power exerted—quite transcendently, however, as regards our comprehension; for there is really no motion whatever. The word *spirit* had been used before, as in reference to the agency of God, but only in a remoter and more tropical sense, as the word Father had been; the conception of a divine personality, or impersonation, called the Holy Spirit, was unknown. We may imagine otherwise, in one or two cases, as when David prays, "Take not thy holy spirit from me," but I think, without any sufficient reason. Now, the Divine Power, in souls, is to be developed under the form of a personal Sanctifier, related, in a personal way, to the Father and the Son, as they to each other. He is conceived, sometimes, as sent by the Father; sometimes, as proceeding from the Father and the Son; sometimes as shed forth from the Son in his exaltation; always as a Divine Agency, procured by the Son, and representing, in the form of an operation within us, that grace which he reveals as feeling and intention towards us.

And here, again, just as the Logos is incarnated in the flesh, so the Spirit makes His advent under physical signs, appropriate to His office, coming in a rushing mighty wind; tipping the heads of an assembly with lambent flames; evidencing his power in souls, by opening the lips of men, and playing those utterances which are, themselves, expressions of the mind within; endowing men with gifts above their human capacity. Now, the Absolute Being, of whom we could predicate no motion or proceeding, becomes a Vital Presence, residing ever with us, to work in us all that we need, and strengthen us to that which none but a divine power can support. What we should not dare to hope, and could not otherwise conceive--the Eternal Life, declared and manifested by Christ, liveth in us.

Thus we have three persons, or impersonations, all existing under finite conditions or conceptions. They are relatives, and, in that view, are not infinites; for relative infinites are impossible. And yet, taken representatively, they are each and all, infinites; because they stand for, and express the Infinite, Absolute Jehovah. They may each declare, 'I am He;' for what they impart to us of Him, is their true reality. Between them all together, as relatives, we are elevated to proximity and virtual converse with Him who is above our finite conditions,—the Unapproachable, and, as far as all measures of thought or conception are concerned, the Unrepresentable God.

The Father plans, presides, and purposes for us; the Son expresses his intended mercy, proves it, brings it down even to the level of a fellow-feeling; the Spirit works within us the beauty he reveals, and the glory beheld in his Life. The Father sends the Son, the Son delivers the grace of the Father; the Father dispenses, and the Son procures the Spirit; the Spirit proceeds from the Father and Son, to fulfill the purpose of one, and the expressed feeling of the other; each and all together dramatize and bring forth into life about us that Infinite One, who, to our mere thought, were no better than Brama sleeping on eternity and the stars. Now, the sky, so to speak, is beginning to be full of Divine Activities, heaven is married to earth, and earth to heaven, and the Absolute Jehovah, whose nature we before could nowise comprehend, but dimly know, and yet more dimly feel, has, by these outgoings, waked up in us, all living images of His love and power and presence, and set the whole world in a glow.

There is, then, according to the view now presented, a real and proper trinity in the scriptures; three persons, Father, Son, and Holy Ghost,—one God. If it be objected that the word *trinity* is not here, neither is the term *free agency*. There certainly can be no harm in the use of such terms as mere terms of convenience, if we are careful not to derive our doctrine from them. That there is, in the scriptures, a three-foldness, which contains the real matter of a trinity, is to me undeniable, and, if I am right in the views now presented, it must be of the highest consequence to religion, that this trinity be admitted, cordially accepted, lived in as a power—a vitalizing element offered to our souls, as the air to the life of our bodies. Every human soul that will adequately work itself in religion, needs this trinity as the instrument of its working; for, without this, it is neither possible to preserve the warmth, nor to ascend into the true greatness of God.

Neither is it any so great wisdom, as many theologians appear to fancy, to object to the word *person;* for, if anything is clear, it is that the Three of scripture do appear under the grammatic forms which are appropriate to person—I, Thou, He, We, and They; and, if it be so, I really do not perceive the very great license taken by our theology, when they are called three persons. Besides, we practically need, for our own sake, to set them out as three persons before us, acting relatively toward each other, in order to ascend into the liveliest, fullest realization of God. We only need to abstain from assigning to these divine persons an interior, metaphysical nature, which we are nowise able to investigate, or which we may positively know to contradict the real unity of God.

Do you then ask, whether I mean simply to assert a modal trinity, or three modal persons ?—I must answer obscurely, just as I answered in regard to the humanity of Christ. If I say that they are modal *only*, as the word is commonly used, I may deny more than I am justified in denying, or am required to deny, by the ground I have taken. I will only say that the trinity, or the three persons, are given to me for the sake of their external expression, not for the internal investigation of their contents. If I use them rationally or wisely, then, I shall use them according to their object. I must not intrude upon their interior nature, either by assertion or denial. They must have their reality to me in what they express when taken as the wording forth of God. Perhaps I shall come nearest to the simple, positive idea of the trinity here maintained, if I call it an Instrumental Trinity, and the persons Instrumental Persons. There may be more in them than this, which let others declare when they find it. Enough, meantime, for me, that there is this ;—that in and through these living persons, or impersonations, I find the Infinite One brought down even to my own level of humanity, without any loss of His greatness, or reduction of His majesty. And if they help me to this, I see not anything more of so great consequence for them to give me, even if I could read their most interior nature, and resolve all problems concerning them. I perceive, too, that God may as well offer Himself to me, in these persons, as through trees, or storms, or stars;—that they involve as little contrariety, as few limitations, and yield as much more of warmth as they have more of life. I discover, also, that this threeness helps me the more, and lifts me the higher, because it baffles me. If I think it more philosophical and simple to conceive God only as one person, that person will really be a finite conception, unwittingly, though very absurdly, taken as Infinite. And then, as the God shrinks, the mind freezes. The simplicity it so much admired, after all, brings disappointment. The ease of this philosophic unity is itself a great fault; for it is as if we had God's measure, and saw His boundaries. He is too clear to be Infinite; and, what is even worse, too clear to have His warmth in the soul. We do not rise to the Infinite by simple thought or direct contemplation, we are borne up to that height only by a resultant motion, between relative and partially repugnant forces, such as we find in the three persons of scripture. Through a certain feeling of multiplicity and vagueness, we are able to realize God dynamically, as we could through no definite conception of Him. Represented as three, God is yet one—the more magnificently one, because He is three. The soul has her sublimation, because she is held in a maze, and God is warm, because He is a mystery. Meanwhile, if our feeling is, at any time, confused by these persons or impersonations, we are to have it for a fixed, first truth, that God is, in the most perfect and rigid sense, one being—a pure intelligence, undivided, indivisible, and infinite ; and that whatever may be true of the Father, Son, and Holy Ghost, it certainly is not true that they are three distinct consciousnesses, wills, and understandings. Or, speaking in a way more positive, they are instrumentally three—i. e. for, and as related to, our finite apprehension and the communication of God's incommunicable nature.

But some one, I suppose, will require of me to answer whether the three persons are eternal, or only occasional and to be discontinued ? Undoubtedly the distinction of the Word, or the power of self-representation in God thus denominated, is eternal. And in this, we have a permanent ground of possibility for the threefold impersonation, called trinity. Accordingly, if God has been eternally revealed, or revealing Himself to created minds, it is likely always to have been and always to be as the Father, Son, and Holy Ghost. Consequently, it may always be in this manner that we shall get our impressions of God, and have our communion with Him. As an accommodation to all finite minds in the universe, it may be the purpose of Jehovah to be known by this divine formula forever. That which most discourages such a belief is the declaration of Paul—"When all things shall be subdued unto him, then shall the Son also himself be subject unto him that did put all things under him, that God may be all and in all." I will not go into a discussion of these very remarkable words ; for I do not care to open God's secrets before the time. Let the future bring the future, and I know it will not be amiss when it comes. Enough for me, now, that by these dear names, my God proves His warmth, and pours His fullness into my heart—that, without them, torpor settles on my religious nature, and the boasted clearness of a God made level to reason, is the clearness of a wintry day.

I suppose the position I have taken would be more acceptable to some, were I to throw in the intimation given by Neander, when ascribing a similar view to the apostles. Thus he says that the trinity "has an essentially practical and historical significance and foundation; it is the doctrine of God revealed in the humanity, which teaches men to recognize in God, not only the original source of existence, but of salvation and sanctification. From this trinity of revelation, as far as the divine causality images itself in the same, the reflective mind, according to the analogy of its own being, pursuing this track, seeks to elevate itself to the idea of an original triad in God, availing itself of the intimations which are contained in John's doctrine of the Logos and the cognate elements of the Pauline theology." If now it be inquired whether, beginning with a doctrine of trinity, produced by the process of revelation, and adequately accounted for as necessary to that process, I would then turn to hunt for some "analogy" in myself, and try to climb up thus, through myself, into a discovery of an original triad in God—convincing myself, also, that John and Paul give "intimations" of such a triad, I frankly answer, no. The expression of such a hope might comfort some who would otherwise be disturbed, but it will only mislead a much greater number, who had better keep their discretion. If God has given us an instrumental triad, which is good for its purposes of revelation, there can be no greater fraud upon it than to set ourselves to the discovery of an original triad back of it, that has no instrumental character, and has nothing to do with revelation. It is just the way to confuse and lead us off from every proper use and construction of the trinity God has given us. In just this way it is, too, that the trinity has been made a source of so great controversy and so little profit, in all past ages—it has been turned into a metaphysical problem, and its instrumental character, as the representative development of God, has, of necessity, been hidden from the view. Besides, what wisdom are we likely to arrive at, better than the shadowy vagaries others, in past ages, have conjured up, by hunting our human spirit through, to find some Platonic triad there, which shall solve the trinity of persons in God? Let us rather baptize our over-curious spirit into the name of the Father, and of the Son, and of the Holy Ghost, and teach it quietly to rest in what of God's Infinite nature it may there receive. We talk of simplicity, often, when upon this matter of trinity—as we rightly may. O, that we had simplicity enough to let God be God, and the revelation He gives us, a revelation!—neither trying to make Him a finite person after our own human model, nor ourselves three that we may bring our humanity up to solve the mysteries of His Absolute, Infinite substance! There is no so true simplicity as that which takes the practical at its face, uses instruments as instruments, however complex and mysterious, (for what is more so than a man's own body,) and refuses to be cheated of the uses of life, by an over-curious questioning of that which God has given for its uses.

This view of Christ and the trinity differs, I am aware, in some respects, from that which is commonly held; but I hope the difference will not disturb you. I have known no other since I began to be a preacher of Christ, and my experience teaches me to want no other. If it has delivered me from agonies of mental darkness and confusion concerning God, which, at one time, seemed insupportable, it cannot be wrong to hope that God will make the truth a deliverance equally comfortable and joyful to some of you.

Observe, too, in closing, what an outlay God has made to communicate or manifest Himself to our race. In His own Absolute nature, God is a being so vast that, when I drew out the conception of Him as existing in Himself, I presume it was somewhat painful to you, so remote was it from all your own personal modes of being and life, as a finite creature. And yet it will be difficult for any one to dispute the necessity of such a conception of God, when taken as Absolute, and as viewed by abstract thought or contemplation. But what have we seen? This Transcendent Being struggling out, so to speak, into the measures of human knowledge, revealing Himself through the petty modes and molds of our finite nature! He fills the whole universe with actions and reactions, such as will bring us into lively acquaintance with Him. He comes into the human itself, and melts into the history of man through agonies, sorrows, and tears. He kindles heaven and earth into a glow, by the relative activities of Father,

Son, and Holy Ghost. And for what? Simply to communicate Himself, to express His nature and His feeling What, then, does our everlasting God and Father plan for, but to bestow Himself upon us? And it is in this view, that the Blessed Three come to me with a sound so dear, and a burden of love so rich. I see therein how earnestly my God desires to be known and possessed by me,—by you as truly, by all, by every human creature. What breathing man is there of you, around whom the Triune is not circling here as a day of light and love? The Incommunicable is communicated, brought down even to be fellow to you, that you may know Him and love Him! He waits to be received, to clear away youi darkness, to purge you from your sin, and be in you the fullness of Him that fil eth all in all.

A

DISCOURSE

ON THE

ATONEMENT,

DELIVERED BEFORE

THE DIVINITY SCHOOL

IN

HARVARD UNIVERSITY,

JULY 9, 1848.

THE ATONEMENT.

You have called me to occupy, this evening, a singular and, in the same view, difficult and responsible office. Which office, however, I most readily undertake, because I seem to have a subject and a duty appointed me also.

It cannot be improper, in the circumstances, to say that when your letter came, inviting me to perform this exercise, I had just emerged from a state of protracted suspense, or mental conflict, in reference to what is called, theologically, the doctrine of Atonement; that is, of the life and death of Jesus Christ, as the Saviour of the world. The practical moment of Christ's work had been sufficiently plain, but the difficulty had been to bring its elements into one theologic view. The subject had for many years been hung up before me, and I had been perusing it on all sides, trying it by manifold experiments, and refusing to decide by the will, what could only be cleared by light, till now, at last, the question had *seemed* to open itself and display its reasons. And when your letter was laid upon my table, I was at that moment engaged in projecting a discourse that should embody, what I dared, somewhat enthusiastically, to hope might

16*

prove a true solution of this momentous, but very difficult subject. Instigated by the same incautious warmth, I accepted the occasion offered, as offered not to me, but to my subject, and forthwith set apart one to the uses of the other.

If, now, a short interval of time and a formal preparation of the subject have somewhat sobered my confidence, if I no longer dream of the possibility that I may solve so great a question to the satisfaction of any one, I do yet cherish a hope that the view I may offer will lead to a reinvestigation of the whole question, and thus, at length, towards a reconstruction of our present theological affinities; or, if this be too much, towards a reduction of our present theological antipathies. Or, again, if this be too much, it will at least be something, if I am able to go directly down into the arena and take up, in manful earnest, the old first question over which our fathers panted in the dust of controversy, discussing it anew by your permission, and without offence to your Christian hospitalities. For it would be a public shame, even to Christianity itself, if I were to come before you on such an occasion as this, and in such a theologic relation, here to speak as one that is cautiously imprisoned within the limits of some neutral subject, neither trusting you, nor daring for myself, to hazard the mention of any point in litigation between us. I consider it also to be only a just compliment, in return for the very unexampled courtesies I am accepting, to assume that your spirit is as broad as your invitation; that you have called me to speak, because you desired to hear me speak my own sentiments, and not to see how well I can accommodate any favorite opinion held by yourselves.

The text I had chosen for my discourse, at the time referred to, was :—

1 John, i. 2.—"*For the Life was manifested, and we have seen it, and bear witness, and shew unto you that eternal life which was with the Father, and was manifested unto us.*"

This particular passage of scripture has seemed to me to offer one of the most comprehensive and most deliberate announcements of the doctrine of Christ, that is anywhere given in the sacred writings, with the advantage that it is yet so far unoccupied as not to have become a technic, under the wear of any theory. In the verse previous, the writer opens by setting forth the fact, as I suppose, of a divine incarnation in the person of Jesus. By the Word, or Word of Life, that peculiar power in the Divine nature by which God is able to represent Himself outwardly in the forms of things, first in the worlds and now in the human person, which is the liveliest type of feeling possible, and closest to God—by this Word of Life, God has now expressed Himself. He has set forth His Divine feeling even to sense and as a fellow-feeling —He has entered into human history, as one of its biographic elements. We have seen, looked upon, handled what may thus be known of Him. Then, he adds—throwing in a parenthesis which is to be a solution of the whole evangelic history—"for the Life was manifested, and we have seen it, and bear witness, and shew unto you that Eternal Life, which was with the Father and was manifested unto us."

Observe three points in this very peculiar language. First, there is a manifestation of something, the mission of the Word is looked upon inclusively as a manifestation, that is, a coming into visibility of something before invisible. Secondly, it is the Life that was manifested—not life generally speaking, but *the* Life. And, thirdly, as if to distinguish it in a yet more definite manner, it is called *that* Life, that Eternal Life, that Eternal Life that was *with* the Father, and was manifested unto us.

Taking, now, these three terms, in connection with the assumption, elsewhere made, that our human race, under sin, are alienated from the life of God; also, with the declaration of Christ, that, as the Father hath life in Himself, so he hath given to the Son, as the world's Redeemer, to have life in himself; and, again, with that deep utterance of joy sent forth by an emancipated soul;—"for the law of the spirit of life in Christ Jesus, hath made me free from the law of sin and death"—taking the text, I say, in connection with these others, as commentaries, we have a good synoptic view, it seems to me, of the doctrine of the Messiah.

It is not that Christ is a man, a human teacher, who is sent to reform us by his words and his beautiful human example, but it is to this effect:—All souls have their proper life only in the common vivifying life of God. Sin, being a withdrawal into self and self-hood, separates them from the life, and, as far as their own freedom is concerned, denies all influx of the Divine into their character and their religious nature. Passing thus into a state of negation, as regards the Divine all-sustaining life, they become imprisoned in darkness, unbelief, idolatry, and a general captivity to sense. And now the Life is manifested in sense; in Christ is life, and the life is the light of men. Christ enters into human feeling, by his incarnate charities and sufferings, to re-engage the world's love and reunite the world, as free, to the Eternal Life. To sum up all in one condensed and luminous utterance, every word of which is power, *God was in Christ, reconciling the world unto Himself.* The apostle says nothing here, it will be observed, of reconciling God to men, he only speaks of reconciling men to God. Had he said "the Life of God was manifested in Jesus Christ, to quicken the world in love and truth, and reunite it to Himself," he would have said the same thing under a different form.

I am well aware that, in offering such a statement, as the true doctrine of Christ and his work, I affirm nothing that is distinctively orthodox, and shall even seem to rule out that view of Christ as a *sacrifice*, an *expiation for sin*, a *vicarious offering*, which, to the view of most orthodox Christians, contains the real import of his work as a Saviour. It will be found, however, that I am proceeding exactly in the line of the scriptures, and I trust also it will appear, before I have done, that the scriptures advance two distinct views of Christ and his work, which are yet radically one and the same.

I. A subjective, speculative—one that contemplates the work of Christ in its ends, and views it as a power related to its ends.

II. An objective, ritualistic—one that sets him forth to faith, instead of philosophy, and one, without which, as an Altar Form for the soul, he would not be the power intended, or work the ends appointed.

Thus, when it is inquired, as in the first form specified, for what end did Christ come into the world, we have a class of terms in the scripture which can scarcely get any proper meaning, if what is said under the second form is considered to be the whole doctrine of Christ. The converse also is equally true. The real problem is to find a place and a meaning for *all* that is said concerning him—to effect a union of the two sides.

As examples of the manner in which the scriptures make answer, when the question is, for what ends did Christ come into the world, we have the following:—

"To this end was I born, and for this cause came I into the world, to bear witness to the truth,"—a passage that is remarkable as being the most direct, specific, and formal statement Christ ever made of the object of his Messiahship; and here he says, that he came to bring truth into the world.

"I am the way, the truth, and the life;"—"I am the light of the world,"—are declarations of a similar import.

"Unto you, first, God having raised up his Son Jesus, sent him to bless you, in turning away every one of you from his iniquities." "Who gave himself for us, that he might redeem us from all iniquity, and purify unto Himself a peculiar people, zealous of good works,"—where the end of his mission is declared to be a moral effect, wrought in the mind of the race.

For this purpose, the Son of God was manifested, that he might destroy the works of the devil"—a passage declaring the precise object of the incarnation as affirmed in my text; and, as the work of the devil is not the punishment, but the corruption of his followers, we are brought to the same conclusion as before.

In all these citations, we have so many echoes of the one just produced, as the grand, comprehensive doctrine of Christ's work, or mission:—GOD IN CHRIST, RECONCILING THE WORLD UNTO HIMSELF. And I affirm, without hesitation, that whenever the question is about *the end* of Christ's work, that end to which he stands related as the wisdom and power of God, the answer of the scripture will be, that he comes to renovate character; to quicken by the infusion of the divine life; in one word, that he comes to be a Saviour, as saving his people from their sins.

Then, again, to show that a view is offered of Christ, in the writings especially of the apostles, which is wholly different from this, one that speaks of him as a propitiation, a sacrifice, as bearing our sins, bearing the curse for us, obtaining remission by his blood, is altogether unnecessary. In the Epistles to the Romans, the Galatians, the Hebrews, those of Peter and John, this altar view or form of Christ, appears even as the eminent, or super-eminent truth of the gospel.

Omitting, therefore, because it is unnecessary, to offer any particular citations to this effect, I will simply refer you to a passage that is remarkable, as being an instance where one view runs into the other, and the altar form becomes, in the issue, a renovating power. The eighth chapter of the Epistle to the Hebrews opens with a look toward sacrifice, describing Christ as a "priest" "having somewhat to offer," but still as "having obtained a more excellent ministry" than the priests of the law, and brought in for us a "better covenant." How better? Because it has a more transforming power in the life, because it fulfills a better and higher design, writing the law in the heart—"*I will put my laws into their mind, and write them in their hearts.*" Here the objective, ritual view passes into the subjective, and reveals the fact that it has and was designed to have a renovating power in character;—thus, becoming a "new" and "better covenant." Accordingly, I design to show that, if the first or subjective view of Christ, that in which I state the end and aim of Christ's work, is true, that end or aim could not be effectively realized without the second, or objective view, in which his whole work is conceived in the altar form, and held forth to the objective embrace and worship and repose of faith.

I am well aware of the insufficiency and necessary obscurity of these brief statements. I offer them only to give a general indication of the course and scope of my argument. And you will not require of me to be as intelligible here, as at the close; for it will be the principal object, or work of my discourse, to set forth and bring into unity this double, subjective-objective view of Christ and his work.

But before I engage more immediately in the effort thus undertaken, it may be useful to glance, a moment, at some of the opinions that have been held or advanced, at different times, concerning the nature and import of the atonement. A historic review of the whole subject would be useful, but this, the limitations I am under forbid. The first churches appear to have had no theoretic view of the work of Christ,—they only received him as the love of God, the sacrifice that brought them into peace, and united them again to the life of God. Irenæus is said to have opened the dogmatic history of the subject, or made a beginning of speculative theology in it, by representing the death of Christ as a ransom paid to the devil, to buy us off from the claims he had upon us. From that time to the present, it has ever been held, on the orthodox side of the Church, to be a redemptive offering paid to God,—not, however, in any such form as indicates the existence of a settled and uniform opinion of the subject. There is a general concurrence in the words *vicarious, expiation, offering, substitute,* and the like, but no agreement as to the manner in which they are to get their meaning. Sometimes, the analogy of criminal law is taken; and then our sins are spoken of as being transferred to Christ, or he as having accepted them to bear their penalty. Sometimes the civil or commercial law furnishes the analogy; and then our sins, being taken as a debt, Christ offers himself as a ransom for us. Or, the analogy of the ceremonial law is accepted; and then Christ is set forth as a propitiatory, or expiatory offering, to obtain remission of sins for us. Regarding Christ as suffering for us, in one or another of these scripture forms or figures, taken as the literal dogmatic truth, we have as many distinct theories. Then, again, different as these figures are from each other, they will yet be used interchangeably, all in the sense of one or another of them. And then, again, to double the confusion yet once more, we have two sets of representations produced under each, accordingly as Christ is conceived to offer himself to Jehovah's justice, or as Jehovah is conceived Himself to prepare the offering, out of His own mercy.

On the whole, I know of no definite and fixed point, on which the orthodox view, so called, may be said to hang, unless it be this, viz., that Christ suffers evil as evil, or in direct and simple substitution for evil that was to be suffered by us; so that God accepts one evil in place of the other, and being satisfied in this manner, is able to justify or pardon.

As to the measure of this evil, there are different opinions. Calvin maintained the truly horrible doctrine that Christ descended into hell, when crucified, and suffered the pains of the damned for three days. A very great number of the Christian teachers, even at this day, maintain that Christ suffered exactly as much pain as all the redeemed would have suffered under the penalties of eternal justice. But this penal view of Christ's death has been gradually giving way, till now, under its most modern, most mitigated and least objectionable form, he is only said to have suffered under a law of *expression.*

Thus, God would have expressed a certain abhorrence of sin, by the punishment of the world. Christ now suffers only as much pain as will express the same amount of abhorrence. And considering the dignity of the sufferer, and his relations to the Father, there was no need of suffering the same, or even any proximate amount of pain, to make an expression of abhorrence to sin, that is, of justice, equal to that produced by the literal punishment of the race. Still, it will be seen to be a part of this more mitigated view, that Christ suffers evil as evil, which evil suffered is accepted as a compensative expression of God's indignation against sin. Accordingly, in the agony of Gethsemane, and when the Saviour exclaims, in his passion, "My God! my God! why hast thou forsaken me!" it will be taken for literal truth, that the frown of God, or Divine Justice, rested on his soul.

It will probably be right, then, to distribute the views of those who are accepted, now, as orthodox teachers, into two classes; one who consider the death of Christ as availing, by force of what it *is;* the other, by force of what it *expresses;* the former holding it as a literal substitution of evil endured, for evil that was to be endured; the latter holding it as an expression of abhorrence to sin, made through the suffering of one, in place of the same expression that was to be made, by the suffering of many.

As regards the former class of representations, we may say, comprehensively, that they are capable, one and all, of no light in which they do not even offend some right moral sentiment of our being. Indeed, they raise up moral objections with such marvellous fecundity, that we can hardly state them as fast as they occur to us.

Thus, if evil remitted must be repaid by an equivalent, what real economy is there in the transaction?

What is effected, save the transfer of penal evil from the guilty to the innocent?

And if the great Redeemer, in the excess of his goodness, consents, freely offers himself to the Father, or to God, to receive the penal woes, or some sufficient part of the penal woes of the world, in his own person, what does it signify, when that offer is accepted, but that God will have his modicum of suffering somehow—if he lets the guilty go, will yet satisfy himself out of the innocent? In which the divine government, instead of clearing itself, assumes the double ignominy, first of letting the guilty go, and secondly, of accepting the sufferings of innocence! In which, Calvin, seeing no difficulty, is still able to say, when arguing for Christ's three days in hell, —"it was requisite that he should feel the severity of the divine vengeance, in order to appease the wrath of God, and satisfy his justice." I confess my inability to read this kind of language without a sensation of horror; for it is not the half-poetic, popular language of scripture, but the cool, speculative language of theory, as concerned with the reason of God's penal distributions.

And yet this objection is aggravated, if possible, by another representation, that Christ did not suffer willingly, or by consent, save in the sense that he obeyed the command by which it was laid upon him to suffer! Thus a distinguished American writer, in his treatise on this subject, written only thirty years ago, says,—"The Father must command him to die, or the stroke would not be from His own hand,"—carrying still the analogy of punishment, so far as to suppose, that, like all penal inflictions, Christ must die under "authority" of God, in order that his death should have any theologic value. It is quite useless to ask, in this connection, what becomes of the deity of the Son, when he is thus under the authority of the Father; for he is not merely under it as being in the flesh, as the scriptures speak, but it is "authority" that sends him into the flesh. To profess the real and proper deity of Christ, in such a connection, is only to use words as instruments of self-deception—his deity, after all, is not believed, and cannot be where such a doctrine is held.

Then, again, according to the same view, Christ is also God and ruler of the world, in his own person. Would any king, then, be in a fair way to maintain justice in his kingdom, if he took all the penalties of transgression on himself? Or if it be said that the human nature only of Jesus suffered, then we have the brief pangs of one human person accepted, in strict justice, as the equivalent of all the penalties of all human transgression, since the world began!

Again, there can be no such thing as future punishment or retribution, in this view, without involving a charge of injustice. For if justice be exactly vindicated, and the terms of the law exactly satisfied, to punish after that is plainly to exact double justice—which is injustice.

Again, it is a fatal objection to this view, that it sets every transgressor right before the law, when, as yet, there is nothing right in his character; producing, if we view it constructively, and not historically, (for historic and speculative results do not always agree,) the worst conceivable form of licentiousness. For, if the terms of the law are satisfied, the transgressor has it for his right to go free, whether he forsake his transgressions or not. As far as any mere claims of law or justice are concerned, he may challenge impunity for all the wrongs he has committed, shall commit, or can commit, while his breath remains!

In the second and more mitigated class of orthodox opinions, a very important and really true position is, at last, reached; viz.,—that the value of Christ's life and death is measured by what is therein expressed. Only it is needed, now, to go a step farther, investigating what he expresses, how or under what esthetic conditions the expression is made, and the object for which it is made —whether it be to express God's character and bring the Eternal Life into visible evidence and social relation; whether to sanctify and set in honor, before mankind, the broken law of God; whether to bring God as a renovating power into union with our human nature; whether, possibly, it be not rather to accomplish all these ends, and that, too, without any imposition or endurance of evil in the penal form of evil, any suffering or pain which is undertaken for effect, as being a direct exhibition of God's justice, or judicial abhorrence to sin.

The objections I have to this more mitigated theory, are these:—

First, it assumes that, as punishment expresses the abhorrence of God to sin, or what is the same, his justice, he can sustain his law and lay a ground of forgiveness without punishment, only by some equivalent expression of abhorrence—an assumption that is groundless and without consideration, as I may cause to appear in another place.

Secondly, this latter seems to accord with the former view in supposing that Christ suffers evil as evil, or as a penal visitation of God's justice, only doing it in a less painful degree; that is, suffering so much of evil as will suffice, considering the dignity of his person, to express the same amount of abhorrence to sin, that would be expressed by the eternal punishment of all mankind. I confess my inability to see how an innocent being could ever be set, even for one moment, in an attitude of displeasure under God. If He could lay His frown, for one moment, on the soul of innocence and virtue, He must be no such being as I have loved and worshipped. Much less can I imagine that He should lay it on the head of one, whose nature is itself co-equal Deity. Does any one say that He will do it for public governmental reasons? No governmental reasons, I answer, can justify even the admission of innocence into a participation of frowns and penal distributions. If consenting innocence says, "let the blow fall on me," precisely there is it for a government to prove its justice, even to the point of sublimity; to reveal the essential, eternal, unmitigable distinction it holds between innocence and sin, by declaring that as under law and its distributions, it is even impossible to suffer any commutation, any the least confusion of places.

All the analogies invented or brought from actual history, to clear this point, are manifestly worthless. If Zaleucus, for example, instead of enforcing the statute against his son, which required the destruction of both his eyes, thinks to satisfy the law by putting out one of his own eyes and one of his son's, he only practices a very unintelligent fraud upon the law, under pretext of a conscientiously literal enforcement of it. The statute did not require the loss of two eyes; if it had, the two eyes of a dog would have sufficed; but it required *the* two eyes of the criminal—that he, as a wrong doer, should be put into darkness. If the father had consented to have both his own eyes put out, instead of his son's, it might have been very kind of him, but to speak of it as public justice, or as any proper vindication of law, would be impossible. The real truth signified would be, that Zaleucus loved public justice too little, in comparison with his exceeding fondness for his son, to let the law have its course; and yet, as if the law stood upon getting two eyes, apart from all justice, too many scruples to release the sin, without losing the two eyes of his body, as before he had lost the eyes of his reason.

According to the supposition, the problem here is to produce an expression of abhorrence to sin, through the sufferings of Christ, in place of another, through the sufferings of the guilty. Now the truth of the latter expression consists in the fact that there is an abhorrence in God to be expressed. But there is no such abhorrence in God towards Christ, and therefore, if the external expression of Christ's sufferings has no correspondent feeling to be expressed, where lies the truth of the expression? And if the frown of God lies upon his soul, as we often hear, in the garden and on the cross, how can the frown of God, falling on the soul of innocence, express any truth or any feeling of justice?

Thirdly, if Christ be himself, in the highest and truest sense, the Eternal Life, God manifested in the flesh, then every expression of justice or abhorrence to sin, which is made by his death as a mere endurance of evil, is involved in yet greater obscurity and confusion. He says, himself, that all power is given unto him in heaven and on earth. He is, in fact, the embodiment, as he is the representation of God and divine government; he must be taken, in all that he does, as doing something which is properly referable to God. No theory of three metaphysical natures, called persons, in God, can at all vary this truth. The transactions of Christ must still be taken as transactions of God. The frown, then, if it be said to be *of* God, is quite as truly *on* God. The expression of justice or abhorrence is made by sufferings that are endured, not out of the circle of divine government, but in it. And thus we have a government realizing its penal distributions or their equivalents, that is, its justice, its significations of abhorrence, wholly within itself and apart from all terms of relation, save as the subjects, so called, arc to be spectators! Whatever speculations we may hold, in regard to modes of expression, can we hold such a view of divine government without some uncomfortable suspicion of mistake in it?

Once more, it is to be noticed, as a law of expression, that when evil is endured simply and only for what it expresses, it expresses nothing. If a man wades out upon some mountain, in the snows of a wintry night, to carry food to a perishing family, then what he encounters of risk and suffering, being incidentally encountered, is an expression of charity. But if he calls upon us to observe his charity expressed in what he will suffer, and, waiting for a stormy night, goes forth on the same expedition to the mountain, he expresses nothing but ostentation. So if Christ comes into the world to teach, to cheer, to heal, to pour his sympathies into the bosom of all human sorrow, to assert the integrity of truth, and rebuke the wickedness of sin, in a word, to manifest the Eternal Life and bring it into a quickening union with the souls of our race, then to suffer incidentally, to die an ignominious and cruel death rather than depart from his heavenly errand, is to make an expression of the Heart of God, which every human soul must feel. And this expression may avail to sanctify the law before us, even though there be no abhorrence expressed in his sufferings. But, if Christ comes into the world invoking, as it were, the frown of God, and undertaking to suffer evil from God, that he may express God's justice, or His abhorrence of sin, then he expresses nothing. The very laws of expression, if I understand them rightly, require that suffering should be endured, not as purposed, or as evil taken up for the expression of it, but that the evil be a necessary incident encountered *on the way* to some end separate from expression,—some truth, benefaction, or work of love.

Having stated frankly these objections to the common orthodox views of atonement, whether resting the value of Christ's death in what it *is*, or in what it *expresses*, it may be expected that I should renounce all sympathy and connection with them. This I have never been able to do. For if they are unsatisfactory, if the older and more venerable doctrine is repugnant, when speculatively regarded, to the most sacred instincts or sentiments of our moral nature, and dissolves itself at the first approach of rational inquiry, is it nothing remarkable, is it not even more remarkable, that it should have supported the spirit of so many believers and martyrs, in so many trials and deaths, continued through so many centuries? Refuted again and again, cast away, trampled upon by irreverent mockeries, it has never yet been able to die—wherefore, unless there be some power of divine life in it? So I have always believed, and I hope to show you, before I have done, where it is, or under what form it is hid; for I shall carry you into a region, separate from all speculation, or theologizing, and there, what I now dismiss, I shall virtually reclaim and restore, in a shape that provokes none of these objections. All that is real and essential to the power of this orthodox doctrine of atonement, however held, I hope to set forth still, as the DIVINE FORM of Christianity, assigning it a place where it may still reveal its efficacy, standing ever as an Altar of penitence and peace, a Pillar of confidence to believing souls.

We come now to the double view of the atonement, or work of Christ, which it was proposed to establish And,

I. The subjective, that which represents Christ as a manifestation of the Life, thus a power whose end it is to quicken, or regenerate the human character.

Here, as it has been already intimated, the value of Christ's mission is measured by what is expressed. And if so, then it follows, of course, that no dogmatic state ment can adequately represent his work; for the matter of it does not lie in formulas of reason, and cannot be comprehended in them. It is more a poem than a treatise. It classes as a work of Art more than as a work of Science. It addresses the understanding, in great part, through the feeling or sensibility. In these it has its receptivities, by these it is perceived, or perceivable. Moving, in and through these, as a revelation of sympathy, love, life, it proposes to connect us with the Life of God. And when through these, believingly opened as inlets, it is received, then is the union it seeks consummated Were it not for the air it might give to my representations, in the view of many, I should like, in common with Paul, (Phil. i. 9, 10.) to use the word *esthetic*, and represent Christianity as a power moving upon man, through this department of his nature, both to regenerate his degraded perception of excellence, and also to communicate, in that way, the fullness and beauty of God.

Hence, it would not be as wild a breach of philosophy itself, to undertake a dogmatic statement of the contents of a tragedy, as to attempt giving in the same manner the equivalents of the life and death of Jesus Christ. The only real equivalent we can give is the representation of the life itself. It is not absurd, however, to say something about the subject, if only we do not assume the adequacy of what we say—we could offer some theoretical views of a tragedy, but our theoretic matter would not be the tragedy. No more can we set forth, as a real and proper equivalent, any theoretic matter of ours concerning the life and death of Jesus Christ, which is the highest and most moving tragedy ever acted in this mortal sphere; a tragedy distinguished in the fact that God is the Chief Character, and the divine feeling, moved in tragic earnest—Goodness Infinite manifested through Sorrow—the passion represented.

Beginning, then, with the lowest view our subject permits, it is obvious that the life of Christ, considered only as a perfect being or character, is an embodiment in human history, of a spirit and of ideas, which are sufficient of themselves to change the destinies of the race, and even their capabilities of good. Is it too much for me to assume that Christ was such a character? Is it intimated that a very close, microscopic inspection has revealed, as some imagine, two or three flaws in his life? Be it so; I want no other evidence that he was a perfect and sinless being. Sin is never revealed microscopically, but, wherever it is, it sets its mark, as we set our flag on a new-discovered island. Show me, therefore, a character that is flawed only microscopically, and I will charge the flaws to the microscope or even to the solar beam, rather than to it. Christ, then, I assume, was a sinlessly perfect being. And how great an event, to have had one such perfect life or biography lived and witnessed in the world, and so deposited in the bosom of our human history. Here we have among us, call him either human only, or divine, what the most splendid gifts of human genius had labored in vain to sketch—a perfect life. What feelings, principles, beauties, ideas or regulative ideals, are thus imported into the world's bosom! Only to have seen one perfect life, to have heard the words and received the pure conceptions of one sinless spirit, to have felt the working of his charities, and witnessed the offering of his sinless obedience, would have been to receive the seeds of a moral revolution that must ultimately affect the whole race. This was true even of a Socrates. Our world is not the same world that it was before he lived in it. Much less the same, since the sinless Jesus lived and suffered in it. Such a character has, of necessity, an organific power. It enters into human thought and knowledge as a vital force; and, since it is perfect, a vital force that cannot die, or cease to work. It must, of necessity, organize a kingdom of life, and reign. The ideas it has revealed, and the spirit it has breathed into the air, are quick and powerful, and must live till the world itself is no more. The same sun may shine above, the same laws of nature may reign about us, but the grand society of man embodies new elemental forces, and the capacity, at some time or other, of another and a gloriously renovated state. The entering of one such perfect life into the world's history changes, in fact, the consciousness of the race; just as the most accomplished, perhaps, of all modern theologians assumes, when he undertakes to verify the truths of the gospel out of the contents of the religious consciousness of the Christian nations, as compared with the ancient consciousness, or that of heathen nations.

Again, the appearing of Jesus, the Messiah, has a much higher significance and power when taken as the manifestation of the Life—the incarnate Word, God expressed in and through the human.

I am obliged here, as in the general treatment of my

subject, to assume a view of Christ's person, which you may not all be ready to admit. Any one, however, may go with me, who earnestly believes that in Christ the Life was manifested. I may use language that implies a different view of Christ's person, but as far as the doctrine of this particular subject is concerned, whoever can look upon Christ as a proper and true manifestation of God, a peculiar being distinguished from ordinary men, by the fact that a properly divine import is communicated by his life, (which, of course, makes the mere human import a matter of inferior consequence,) may well enough admit whatever I shall advance, and harmonize it, for himself, with his own particular view.

Regarding the world, then, even as an upright and sinless world, how great an event is it that the Eternal is incarnated in their history, that the King is among them, expressing, by the mysterious identification of his nature with theirs, a mystery yet more august—the possible union of their nature with His! How memorable his words, teachings, works, and condescensions! And when he withdraws into the deep recesses of spirit again, what name will be dear to them as the name of their Christ! His appearing is a new epoch in their history. He will live in their hearts, life within life. A divine light from the person of their Emanuel will stream through their history. Their words will be sanctified by his uses. Their works will be animated by his spirit. A divine vigor from the Life manifested among them will penetrate their feeling, elevating their ideas and purposes, and even their capacity of good itself.

But if we are to understand the full import of Christ's mission, we must go farther. He is not merely a perfect life embodied in history. He is not merely the Eternal Life manifested in a good and upright history. We must regard him as the Life manifested in an evil history, or that of an alienated and averted race. He finds us under sin, captives imprisoned by evil, and he comes to be our liberator. Accordingly, we are now to see in what manner he addresses himself to the moral wants and disabilities of a state of sin.

And here, glancing first of all at human society, we discover the appalling fact that sin, once existing, becomes, and even must become, a corporate authority—a law or Ruling Power, in the world, opposite to God. Entering into the fashions, opinions, manners, ends, passions of the race, it molds their institutions, legislates over their conduct, and even constructs a morality by standards of its own. And thus, acting through the mass, it becomes a law to the individual, crowning Lust and Mammon as gods, harnessing nations to the chariot of war, building thrones of oppression, kindling fires of persecution, poisoning the fountains of literature, adorning falsehood with the splendors of genius, sanctifying wrong under the plausible names of honor and fashion. Thus, or by all these methods, sin becomes a kind of malign possession in the race, a prince of the power of the air, reigning unto death. To break the organic force of social evil, thus dominant over the race, Christ enters the world, bringing into human history and incorporating in it as such, that which is Divine. The Life manifested in him becomes a historic power and presence in the world's bosom, organizing there a new society or kingdom, called the kingdom of heaven, or sometimes the church. For the church is not a body of men holding certain dogmas, or maintaining, as men, certain theologic wars for God; but it is the Society of the Life, the Embodied Word. Thus it is expressly declared to be the body of Christ, the fullness of him that filleth all in all. Hence our blessed Lord, just before his passion, considering that now the organic force of evil was to be broken, said, now is the judgment of this world, now is the prince of this world cast out. The princedom of evil is dissolved—the eternal Life, manifested in the world, organizes a new society of life, breaks the spell forever of social evil, and begins a reign of truth and love that shall finally renew the world.

While the social authority of evil is thus broken, there is also a movement on the individual, to clear the disabilities which sin has wrought in his nature, and withdraw him from the internal bondage of evil.

God is the light of our spiritual nature. Sin withdraws itself from God. Hence the condition of sin is a condition of blindness and spiritual darkness. The moral conceptions are dulled. The man lives in his senses and becomes a creature of sense. His religious ideas, separated from faith or by unbelief denied, still maintain their activity as vagaries, after they have lost their verity; and, haunted by these vagaries, he finds no rest till the God whose conception he has lost, is replaced by such as he can invent for himself. Hence the infallible connection of sin and idolatry. The glory of the incorruptible God is necessarily lost. Actuated still by a dim religious instinct, whose object and throne of worship are no longer seen, he fashions gods through the smoke of his own lusts—cruel and deceitful monsters, of course, for a God of love cannot be conceived through clouds of animosity and tempests of wrath.

What, now, shall cure this blinded condition of the race? How needful that God should meet them in the element where their soul lives, that is, in their senses. It is not so much an absolute religion—not doctrines or precepts or arguments that they want, but a production of the divine in the human, a living Presence, a manifestation of the Life. Therefore the Word is made flesh and dwells with men. The true light now shineth. God, who commanded the light to shine out of darkness, hath shined in our hearts, to give the light of the knowledge of the glory of God in the face of Jesus Christ. God is here, in act, word, power, filling the molds of history, and visiting the blinded world in the palpable forms of life itself. The understanding that was darkened, being alienated from the life of God, beholds once more a light in the manifested life. Even the atheist feels a Presence here, whose simple and pure shining, as it provokes no argument, suffers no answer. While the understanding is blockaded by doubt, a God streams into the feeling, and proves His reality to the heart. The torpors of logic are melted away by the warmth of the life, and he knows God as love, before he finds him as the absolute of the reason. Thus it has been also with idolatry. No speculations or abstractions about God have ever been able to correct or overthrow idolatry.

But how many idolatrous nations have yielded to the wondrous power that has invaded their feeling from the life and cross of Christ! The Word made flesh is the true light to them. The historic Christ fills them with God as a higher sense. The divinity, in him, floods their feeling, and they receive God as a Power, before they conceive his philosophic Idea.

The manifestation of the Life also revives in man, as a sinner, the consciousness of himself. It is one of the paradoxes realized by sin, that, while it makes a man every thing to himself, it makes him also nothing. It smothers the spark of conscious immortality. This world is practically all to him. The grave is dark, and he has no faith to throw a light across on spiritual realities beyond it. But when he that was in the form of God comes into the human state, when we see one here who visibly is not of us, when he opens here a heart of love, and floods the world with rivers of divine feeling, when we trace him from the manger over which the hymns of heaven's joy are ringing, to the cross where his purpose to save embraces even death for man; and then, when we see that death cannot hold him, that he bursts into life again as a victor over death—following such a history transacted, in our view, we begin also to conceive the tremendous import of our own, the equally tremendous import also of our sin. If God, to renew the soul moves a plan like this, what is it to be a soul, what to desecrate and destroy a soul? The conscious grandeur of his eternity returns upon the transgressor and he trembles in awe of himself—himself the power of an endless life.

Suppose, now, to advance another stage, that a man under sin becomes reflective, conscious of himself and of evil, sighing with discontent and bitterness, because of his own spiritual disorders. Conceive him thus as undertaking a restoration of his own nature to goodness, and the pure ideal of his conscience. What can he do without some objective power to engage his affections, and be a higher nature, present, by which to elevate and assimilate his own? Sin has removed him from God; withdrawing into himself, his soul has become objectless, and good affections cannot live, or be made to live, where there is no living object left to warm and support them. He can rise, therefore, by no help from his affections, or through them. Accordingly, if he attempts to restore himself to that ideal beauty and purity he has lost, he is obliged to do it wholly by his will; possibly against the depressing bondage of his affections, now sunk in torpor and deadness, or soured by a protracted, malign activity. Having all this to do by his will, he finds, alas! that if to will is present, how to perform is not. He seems, to himself, like a man who is endeavoring to lift himself by pulling at his feet. Hence, or to remove this disability, God needs to be manifested as Love. The Divine Object rejected by sin and practically annihilated as a spiritual conception, needs to be imported into sense. Then, when God appears in His beauty, loving and lovely, the good, the glory, the sunlight of soul, the affections, previously dead, wake into life and joyful play, and what before was only a self-lifting and slavish effort becomes an exulting spirit of liberty. The body of sin and death that lay upon the soul is heaved off, and the law of the spirit of life in Christ Jesus—the Eternal Life manifested in him, and received by faith into a vital union—quickens it in good, and makes it free.

But there is yet another difficulty, over and above the deadness and the moral estrangement of the affections; I speak of the fearful and self-accusing spirit of sin. Reason as we may about human depravity, apologize for men, or justify them as we may, they certainly do not justify themselves. Even in the deepest mental darkness concerning God, stifled, we may almost say, as regards their proper humanity, under the sottish and debasing effects of idolatry, still we see the conscience struggling with guilty fears, unable to find rest. An indescribable dread of evil still overhangs the human spirit. The being is haunted by shadows of wrath and tries all painful methods of self pacification. Vigils, pilgrimages, sacrifices, tortures, nothing is too painful or wearisome that promises to ease the guilt of the mind. Without any speculations about justification, mankind refuse to justify themselves. A kind of despair fills the heart of the race. They have no courage. Whether they know God or not, they know themselves, and they sentence themselves to death. If they have only some obscure notions of a divine Being, then they dread the full discovery of Him. If He lurks in their gods, they fear lest their gods should visit them in vengeance, or plague them by some kind of mischief. The sky is full of wrathful powers, and the deep ground also is full. Their guilty soul peoples the world with vengeful images of its own creation.

And here, now, if we desire to find it, is the true idea of Christian justification. We discover what it is by the want of it. Justification is that which will give confidence, again, to guilty minds; that which will assure the base and humiliated soul of the world, chase away the demons of wrath and despair it has evoked, and help it to return to God in courage, whispering still to itself—soul be of good cheer, thy sins are forgiven thee.

And this result is beautifully prepared by the advent of Christ, as well as by the crowning act of his death. God thus enters humanity as the Word made flesh, and unites himself to it, declaring by that sign, that he is ready to unite it unto himself. We perceive also and hear that he has come, not to condemn the world, but to save it. No storm wraps him about when he comes. The hymn that proclaims him, publishes—"peace on earth." He appears in a form to indicate the gentlest errand and the closest approach to our human lot; one, too, that never appalls the guiltiest—the form of a child. In his ministry he sometimes utters piercing words, still he is a friend, even a brother to the guilty. He calls the heavy-laden to come unto him, and promises rest. In short, he lives confidence into the world. Apart from all theologic theories, we know, we see with our eyes, that God will justify us and give us still his peace. And then, when we truly come unto him, believing that Christ the Word is He, when, forsaking all things for him, we embrace him as our life, then are we practically justified. It is impossible for us to fear. No guilt of the past can disturb us; a peace that passeth understanding fills our nature. Being justified by faith, we have peace with God through our Lord Jesus Christ.

Or, if we advert, in this connection, to the sufferings and death of Christ, we shall see how these, without the imputation of any penal quality or frown of God upon his person, have a special efficacy in fortifying our assurance or hope of justification with God. Dismiss all speculation about the mode, possibility, interior reality of this suffering; understand that God, having proposed, in this manner, to express His love, all logical, theological, ontological, physiological questions are, by the supposition, out of place. Come, then, to the spectacle of Christ's suffering life and death, as to a mystery wholly transcendent, save in what it expresses of Divine feeling. Call what of this feeling you receive the reality—all else the *machina Dei* for the expression of this. With deepest reverence of soul, approach that most mysterious sacrament of love, the agony of Jesus; note the patience of his trial, the meekness of his submission to injustice, and the malignant passions of his enemies; behold the creation itself darkening and shuddering with a horror of sensibility at the scene transpiring in his death; hear the cry of the crucified—"Father, forgive them, for they know not what they do;" then regard the life that was manifested, dropping into cessation, and thereby signifying the deposit of itself in the bosom of that malign world, to whose enmity it is yielded—who, what man of our race beholding this strange history of the Word, will not feel a new courage enter into his soul? Visibly, God is not the implacable avenger his guilty fears had painted. But he is a friend, he is love. And so great is this change, apart from all theology, that I seem even to see another character produced by it, in the Christian nations. They dare to hope. God is closer to them and in a way to inspire courage. They are not withered, humiliated even to baseness, under those guilty and abject fears that take away at last the spirit of other nations. It is not that they have all a theory of justification by faith, but that their current conceptions of God are such as the history of Jesus, the suffering redeemer, has imparted. They have a feeling of something like justification, even if they never heard of it—a feeling, which, if it were to vent itself in language, would say—Therefore we are freely justified by grace. It is not that the suffering appeases God, but that it expresses God—displays, in open history, the unconquerable love of God's Heart.

But what, in this view, some will ask, becomes of the law and justice of God? First, we have Christ, interrupting the flow of justice by delivering men, or assisting them to deliver themselves from the penal consequences of transgression; from the blindness, bitterness, deadness, and other disabilities it produces. Secondly, there is made out, or given to men, a confidence equally repugnant to justice, that God will freely accept, embrace, and even justify the transgressor who forsakes his sin. Where, now, it will be asked, is government? What becomes of law? And since God's love of right, or what is the same, his justice, was evidenced by his law and the penalties added to enforce it, what shall save the obligation of the law; what, indeed, shall displace the ambiguity that shades the divine character itself? Hence the necessity, it is argued, of some vicarious suffering, or expression made by suffering, that shall vindicate the law as effectively as the penalties remitted would have done, and thus shall save the moral rigor of God's integrity, in the view of his subjects.

But, granting this, it does not follow that the new vicarious expression of God must be made by a process equally vindictive with punishment; or that God's abhorrence to sin must be poured out upon Christ's own person. Neither does it follow, as our theories of vicarious atonement generally assume, that the grand judicial and penal demonstration, supposed to be necessary is wanted before the high court of the universe to answer the public ends of government there. We may, doubtless, assume to know that all the transactions of God, in all his worlds, constitute, when taken together, a sublime and perfect unity; and that, when they are mutually known in worlds now sundered, they will be received as displays of His "manifold [that is, various, diversified] wisdom," and the adorable fertility and grandeur of His government. And so each part of the universe, by the contribution of its own particular history, will exalt and fortify the admiration of all towards the common Lord and King. But as regards the effect of Christ's death, taken as a central spectacle in the universe, and designed to impress the minds of God's other subjects, and fortify His sway in other worlds, manifestly we know nothing of it; and all that is advanced by our theologians in regard to it, is to be taken only as evidence that the traditional effects of the Ptolemaic system continue for so long a time in theology, after they have disappeared from the almanac. If a vindication of God's law is wanted, in order to the offer of forgiveness, it is wanted here, and for effect in this world. And if we narrowly inspect the case presented, we shall be at no loss in regard to the real ground of such a necessity. For it is even a fundamental condition, as regards moral effect on our character, that, while courage and hope are given us, we should be made, at the same time, to feel the intensest possible sense of the sanctity of the law, and the inflexible righteousness of God. What we need, in this view, is some new expression of God, which, taken as addressed *to us*, will keep alive the impression in us, that God suffers no laxity. In a word, we must be made to feel, in the very article of forgiveness, when it is offered, the essential and eternal sanctity of God's law—His own immovable adherence to it, as the only basis of order and well-being in the universe.

As to the manner in which this desired result is effected, since it presents the hinge question at issue between Unitarianism and orthodoxy, I will dilate upon it here as the gravity of the question demands.

On one side, it is affirmed that God could not forgive sin, either without an equivalent suffering, or an equivalent expression of abhorrence to sin made by suffering, in the place of punishment. On the other side, since this doctrine, in either form of it, seems to involve some thing offensive to our moral sense, or repugnant to our ideas of God, it is affirmed that God, out of His simple goodness or paternity, can forgive, and will forgive every truly penitent sinner. Satisfied with neither doctrine, for the reasons urged by one against the other, and, perhaps I should say, with both, for the reasons urged by each in its own behalf, I venture to suggest, as the more real and reasonable view, that, in order to *make men penitent,* and so to want forgiveness—that is, to keep the world alive to the eternal integrity, verity, and sanctity of God's law—that is, to keep us apprized of sin, and deny us any power of rest while we continue under sin ; it was needful that Christ, in his life and sufferings, should consecrate or reconsecrate the desecrated law of God, and give it a more exact and imminent authority than it had before—this, too, without anything of a penal quality in his passion, without regarding him as bearing evil to pay the release of evil, or as under any infliction or frown of God, and yet doing it by something expressed in his life and death.

I will name, in this view, four methods in which Christ is seen to have brought the law closer to men's souls, and given it even a more sacred rigor and verity than it had before his advent.

1. By his teachings concerning it. John the Baptist had an altogether different conception of Christ, from that which is entertained by our modern Christian world. He looked upon the advent of Jesus as the advent of a new and more fearful revelation of God. Now he was coming to lay the axe to the root of every unfruitful tree, coming with the fan in his hand to sift out the pure wheat

of character, and burn up the chaff of religious pretense and hypocrisy, as in a fire.

Accordingly, there is no chapter in the Old Testament, where the law of God is held up in such terms of rigor and exactness, as it is in the sermon on the mount, the very first exposition that Christ made of his mission. Eternity was before seen only under a veil. It had been revealed more by implication than by express teachings. Here it is visibly set open by Christ, and the law of God, so much occupied before with outward service, so exclusively maintained by temporal penalties, is now spiritualized in every statute, rolled back upon the very thoughts and motions of the heart, and uttered there, under the sanction of eternal retributions. Christ even declares that no jot or tittle of the law shall pass away —that he comes, on the contrary, to fulfill the law; that is to fill it out, bring it into spiritual application, and maintain it by the distributions of a future state. I am well aware that what I here advance is specially repugnant to certain modern assumptions concerning Christianity, as a scheme of mere humanities apart from government; a scheme all leniency and accommodation. I go into no issue here on this question. I only say, what is obvious to any one, on simple inspection, that the law of Christianity is as much more stern in the form Christ gives it, and its distributions as much more appalling, as the precept is deeper, and the eternity of its reign more open to view. If any one has an explanation to give, whether of this or the Old Testament severities, the way is open; only be it agreed that Christianity as set forth by Christ, instead of pretending to be a looser, more accommodating faith, is, in fact, a law-system more exact and appalling. It expresses the mercy and love of God, the freedom, tenderness, and impartiality of his compassions, and just as much more intensely, the truth compels me to say, the holiness, exactness and sacred rigor of his law.

This I say as by direction; for I feel that nothing could be more unacceptable to the judgments of this age of the world. I say it also with some proper sense, I trust, of the possible aberration of the judgments of the age; for every age has its own drift and fashion, in which, though it be infallible to itself, it is often found, by those that come after, to have seized upon assumptions that God had never yielded, to have constructed a wisdom which human society could not bear, and time refused to audit. Believing, therefore, that Christianity is wiser than the age, I prefer to let it stand in that stern aspect it assumes for itself, and offer its mercy to man out of cloud and darkness which I know not how to clear. Most assuredly there is no look of laxity or inexactness in it or its law. It is nowhere in the vein of indifference, or false pity to man.

But there is a deeper expression in the life and death of Christ than any that is offered by his mere words. And it is here, especially, that he fulfills the office of a sacrifice, of which so much is said in the scripture; which, if we investigate, we shall find that he sanctifies the law before which he offers forgiveness, in three other distinct methods, analogous to those by which the ritual sacrifices became effectual—(2.) by obedience, (3.) by expense and painstaking (4.) by the offering of his Life, as a sacred contribution.

To each of the methods thus numerically indicated, I will recur, in successive illustrations, after I have sufficiently examined the ritual economy of sacrifice to become possessed of the analogies it offers.

The institution of sacrifice is most reasonably regarded as a positive institution, originally appointed by God. We find the rite in use at a time when marriage, a far less artificial institution, is represented as being received by God's appointment, and when he himself was introducing, by his lessons, the culture of the ground and even the dress of the body. It was most natural, too, that, when he was teaching the guilty, fallen pair their severance from him, by removing them from their paradise, he should also teach them by what rites of penitence and worship they might be purified and restored to union with him. We also find a positive statute enacted, at a very early period, forbidding the eating of blood, the object of which is to make it a sacred thing for the uses of the altar. Afterwards, undeniably, the system of sacrifice was carefully elaborated by the minutest and most specific positive statutes. Besides, which to me is most convincing of all, there is a certain fore-looking in this ritual, and then, when Christ appears, a certain retrospection, one answering to the other, one preparing words and symbols to express the other, and a beautiful and even artistic correspondence kept up, such as argues invention, plan, appointment, and indicates a Divine counsel present, connecting the remote ages of time, and weaving them together into a compact and well-adjusted whole. And if the redemption of man is the great work of the world, that in which all existences here find their highest import, as most assuredly it is, then what may better occupy the wisdom and the greatness of God, than the preparation of so great a work?

The matter and manner of the sacrifice are familiar to us all—the going up to Jerusalem, driving thither, or purchasing there, a choice, unblemished animal; the confession of sin upon his head before the altar; the solemn formalities of the slaughter and preparation of the sacrifice; the sacred blood sprinkled before the vail that is closed against unholy feet, the horns of the altar touched with blood, and the remainder poured out before it on the ground; then the fire kindled and the smoke of the victim, made a total loss for sin, rolling up before the eyes of the worshipper to heaven. And then he returns again to his tribe, thinking, on the way, of the journey he has undertaken for his sins—as he went up thinking of the sins that required him to go.

What, now, is the real meaning or value of this transaction? The ceremony is proposed to be connected with the remission of sins—how thus connected?

It is not that God has been appeased by the smell of the sacrifice. It is called an atonement, or propitiation, but it cannot be supposed that God is pacified in any way by the sacrifice.

It is not that the worshipper has embraced the atonement of Christ, typified in his sacrifice, as we sometimes hear. He had no such conception. Even the sacred prophets themselves, we are told, were guessing *what,* as well as what manner of time, the Spirit that was in them did signify when they spoke of Christ and his day. Nay, his own disciples, explicitly taught by himself, could not understand the import of his death till they were specially illuminated. Doubtless the worshipper had sometimes, and ought always to have, exercised faith in God, as a forgiver of sin; and, as God is Christ and Christ is God, there was exercised, of course, a virtual, but not formal faith in the Christ of the future.

It is not true or supposable, as needs to be specially noted, that the animal offered is punished for the sins of the worshipper. No hint or trace of any such impression can be found. Nor can it be argued from the confession of sins upon the head of the victim; for, when the scape-goat is employed, the confession upon his head is even more formal, and yet the animal is only driven away into the wilderness to signify the clearing of sin, its forgiveness and removal forever. Besides, if there were any idea of punishment connected with the sacrifice, if the death of the animal had a penal character, because of the sins supposed to rest on it, then something would be made of the suffering inflicted; which we know was never thought of, and made no part of the transaction. The animal was simply dispatched, as when slaughtered for the table, and it nowhere appears, in the whole range of Hebrew literature, that any one ever thought of the sufferings of the animal, as entering at all into the real moment of the transaction.

We come now to that in which the real value of the sacrifice did consist. The institution had, of course, a historic value as connected with the future life and work of the incarnate Redeemer; for in it are prepared correspondences and, so, types or bases of language, in which that more spiritual grace may be represented. I had also a value, considered as part of a great national religion, in which public remembrance of sin is made every year. It was also, as a rite, to have a renovating power over the character, somewhat as the manifested Life in Christ Jesus is designed to have; only in a vastly feebler and inferior degree. And therefore, in cases where it had no such effect, it was openly declared, on the part of God, to be an abomination to him, and as such to be rejected. The value of the sacrifice lay chiefly, however, in the power it had over the religious character—the impressions, exercises, aids, and principles, which, as a liturgy, it wrought in the soul of the worshipper. And among these, as connected especially with the remission of sins, was the impression it cherished of the sanctity of violated law; for, as I have said already, it is on the ground of that impression secured, both that forgiveness will be wanted, and may be safely offered.

We come back, then, from our excursion, to the three points above stated, to show how both Christ and the ritual sacrifice do, in correspondent methods, sanctify the law, or deepen the impressions held of its sanctity, in the minds of those who are exercised under them. Resuming our course of argument, I observe—

2. That Christ, coincidently with the ritual sacrifice, fortifies and sanctifies the law through his obedience. God appointed for the Hebrew nation a great public rite, one that required them, every year, to go up to the capital city, and there, in a vast assemblage of worshippers, offer their sacrifice for sin. The design evidently was that as every man, by his sin, weakens the sense of obligation,

and desecrates the authority of God, so by this grand public acknowledgment of God's authority, they should give their testimony to the sacredness of His will. What people, consenting, every year, at God's command, in such an ordinance—men of all ranks and characters leaving their homes and going up to the religious capital, there to make a public confession of their sin—would ever be in danger of holding a loose opinion of God's authority, or the sanctity of obligation, however freely their sins are forgiven?

The same impression is made, and far more deeply, by the obedience of Christ; for, considering who he is, there is more of meaning in his obedience than there is in the obedience of many nations. Regard him as coming under the desecrated law—which he does in the mystery of his incarnation; then consider the import of his life, taken in the simple aspect of a free, faithful, loving, unfaltering obedience—obedience unto death. And then, if the speculative instinct rushes in to insist on the absurdity of obedience in a being whose nature is essential deity, let it be enough to reply that there is no being in the universe, of whom obedience can be predicated in so vast a sense as of God. For though God is under no obligations to another, he is yet under obligations to goodness to devise, do, bear, forbear, suffer, all which the conception or idea of infinite goodness and love contains. He is really under the same law of obligation that we were under and cast off, and it is the glory and greatness of his nature that he delights eternally to acknowledge this law. Christ is the manifested Life revealing this everlasting obedience of the divine nature.

All that he does and suffers is but an expression of the homage, rendered by God himself, to that which we reject; and the only object of his mission is to bring us back into a like free obedience to the same lovely requirement. His poverty and patience, his weary, persecuted life, his agony, his cross, his death—exclude from these all thought of penal suffering or vindictive chastisement, regard him simply as supporting, thus, the call of duty, and signifying to mankind the self-renouncing and sublime obedience of the divine nature—what an expression of love to the right, and homage to law! How sacred now is law!—how sacred, yet how lovely! Why, the punishment of all mankind, even for eternity, could not signify as much.

3. Christ, coincidently with the sin offering, sanctifies the law through expense and painstaking. The sacrificer must come bringing the best and choicest of his flock, a lamb or a bullock without blemish. He must be absent from home, and leave his business behind, for whole days—all in the way of expense and painstaking for his sins. And, in one view, the expense he makes is wholly useless—a dead loss. The victim, the choice animal that was reared so carefully, is wholly burnt up, changed into smoke before his eyes—all under the law and by the law, desecrated by his sins. God will not even let him give it to charitable uses, lest he should be thinking of merit, when he ought to be thinking of his sins. It must go to smoke and simple destruction, and then the sacrifice will move his conscience. He will feel that the stern mandate of God is upon him. It will be as if he came to salve the violated law, by a willing loss of time and

property, laying his humble acknowledgments and dropping his tears upon the breaches and scars his sins have made.

So, also, Christ, by the sorrow and suffering of his painstaking life, accomplished a like result. Regarding him, not as acting here before the law, in some abstract way, or with a view to some governmental effect in other and remote fields of being, but as being engaged simply to win us back to newness of life, and restore us to union with God, it results that, by his sufferings, he does express the intense love of God to His law, and also impress in our souls a most deep and subduing sense of its value and sacredness. And this he does, not by saying, "see me suffer," or "see what sufferings the Father lays upon me;" for by that volunteering of naked suffering, according to the known laws of expression, nothing would be expressed, as I have already shown. This suffering is expressive, because it is incidental to an effort to reveal the love of God, and bring the eternal Life into the closest possible proximity to our human hearts. And the suffering we speak of has its power, not as answering to the sufferings of the victim in the sacrifice, for nothing is made of the sufferings of the victim, but as answering rather to the expense and painstaking and solemn preparation of the whole ceremony.

If we look upon it as the very end and aim of Christ's mission, to recover man to God and obedience; or, what is the same, to re-establish the law as a living power in his heart; then, of course, everything he does and suffers, every labor, weariness, self-denial and sorrow becomes an expression of his sense of the value of the law—every pang he endures, declares its sacredness. So that if he offers pardon, free pardon, to every transgressor, we shall never connect a feeling of license, but shall rather feel a sense of the eternal sanctity of the law, and have a more tremulous awe of it in our conscience, than we should if every transgressor were held to punishment by the letter of it. Indeed, if that were the doctrine, we should reason away and reject the doctrine as incredible; so that it would have no verity, and, of course, no sacredness at all. Whereas, having seen, in the painstaking, suffering life of Jesus, what God will do for the practical establishment of his law, we are seized with a deep and awe-felt conviction, that if we do not return to it according to his call, there is yet something different that must assuredly follow. All this, you perceive, without anything said of a penal quality, in the sufferings of Christ. No evil is laid upon him as evil, by the Father, to be endured retributively. He only suffers the ills that lie in his way, and endures the violence that human malignity and cruelty heap on his head.

But this, it will be apprehended by some, destroys the whole import of such scenes as the agony and the crucifixion. It may require a different construction of these scenes, but I hope it will not be too hastily concluded that a different construction robs them of their sacred import and power. It is imagined, by many, that what is called the "agony" of Jesus, was caused by the penal attitude in which he found himself before the Father, and the consequent sense of desertion he felt. What account, then, shall we make of this very wonderful and peculiar passage in his history? Evidently it is not from any

20

human fear that he suffers ; for the pathology observed is not that of fear—there is no pallor, the blood does not fly the skin, retreating as in fear on the springs of life, but it is forced even through the skin, as was never observed, it must be granted, in any case of mere human suffering. It was not that the soul of the sufferer was racked, by a sense of the withdrawment of the Father. How could the Father withdraw from so great excellence and purity, under so great a burden of sorrow—what end could it serve, thus to falsify his character? Besides, it was only just now that Christ was saying,—"therefore doth my Father love me, because I lay down my life for the sheep,"—also, directly to the Father,—"I have glorified thee on the earth, now I come to thee." It is also represented, by Luke, that an angel is sent to strengthen and support him—sent by the Father to support him under His own displeasure! Sometimes the exclamation, which he uttered afterwards, on the cross, is made to assist the interpretation of the agony also—"My God! my God! why hast thou forsaken me!" But this is only the language of intense suffering, an interjection, so to speak, of anguish. Besides, it appears to have had a current use ; for we find it more than once in the poetic writings of the Old Testament. Thus, Isaiah represents Zion as crying out in distress,—"the Lord hath forsaken me;" when God immediately responds,—"I have graven thee upon the palms of my hands." To take this language of passion, this common outcry of distress, and hold it in a cool, historic, or dogmatic sense, is to violate all dignified laws of interpretation. Besides, we are to observe that, between this agony and the trial

—probably before Christ leaves the garden—we hear him saying, "thinkest thou that I cannot now pray to the Father, and he shall, presently, give me more than twelve legions of angels?" Was he, then, deserted of the Father?

Rejecting this interpretation of the agony, we take up the 13th and following chapters of John's gospel, which contain his farewell and his parting prayer, and there we see that the whole day previous had been a day of unutterable sorrow and sadness both to himself and his disciples. They had all been struggling in a kind of agony from the early morning, it will be seen, down to the moment when they entered the garden; and the disciples were so spent that they could not retain their consciousness;—"He found them sleeping for sorrow." He only could not sleep, for the cup that was before him and might not pass from him. But why is he wrenched by this so peculiar agony? Consider, I answer, that, in the outward humanity of Jesus, there is held, in some close and mysterious union, a divine nature; and then will our physiologists or physicians tell us how long a vehicle so slender is to support the tremendous reaction of compassions and struggles of feeling that are so deeply toned! or, when the vehicle breaks under the burden, by what pathological signs it will be discovered! Besides, this divine-human being, whose interior nature we are forbidden to investigate, is unquestionably a sinless character, a being in the exactest internal harmony, that of purity, innocence, and life. He has never felt a throb of sinful disturbance, or shaken with one chill of death, since he came forth as a "Holy Thing," into our world. Now, that which is itself the type and fruit of sin, bodily death, is at hand to be experienced. Will any psychologist or theologian tell us exactly how he ought to feel, whether he will suffer less than a man, or more? If innocence shudders at the thought of wrong, more than a soul that is dulled and half disintegrated by the consciousness of wrong, may it not, for the same reasons, shudder with a more intense horror, before the prospect of that complete disintegration or tearing asunder, which is the natural doom of wrong? If, too, a massive engine may shake, or even sink a frail and poorly timbered vessel; or if a gigantic, masculine soul, knit to the body of a feeble and delicate woman, and, in that, called to suffer martyrdom, might possibly cause it to shudder and shake with a more insupportable horror, than the delicate, feminine soul appropriate to its measure would do, what kind of demonstration shall be expected, when the Incarnate Word is summoned to die? I only inquire, you observe—I assert nothing for the very sufficient reason that I know nothing. Enough for me, that my Redeemer, my most painstaking Saviour, falters not. Enough for me, that in that bloody sweat, falling on the desecrated earth, I see the love God has for love, the unspeakable desire He feels to win us back from sin, to re-establish the order of His realm, and hallow, for eternity, in our hearts, the sanctity of His violated law. No conception of a penal agony, or a penal cross could signify as much.

4. The law of God is yet more impressively sanctified by Christ, if possible, in the article of his death, considered as counterpart to the uses of blood in the ritual. The admirable ingenuity of the ritual, in this particular feature

of it, and also the intense force it had, as an artistic plan, to impress on the mind a sense of the holiness of God's character and the sacred authority of His government, must appear, I think, to every one who rightly apprehends it. The plan hangs on a sense produced of the essential sacredness of blood. At the very first institution, probably, of sacrifices, (for we trace it as early as the times of Noah,) the eating of blood was prohibited, on the ground that the blood is the life, and that life is a sacred thing. There was, in fact, no greater crime than the eating of blood. It was capitally punished. Even a stranger was put to death without mercy, who had been guilty of the crime. Now the whole object of this prohibition was to invest the element of blood with sacredness, for the uses of the altar. Thus Moses, in the 17th chapter of Leviticus, which I will venture to suggest is the one text, above all others, to open the true idea and import of sin-offerings, says, "For the life of the flesh is in the blood, and I have given it to you, upon the altar, to make an atonement for your souls; for it is the blood that maketh an atonement for the soul; therefore, I said unto the children of Israel, no soul of you shall eat the blood."

In this manner the element of blood was invested with the intensest possible sacredness. Then, when the worshipper comes before God, at His altar, there to offer blood and life, for his sin—to see the sacred drops that contain the sacred life sprinkled for him, before the holy of holies, and touched upon the horns of the altar—what is he saying but that only the most sacred thing he knows, even life, can suffice to resanctify the law, violated by his sins? Nay, more, a sacred thing is something that belongs especially to the occupancy and right of God, and the impression was that blood, being the mysterious principle of life, is somehow specially near to the Divine nature—thus, and therefore, sacred. Accordingly, when the man makes an offering of blood for the remission of his sins, doing it by God's command, he professes, in the act, that only something derivable from God, some sacred element yielded by Him, can suffice to cover his sin and hallow again the violated majesty of broken law. Thus maintained, the sense of law cannot perish. The sacred throne of law stands naked ever before the people, and remission becomes a want, under the same process which makes it possible,—possible, too, because the law, still upheld and sanctified in the conscience, makes it a want. Were they simply assured, instead, of God's fatherly benignity and His readiness to forgive sins freely, the assurance would be virtually a declaration of impunity, and a half century of time would suffice to obliterate even the sense of religion.

After thousands of years, spent under this regimen of sacrifice, have wrought into the Hebrew mind, and indeed the mind of the race, this one great maxim—an almost universally accepted maxim of religion—that without shedding of blood there is no remission, Christ appears and closes his sanctified and sublime life, by submission to a violent death. He is not a sacrifice in any literal sense, as we know. There is no altar in his death, no fire is kindled, by no act of religion or priestly rite is he offered up; he is simply murdered by the malice of his enemies. And yet, in another view, as I shall presently show, he is not the less really a sacrifice. Only let it suffice here to notice, that Christ himself called the attention of his disciples, beforehand, to his own blood, as now to be shed, and hereafter to be remembered, as the blood that was shed for the remission of sins. How, for the remission of sins, if there was no altar, no form of sacrifice or offering? The analogy, I answer, is one remove farther back, in that which rendered even the sacrifices themselves significant, viz., that only some sacred thing, something yielded by God, is sufficient to cover the breaches made by our sin. That is, nothing else can so dignify and exalt the authority of God's government and law, as to remove the danger, that the free proclamation of forgiveness, will breed, in men, such a spirit of license, that not even forgiveness will be wanted or accepted.

Thus Christ, we say, is the manifested Life. And the blood that circulates in him, according to the accepted modes of thinking under the ritual, represents, also, that which is inmost in the vitality of his person. Catching the suggestion of Christ concerning his blood, shed for men, and learning, after his death, to conceive more adequately the nature of his divine person, the disciples begin also to see that God has yielded, in his death, something more intensely sacred than they had conceived. Nay, all the most sacred things they have ever known on earth, even the blood of the altar itself, is rather profane than sacred, when compared with the Incarnate Life of Jesus. And this life they now look upon as distilling, in sacred drops, from his cross; falling into the desecrated earth, to permeate and vitalize both it and us, and hallow again before God, His polluted law and realm. Therefore they now say, with a meaning too deep for their words, or for any other words—"Neither by the blood of goats and calves, but by HIS OWN BLOOD he entered in once into the holy place, having obtained eternal redemption for us."

Looking, now, at the death of Christ in this manner, we are made, first of all, to feel, whether we can explain it or not, that it has a marvelous power over our impressions, concerning ourselves and our sins, the law of God and His character. It brings an element of divinity into everything, sheds an air of solemnity and grandeur over everything. It is even more awful to the guilty conscience itself, than the thunders of Sinai. And, then, secondly, we shall be able also, I think, to see that the whole effect, contemplated under the laws of art, is produced by the fact that the Life, thrice sacred, so dimly shadowed before in the victims of the altar, is here yielded, as a contribution from God, to the pacification and reconsecration of His realm. The effect depends, not on any real altar ceremony in his death, but it depends, artistically speaking, on the expressive power of the fact that the Incarnate Word, appearing in humanity, and having a ministry for the reconciliation of men to God, even goes to such a pitch of devotion, as to yield up his life to it, and allow the blood of his Mysterious Person to redden our polluted earth!

I have dwelt more at large on this particular feature of the work of Christ, because it is here that most of our disagreements and difficulties have their spring. My doctrine is summarily this; that, excluding all thoughts of a penal quality in the life and death of Christ, or of any divine abhorrence to sin, exhibited by sufferings laid upon his person; also, dismissing, as an assumption too high for us, the opinion that the death of Christ is designed for some governmental effect on the moral empire of God in other worlds,—excluding points like these, and regarding everything done by him as done for expression before us, and thus for effect in us, he does produce an impression in our minds of the essential sanctity of God's law and character, which it was needful to produce, and without which any proclamation of pardon would be dangerous, any attempt to subdue and reconcile us to God, ineffectual. Meantime, it may comfort some to add, that he does by *implication*, or inferentially, express in all that he does the profoundest abhorrence to sin; for, if he will endure so much to resanctify his law and renew us in the spirit of it, how intensely signified is the abhorrence of his nature to the transgression of his law—more intensely than it would be by the punishment even of us all.

How very exactly these representations correspond with the language of Paul, in what may well be called his standard text, will readily appear. According to the view I have given, whatever power is exerted here vicariously as a ground of forgiveness, is seen to be in the nature of manifestation, or expression, as represented by him. "The righteousness of God, without the law, is *manifested*." He does not say, you will observe, that the righteousness of God is satisfied, or vindictively maintained, but simply that it is manifested. Then, four verses after, he amplifies the same idea—"whom God hath set forth [made conspicuous in the flesh] to be a propitiation [propitiatory, or mercy seat—made so, not by standing in any penal attitude under God, but] by faith in his blood [so that, believing in him as the Sacred Life yielded for us, we may come into peace] to declare [εἰς ἔνδειξιν, more literally for the demonstration, expression, or public show of] his righteousness, for the remission of sins that are past, [not on adequate repayment of their penalty, in sufferings borne by another, but] through the forbearance of God. To declare [demonstrate or express] his righteousness [not hereafter, not before unknown, unimagined worlds in his moral empire, but] at this time [now and before us] that he might be just [righteous—that is, might stand before us in the exactness of his integrity] and the justifier of him that believeth in Jesus," [acquitting and accepting, in peace, all who forsake their sins, in a way of dependence on his gracious interposition.]

But there is yet one other feature of the life and death of Christ, considered as related to our reconciliation to God, which must be distinctly considered—I mean the subduing power it had, in virtue of what is expressed in it, over the human will. I have spoken of ideas, incentives, aids to liberty, justification, all provided in the incarnate life and death of Christ, but we do not really seem to ascend to the true grandeur of the Christian scheme, till we see the divine government prevailing and finally establishing itself in the willing obedience of souls, by an act of submission.

The first stage of government is the stage of law. But law, taken by itself, can establish nothing. There is an *a priori* necessity, and, of course, a historic certainty, that the training of an empire of free beings, and the final and complete union of their will to God, will require a double administration, or a change of administration, such as we find exhibited in the scriptures,—law and grace; the letter that killeth and the spirit that giveth life; justification by works, and justification by faith; bondage and liberty; the old covenant of outward discipline, and the new covenant written in the heart. Nor is it to be thought that such a view involves the opinion that God fails in one plan, and is, therefore, obliged to try again—fails in severity and compulsion, only to succeed, at last, by kindness and love. There is no violation of the unity of reason, as it is called, in this double administration; for to Him it is all one work, equally necessary in both the parts, to the one final result, a freely chosen, but eternally established obedience in His subjects.

Under the first stage, that of commandment, the soul makes her acquaintance with obligation, comes at the terms, so to speak, of her existence, lays her hands upon the iron fences of law that stiffen round her. Will she keep within her inclosures? If we speak of a naked possibility, she doubtless may. But it will be wonderful if she does not sometime yield to the instigation of her curious nature, and try the bad experience of evil. Or if she does not, if she stays within her iron inclosure, only because it is iron, she would seem to be governed in the good she follows, by constraint; which can hardly be regarded as a state of perfected virtue—it is a prudential and even cringing virtue, more than a virtue of liberty.

Accordingly, we look for a lapse, under this first discipline of law. Feeling its bars, as the bars of a cage, about her, the soul begins to chafe against them, and sc she learns the law—first, by attrition against it, and then by bondage under it. This is her fall. Having come to this, law by itself can do no more. The cage cannot reconcile the prisoner. Indeed, the law, taken as an appeal urged home only by penalties, becomes even a hindrance to his recovery. For it is the very misery and death of sin that it enthrones self interest, and makes the man a centre to himself. And, therefore, mere law, goading him still by appeals to self interest, only holds him to that which is the essential bondage and mischief of his condition. To renovate him now in good, requires a new motivity, one that will subdue him to love, and unite him to the good as good, not as profitable—to God's own beauty, truth, loveliness, and glory. To be balked in his self-seeking, to be shown that loss only and death are in the way that he pursues for profit, is not evil, it is means to an end, because it stops him, moves him to reflection. But there needs, just here, to be a captivating, or subduing power displayed, one that shall break his will, take him away from his self-seeking, engage his love, and regenerate the liberty of his fallen affections.

Hence there needs to be a change of administration. He needs, now, to be approached in a different manner Fighting out the war with him, by terms of force and penalty, can do nothing for his restoration. What, then, if the king, not renouncing his throne, nor silencing his legal thunders, should, in some mysterious way, come into the flesh and make his approach to the repugnant and chafing spirit of transgression, through personal feeling, on a level, even, of patience with wrong itself. Let him steal upon the alienated man, by a life that is parallel with his own—a life that is spent between a manger at the beginning and a cross at the end. Let him fall into the truest affinity with the lowest forms of humanity, entering into the feeling of all through what is lowest and most sorrowful in their lot—their wants, losses, and bodily and mental diseases—raining no fires of penalty on the head of their sin, but softening its dismal pains and healing its sorrows.

May I, without defect of reverence, express the deeper truth, that which is the appalling mystery of God in Christ Jesus—mystery, yet philosophy, of this divinest work of God, called redemption—the King Himself here takes the attitude of submission to evil. Requiring of us to vanquish wrong by a patient submission thereto, he does it, not as duty or wisdom only for us, but because it is a first law of power that a malignant or bad spirit will soonest yield to endurance, and is least of all able to endure the meekness of love. Observing this great truth himself, the divine Word is incarnated in the form of a servant, moving now upon the heart of evil from a point below it—attacking sin, not by penalties only, but by submissions rather. The malign spirit rises, bursting forth in a storm of deadly violence against his person. The only perfect being that ever lived in the flesh, he becomes the most insulted and abused being. But loaded as he is with insult, and dragged out to die, he bears the concentrated venom of his crucifiers with a lamb's patience, makes no answer, repels no taunt, complains of no severity. We see him, in fact, descending below our malignity, that it may break itself across his Divine Patience. He outreaches, by his love, the measure of our animosities—the wrong will in us, all the malignities of our devilish passion feel themselves outdone. Evil falls back from its apparent victory, spent, exhausted, conscious, as it never was before, of its impotence. The submission of the Word fairly broke its spirit, and ever since that day has it been falling visibly as Lucifer from heaven. Before this cross, we feel ourselves weak in evil. Into our angry spirit, chafing against the rule of law, there steals a gentler feeling—some secret centurion, hid in the heart's inmost cell, whispers, "truly this was the Son of God." And then embracing, as love, what we had rejected as law, or commandment, we do, in fact, accept all law. And now we have it, not in constraint—it is written in the heart. The letter that killeth is gone, and the spirit that giveth life, uniting us truly and forever to God's own person, we receive back in love all we had rejected in transgression, counting it our freest freedom to be one with Him forever; therefore one, not in the statutes only that He imposes, but in the principles by which He rules.

Thus far I have spoken of Christ, as related to the great end of his mission, viz: the reconciliation of our race to God; or, what is the same, the moral renovation of their character. For this end he expresses God and thus becomes a power—in scripture phrase, the power of God, and the wisdom of God. Or, as the same writer declares, in immediate connection and in terms yet more specific—"Christ, who is made unto us wisdom and righteousness and sanctification and redemption." Not righteousness in one sense, and wisdom and sanctification in another—not imputed righteousness and real sanctification; but a power and spring of all in our hearts—wisdom, righteousness, sanctification and redemption. In one word, union to God, as the essential life of our being and character is restored. And this was the true end of the incarnation.

Accordingly, we are able, just here, to conceive more exactly than before, the real import of the incarnation. It is not that God simply makes a theophany or show of Himself, though a human body. Neither is it that He is one of two residing in this human body—a Divine Soul dwelling with a human. In neither case would He really come into sympathy with our human feeling at all; or, if at all, but feebly; for in the former, the mere accident of his connection with a human body, taken as a type, would signify nothing to our human feeling, and, in the latter, the human soul, being distinguished as a separate nature, having a separate consciousness and suffering by itself whatever is suffered, the Divine heart is even more remote therein from any condition of sympathy with us. All such efforts, therefore, at the interior conception or analysis of Christ, are to be discarded, and we are to accept him as the identification of the divine and the human—the Word *become* flesh. Unquestionably the whole matter of the transaction is mysterious, and will be. Unquestionably the whole import of the transaction is what it expresses. And, in order to the fullest and most vivid power of the expression made, we want no mock solutions interposed; but we want, rather, to behold the Divine brought into our human conditions of sorrow and pain—to accept the Incarnate Word thus, in simplicity, as a brother, looking never beyond what appears. But if we must be wiser, if, penetrating the matter of the transaction just an inch, we are pleased to discover a God acting from behind a human soul, in a human body, we have still as much of mystery left upon our hands as before, and the eternal Life as much more distant from our feeling, as we have more impediments and inanities placed between us.

Besides, what we want, as beings alienated from the Life of God, is to see the possible union of the divine and the human signified to us; for there is to be, and must be a real life-union between the Spirit of God and all the righteous spirits of his kingdom. It is to be no mere collection of good and well shaped atoms, but an organic frame of Life—"I in them and thou in me, that they may be made perfect in One." Therefore it is the total aim of Christianity to destroy the life of self, bring us off from the self-centres about which we revolve in our sins, and set us moving as in God;—that is, to take us away, at last, from our separate contrivings and willings and the life of prudence, and elevate us into a life of perpetual inspiration, whose impulse and perfection are the pure inbreathing of God. Hence the relevancy and sublimity of the incarnation, always to be taken with simplicity as the real union of the divine and the human—beyond which we have no further questions to ask and nothing to say, unless each can say for himself—Christ liveth in me.

Here I close the subjective view of Christ's mission.

Considered as a power moving the spiritual regeneration and redemption of man, this is the conception we form of it. Is it a true conception? I have a degree of confidence that it is. But there is yet another question: is it satisfactory—is it the gospel of Christ? However it may seem to others, for it certainly appears to be a plan not wanting in magnificence, I am still obliged to confess that, taken by itself, it is not satisfactory to me, and I could not offer it as the full and complete gospel of Christ.

I observe, in the scriptures, a large class of representations, such as speak of the *atonement* received by Christ, his *sacrifice*, his *offering*, his *bearing the sins* of many, the holiest opened by his *blood*, the *curse* he became, the *wrath* he suffered, the *righteousness* he provided, which do not seem to have their proper, natural place and significance in the view here presented. I recollect, also, that around these terms of grace, the whole church of God, with but a few limited exceptions, have hung their tenderest emotions, and shed their freest tears of repentance; that by these the righteous good, the saints and martyrs of the past ages have supported the trial of their faith; that before these they have stood, as their altar of peace, and sung their hymn of praise to the Lamb that was slain; and remembering this, I cannot convince myself that they were wholly mistaken, or that they were not receiving here, in the living earnest of their spirit, something that belongs to the profoundest verity and value of the cross. Men do not live in this manner, from age to age and by whole nations, upon pure error. Spiritual life is not fed, thus interminably, upon a gospel that mocks all reality. If their supposed gospel does not stand with reason or theory, it must somehow stand with faith, feeling, and all that is inmost in eternal life. This brings me to the—

II. Department of my subject, that in which I proposed to unfold an objective ritual view, answering to the more speculative and subjective now presented, and necessary, as such, to the full effect and power of Christ's mission.

Few persons are aware how intently our mental instinct labors to throw all its subjects of thought and feeling into objectivity. For we think, in the liveliest manner, only when we get our thoughts out of us, if I may so speak, and survey them as before us. Thus we say of a scene, that it was *pitiful*, or *joyful*, or *delightful*, not because the scene itself was really full of pity, joy, or delight, but because we were so ourselves. Still we do not say it, but we give objectivity to our feeling, passing over our pity, joy, delight, into the scene, and having it for our pleasure to see the feeling there. So we say that a thing is *grateful* to us, when we mean that we are grateful for it; and, in the same manner, we call a man a *suspicious* character, when we only mean that we are suspicious, or may well be suspicious of him. We even throw our own acts into objectivity. Thus the word *attribute* properly denotes an act of *attributing* or *imputing* in us, but we use it as having no subjective reference whatever. We even make our own thinking processes objective, in the same manner, saying, *it occurs to us*, *it appears to us*, when, in fact, we are only describing what transpires within us. Human language, indeed, is full of illustrations to the same effect, showing how it is the constant effort of our nature to work itself, report its thoughts and play its sentiments, under forms of representation that are objective.

Accordingly, it will be found that all the religions the world has ever seen, have taken, as it were by instinct, an objective form. No race of men, so far as I know, have ever undertaken to work their sentiments towards God or the gods artificially; that is, by a reflective operation, or by addressing their own nature, under the philosophic laws of moral effect. The religion has been wholly an outward transaction, not in form a transaction of the soul. It has worked the soul only in a manner somewhat unconscious, or by a kind of silent implication. Ask the worshipper what is the religion, and he will say, it is the sacrifice offered thus or thus, the procession, the vow, the priestly ceremony—some objective pageant or transaction. He probably conceives no such thing as a subjective effect, distinct from what he sees with his eyes; still there is such an effect, and it is only in virtue of this, received in a latent or unconscious manner, that the transaction seen by the eyes has any significance to him.

Such, as we may see at a glance, was the religion of the Jewish people. It stood, not in subjective exercises carefully stated and logically distinguished, but in a carefully exact ritual of outward exercise. Their religion, if closely studied, will be found to consist of artistic matter wholly above their invention—a scheme of ritualities so adjusted as to work sentiments, states, and moral effects in the worshippers, which, as yet, they were unable to conceive or speak of themselves. It had a mystic power wholly transcendent, as regards their own understanding, and one that involved an insight so profound, of the relation of form to sentiment, that God only could have prepared it. Manifestly it was impossible for a people so little exercised in reflection, to make any thing of a religion which consisted in reflecting on themselves, conceiving, then addressing their wants, by intellectual motives. Working thus upon themselves, in the manner of 'Edwards on the Affections,' what could the men whom Moses led out of Egypt have done? But they had their 'Edwards on the Affections' in altars, unblemished bullocks and lambs, bloody sprinklings, smokes rolling up to heaven, and solemn feasts; and counting these to be their religion, beyond which they could hardly manage a religious thought of any kind, there was yet an artistic power in their rites, such that in being simply transacted, they carried impressions, so efficacious in the production of a religious spirit, that many, without the least conception of religion as a subjective experience, were undoubtedly brought into a state of real penitence and vital union with God. Having no philosophy of the moral government of God; without any conception whatever of law, in the higher sense, or of sin, justification, faith, and spiritual life; the ritual came into their feeling when transacted, with a wisdom they had not in their understanding, and their soul received impressions under the artistic objectivities of the altar, which, by reason or intellectual contemplation, they were wholly unable to comprehend. In the progress of their history, they visibly become more reflective, speaking oftener of that which lies in the state of the heart, and the internal aim and principle of the life. Still they had never gone so far, previous to the coming of Christ, as to conceive a purely subjective religion.

Nor is that any proper and true conception of Christianity. Some persons appear to suppose that Christianity is distinguished by the fact that it has finally cleared us of all ritualities or objectivities, introducing a purely subjective and philosophic or ideal piety. This they fancy is the real distinction between Judaism and Christianity. They do not conceive that Christianity rather fulfills Judaism than displaces it—that, while it dismisses the *outward* rites and objectivities of the old religion, it does, in fact, erect them into so many *inward* objectivities, and consecrate them as the Divine Form of the Christian grace for all future time. Thus, instead of a religion before the eyes, we now have one set up in language before the mind's eye, one that is almost as intensely objective as the other, only that it is mentally so, or as addressed to thought. The sacrifices and other Jewish machineries are gone, yet they are all here—indeed they never found their true significance, till Christ came and took them up into their higher use, as vehicles of his divine truth. The scheme of God is one, not many. The positive institutions, rites, historic processes of the ante-Christian ages are all so many preparations made by the transcendent wisdom of God, with a secret design to bring forth, when it is wanted, a divine form for the Christian truth—which, if we do not perceive, the historic grandeur of Christianity is well nigh lost.

Then, also, and for the same reason, is the sublime art of Christianity concealed from us. We do not conceive it as art, but only as a didactic power, a doctrine, a divine philosophy. Whereas a great part of its dignity and efficacy consists in the artistic power of its form as an objective religion—a religion *for* the soul and *before* it, so intensely efficient to operate a religion in it. And this, precisely, is the defect of the subjective view I have presented. It offers no altar Form for the soul's worship, but only something to be received by consideration—such a kind of remedy for sin that, if we had it on hand always to act reflectively, and administer to our own moral disease, it would be well. But that is not the remedy that meets our case. Just as the sick man wants, not an apothecary, but a physician; not a store of drugs out of which he may choose and apply for himself, but to commit himself, in trust, to one who shall administer for him, and watch the working of his cure: so the soul that is under sin wants to deposit her being in an objective mercy, to let go self-amendment, to believe, and in her faith to live.

I shall recur to this point hereafter, when I hope to make it appear that, without this objective side, Christianity would in some points even frustrate itself. But, before attempting this, it will be necessary to go into some illustrations that will show, more exactly, what is meant by the objective form of Christianity.

Many persons are not aware of the manner in which subjective truths, thoughts, sentiments, and changes, often find objective representations, which, though wholly unlike in form, are yet their virtual equivalents. Thus it may be represented, as a subjective truth, that every soul contains in itself a perfect memory, one that garners up every thing of the past, and will, at some future day, be roused to report to us all the acts and thoughts of our past lives. Now, for this, we have a good objective equivalent, when it is represented that God keeps a judgment book, in which he records all our actions. No two representations could be more unlike, and yet they are good equivalents. So we may describe the unquiet and subjectively discomposed state of a transgressor, as being the natural and proper effect of his transgression; but he is very likely, himself, to represent the disturbance he feels objectively, as being the wrath of God. And then, when he is restored and brought into the peace of Christ, he is very likely, for similar reasons, to conceive of Christ as having conciliated God; not of himself, as being reconciled to God. I do not undertake to say that subjective and objective representations, like these, are rigid and exact equivalents one for the other—no two representations of any kind were ever exact equivalents. I only say that one form is a valid and sufficiently accurate substitute, in certain uses, for the other. Both forms will have their advantages. The subjective is commonly more philosophical and literal; the other often carries the true impression, or thought, only by implication; and sometimes the more powerfully, for the very reason that the person using it is wholly unconscious that any such impression or effect is in him. The objective representation is often taken literally, occupying the mind with a form of supposed truth, which is not true, (so also does the subjective) but which envelops a truth or true impression of the highest validity and power.

And this will be found to hold, most especially of those objective forms which are employed artistically, or as elements and terms of moral expression or moral effect. There is no doubt that the Hebrew people, whose religion was so intensely objective, held it in a manner of literality that involved real misconception. They saw nothing in it but the altars, priests, confessions, sprinklings and smoking fires, and these they called their atonement, or the covering of their sin; as if there were some outward value in the things themselves—taken outwardly these were the religion. But, meantime, there was a power in these, by which subjective effects were continually transpiring within them, and the outward value of the rite, which was a fiction, had yet an inward value correspondent thereto, which made the fiction truthful. There was a re-acting power, a power to produce reflex impressions in the rites, by which the law was sanctified; by which they testified and were made to feel repentance for sin; by which they were exercised in faith to receive the remission of sins. They had their religion, as they thought, in their altar, which conciliated God to them; and what they had, as they thought, before their eyes, was a religious experience in their hearts. This, at least, was the plan, though it was possible for them to fail of the true result, as it is for us, under a more reflective and self-regulative form of piety. They were to deposit their soul in the outward rite, and there to let it rest; and then the outward rite was relied upon to be a power in the heart. The plan was, to frame a religion that would produce its results artistically; that is, immediately, without reflection, by the mere liturgic force of forms. Endowed with an artistic power, these forms were to work their impression, in the immediate, absolute way that distinguishes art, and without the interposition of thought, debate, choice, and self-application. Thus the Jew had, in effect, a whole religion present to thought, when he simply looked upon the *blood* of his victim; and yet in a manner so transcendent, in one view so mystical, that when we endeavor to analyze the import of the word *blood*, and tell by what element or elements it becomes thus expressive, we find it difficult, by any circumlocutions that avoid the altar and the sacrificial images, to say any thing that shall exactly represent our impressions. This same artistic force or immediateness of impression, is obviously as much more to be desired in Christianity, as the subjective truths and powers it contains have a vaster moment.

Passing, now, into the domain of Christianity, let us try an experiment on the subjective doctrine already exhibited, and see how far it may be represented in objective equivalents drawn from the ancient ritual. Christ, we have seen, is a power for the moral renovation of the world, and as such is measured by what he expresses. Thus we have seen that by his obedience, by the expense and painstaking of his suffering life, by the yielding up of his own sacred person to die, he has produced in us a sense of the eternal sanctity of God's law that was needful to prevent a growth of license or of indifference and insensibility to religious obligation, such as must be incurred, if the exactness and rigor of a law-system were wholly dissipated, by offers of pardon grounded in mere leniency. The moral propriety, then, or possibility, nay, in one view, the ground of justification, is subjectively prepared in us; viz., in a state or impression, a sense of the sacredness of law, produced in us by Christ's life and death. But we cannot think of it in this artificial way; most persons could make nothing of it. We must transfer this subjective state or impression, this ground of justification, and produce it outwardly, if possible, in some objective form; as if it had some effect on the law or on God. The Jew had done the same before us, and we follow him; representing Christ as our sacrifice, sin-offering, atonement, or sprinkling of blood. Now in all these terms, we represent a work as done outwardly for us, which is really done in us, and through impressions prepared in us, but the more adequately and truly still, for the reason that we have it in mystic forms before us. These forms are the objective equivalents of our subjective impressions. Indeed, our impressions have their life and power in and under these forms. Neither let it be imagined that we only happen to seize upon these images of sacrifice, atonement, and blood, because they are at hand. They are prepared, as God's form of art, for the representation of Christ and his work; and if we refuse to let him pass into this form, we have no mold of thought that can fitly represent him. And when he is thus represented, we are to understand that he is our sacrifice and atonement, that by his blood we have remission, not in any speculative sense, but as in art. We might as well think to come at the statue of Aristides speculatively, interpreting its power by geometric demonstrations, instead of giving our heart to the expression of integrity in the form, as to be scheming and dogmatizing over these words *atonement, sin-offering*, *sacrifice*, and *blood*, which are the divine form of Christianity.

It is only another aspect of the same truth, when Christ is represented, objectively, as our righteousness. As the sacred blood, yielded for sin, stood in place of a righteousness, in virtue of the impressions produced by it, so also does Christ; and as the offering was a liturgic exercise of faith and penitence, so likewise Christ is a power to regenerate character and restore us to righteousness of life. What, then, shall we call him, if not our righteousness; transferring, again, what is only subjective, in us, and beholding it in its objective source—that is, in the form of divine art and expression, by which it is wrought? This is the true attitude of faith; for if, in the utmost simplicity, we thus believe in him, if we take him, objectively, as a stock of righteousness for us, and hang ourselves upon him for supply, we can scarcely fail to have his life and character ingrafted in us. We may take his obedience as accruing to our benefit, we may see our righteousness in him, just as we see our pity in things that we say are pitiful. If we go farther, if we speak of his righteousness as imputed to us, it will not be ill, in case we hold the representation as in art, and not as a dialectic or dogmatic statement.

Or, adverting to the affecting truth that Christ has come between us and our sins in his death, we shall see our sins transferred to him, and regard him as loading himself with our evils. And then, as if we had put our sins upon his head, we shall say that he bears our sins, suffers the just for the unjust, is made a curse for us. All those terms of vicarious import, that were generated under the ritual sacrifice, will be applied over to him, and we shall hold him by our faith, as the victim substituted for our sins. And so, with the humblest and most subduing confessions, we shall deposit our soul tenderly and gratefully in his mercy.

Or we may take the general doctrine affirmed as the subjective verity of the gospel, viz., that God is in Christ reconciling the world unto Himself. Then *all* the sacrificial terms, that represent pacification with God, will come into application at once; Christ will now be called our priest answering for us, our sacrifice, passover, lamb, blood of sprinkling. Here, too, the word *propitiation*, as used (1 John, ii. 2,)—a different word, in the original, from that which we found in the third chapter of the epistle to the Romans—will get its proper objective sense. Viewed thus objectively, Christ will be a propitiation, a piacular, expiatory, vicarious offering, and, embracing him in this altar form, there will be a simplicity in our moral attitude, such as will favor the transforming and reconciling power of his life, as no attempt to apply him artificially and reflectively would do—therefore with a more certain and deeper effect.

Or, if we are occupied more especially with the desire of purification, or with present, actual deliverance from evil and the new purity and cleanness of our heart before God, we shall speak of Christ as a lustral offering that removes our defilement, and declare that the blood of Christ cleanseth from all sin. All things, we shall say, in our deep gratitude, are purged with blood, and without shedding of blood there is no remission

You perceive, in this manner, and as a result of our experiment, that as soon as we undertake to throw the elements of our subjective doctrine into an objective representation, it passes immediately into the view commonly designated by the phrase *vicarious atonement*, only it rather becomes a vicarious religion. And thus, after all, it proves itself to be identical, at the root, with the common Protestant doctrine—identical, I mean, not in any rigid and exact sense, but in such a sense that one is a more didactic and reflective, the other a more artistic representation of the same subject matter. There is no conflict, until we begin to assert the former as the only truth of the gospel, or to work up the latter by itself, into a speculative system of dogma or of moral government. If we say that Christ is here, reconciling men to God, it is, for just that reason, necessary to have a way of representing that God is conciliated towards us. If we say that Christ is a power, to quicken us into newness of life, and bring us out of the bondage we are under to evil, for just that reason do we need to speak of the remission of sins obtained by his blood; for the two seem to be only different forms of one and the same truth, and are often run together in the scriptures—as when the blood of Christ, "who offered himself without spot to God," is said "to purge the conscience from dead works, to serve the living God." The two views are not logically or theologically equivalent, but they are not the less really so on that account. An objective religion that shall stand before me, and be operated or operative for me, excluding all subjective reference of thought, must take such forms, most obviously, as are no logical equivalents of the same, considered as addressing and describing our internal states; for, by the supposition, an objective artistic power is substituted for those methods of address which appeal to consideration, reflection, and self-regulation.

But it will be imagined, I suppose, by some, that the objective religion, the view of vicarious atonement, which, as we have seen, may be generated by a transfer of the speculative doctrine, is only a rhetorical accident—that the apostles and evangelists only took up certain Jewish figures, made ready at their hands, using them to convey the Christian truths. Contrary to this, it is my conviction, and I shall now undertake to show, that God prepared such a result, by a deliberate, previous arrangement. It is the Divine Form of Christianity, in distinction from all others, and is, in that view, substantial to it, or consubstantial with it. It is, in fact, a Divine Ritual for the working of the world's mind. It was not more necessary, indeed, that the Life should find a body, than it is that the power Christ deposits in the world should have an operative vehicle. The Christ must become a religion *for* the soul and *before* it, therefore a Rite or Liturgy for the world's feeling—otherwise Christianity were incomplete, or imperfect.

Let me offer, now, as the proper conclusion of my argument, a few considerations that seem to lead us into such a conviction.

1. It is obvious that all the most earnest Christian

feelings of the apostles are collected round this objective representation—the vicarious sacrifice of Christ, for the sins of the world. They speak of it, not casually, or by allusion, as an apostle converted from under the Roman religion might have alluded to the rites of Mars, or the Vestals; but they do it systematically, they live in it, their Christian feeling is measured by it, and shaped in the molds it offers. And, if we consider how Christ their Lord had himself been crucified by the nation, and in the very name of the national religion; if we recollect that they themselves had renounced the ritual law of Moses; what temptation had they to set Christianity in a form so intensely Jewish? above all, what to set their own most sacred feelings in the molds of an abjured faith? Indeed, it was a part of their very doctrine, that Christ was liberty, and the law a bondage—a compost of beggarly elements. Why, then, does their Christ take the molds of the law, unless there was, after all, some profoundly sacred relationship between the outward rites of one and the spiritual grace of the other?

2. It is expressly declared, in the epistle to the Hebrews, and is tacitly assumed elsewhere, that the old system had a certain relationship to the contents of the new. It was an example and shadow of heavenly things, a figure for the time then present. Not, as the old theologians somewhat childishly conceived, that the types of the Old Testament ritual showed the saints of that age, the Christ to come; but that, by means of this ritual, the national mind was impregnated with forms, impressions, associations, not derivative from nature, which, when the Christian ideas are born, are to become types

or bases of a language to convey them. And, since the ideas to be expressed or embodied, were themselves out of nature; since God, also, is a being who holds his ends in contact, ever, with His beginnings, and His beginnings with His ends, what forbids the belief that the old ritual was appointed, in great part, for a use so sublime—to prepare a sacred language for the sacred and supernatural grace of Christ? Which, again, is rendered very nearly certain, by the manner in which Christ himself speaks of the Mosaic ritual and law. In one view, he came to repeal it and forever displace it. In outward historic fact, he has done so, and yet he solemnly protests—"I come not to destroy the law or the prophets—I am not come to destroy, but to fulfill." In which we plainly see that he regards the old system as having, behind its outward formalities, a deep Christian intent. Therefore, he declares that he came to fulfill this intent, to bring a grace to man, which this only foreshadows, and for which it is appointed by God to be the sacred Form and vehicle.

3. It is conclusive to the same effect, that Christ is represented in terms of the old ritual, before his passion. Passing by the fifty-third chapter of Isaiah, and other similar prophecies, called Messianic, John the Baptist breaks out on the very appearance of Jesus:—"Behold the Lamb of God that taketh away the sins of the world!" Why the Lamb of God, why this very singular relation to the sins of the world? If such figures may have been caught up, after Christ's death, to express the gratitude of the heart, why is Christ accosted in them, when appearing as a mere human stranger, before his

passion, and even before his ministry is begun? John the Evangelist, saturated with the same impressions, finds a remarkable coincidence, in the fact that no bone of Christ is broken on the cross. Nor is there any so remarkable want of dignity in noting such a coincidence, if it be set forth simply as a finger-mark pointing to the great comprehensive truth—Christ our Passover, the old ritual fulfilled in the offering of the Life. Still less, when we come to observe that Christ himself, as if to seal the certainty of a divinely appointed relationship between his sacrifice and the ritual of the nation, brings his ministry to a close, by re-enacting the Passover supper as a Christian rite. In his own flesh and blood he finds the Lamb of the feast. "This is my blood of the new testament, which is shed for many, for the remission of sins." Regarding Christ, now, as being simply a Jew, (which he is in his outward person,) a pious Jew, just about to suffer martyrdom, what could move him to declare that he is a lamb offered for the remission of the sins of the world, and actually to insert himself in the solemn passover supper of his nation, in place of the lamb! We do not understand this very remarkable institute of Christ, until we see that God has been planning, from the first, for an objective religion; that the old rites exist, in part, for this purpose, to be fulfilled, at last, in Christ, and become a holy ritual of thought and feeling—a sacred body, of which Christ is the life and spirit. Embodied thus, in a form of divine art, Christ is set before mankind, to be a religion for them, and become, in that manner, a religion n them.

4. Once more, there is a profound philosophic necessity

that a religion, which is to be a power over mankind, should have this objective character. Christianity, set forth as a mere subjective, philosophic doctrine, would fail, just where all philosophies have failed. Instead of bringing us into the bosom of a divine culture, it would throw us on a work of mere self-culture, producing, it may be, another sect of Pythagoreans, or another Academy somewhat more illustrious than the old, but scarcely a religion; for it is the distinction of a religion, that the soul adheres, by faith, to being out of itself, and lays itself recumbently on causes which are not in its own superintendence. Self-culture, indeed, has nothing to do with religion, whatever be its aim, however sacred the causes we apply to ourselves, until we begin to deposit our soul, so to speak, in God and in forms of exercise and feeling which are offered us by Him. Or, if we say that Christ has undertaken by his mission to bring us a spiritual remedy for our sin, how can it be a sufficient remedy, if it remains for us to apply it to our particular wants and diseases? What man can understand, or detect his own evils by reflective action? For, just as his consciousness cannot hunt his body through, detecting with mesmeric insight the diseases working in each organ, duct, fibre, and secretion; so much less, by conscious reflection, can he read the interior secrets and subtle perversities of his character. The only sufficient remedy for a chronically diseased man, is one that is comprehensive, and will, of itself, feel out his complaints—some new clime, for example, where the air itself, more searching and subtle than consciousness, will find out his diseases, and apply its own remedial force to them all. So if we are left to apply a Christ to the soul reflectively, as a philosophic cause, or remedy, we shall accomplish little, perhaps only nourish a conceit of health, which is worse than any other of our diseases.

It will not be understood that I propose to dismiss, or that I deprecate the use of reflection in matters of religion. In one view, it is the great work of the Christian preacher to bring men to reflection. It is only thus that they are made to understand themselves and the wants of their immortal nature. The sense of sin, the unrest of a mind separate from God, the deep hunger of a soul denied the life of religion—none of these are consciously felt, save under the sober influence of reflection. Still, there is nothing in this of true religion. No man is in the Christian state till he gets by, and, in one sense, beyond reflective action. And precisely here is the fundamental necessity of an objective form or forms of art, in the Christian scheme. While a man is addressing his own nature with means, motives, and remedies, acting reflectively on, and, of course, for himself, he is very certainly held to that which he needs most of all to escape, viz., the hinging of his life on himself, and the interests of his own person. This, in fact, is the sin of his sin, that his life revolves about himself, and does not centre in God. His redemption, his salvation, therefore, is, to be delivered of himself; which he can never be, while tending and cherishing and trying, by subjective applications made to himself, to foment new and better qualities in his heart. What he needs just here, while struggling vainly to lift himself by his own shoulders, is the presentation of a religion objectively made out for him; so that, when he is ready to faint, he may drop himself, by an act of faith and total self-renunciation, into the objective grace provided, there to deposit himself and cease even to be, save in his Saviour. Precisely here it is that Christian liberty begins, and here is the joy of a true Christian experience. It is going clear of self to live in the objective. It is the passing out of self-love into the love of God ; or, what is the same, into a state of faith and devotion, the fundamental distinction of which is that the man is moving outward, away from his own centre towards God, to rest on God, and live in God. I do not say here, it will be observed, that no one can have a true Christian experience, who does not find it in the embrace of Christ as a sacrifice, or a vicarious religion. I only affirm, that no one ever becomes a true Christian man, who does not rest himself in God, or give himself over to God, in objective faith and devotion, somehow. He may do this, regarding simply the essential truth and goodness of God as revealed in Jesus Christ ; he is only liable here—since he knows that God is thus approaching him, to move as a power upon his love—to fall back, or rather stay upon the old hinge of self and self-devotion, which is the radical evil of his character. Hence, while he is softened to feeling, by the love of God thus expressed, he wants a place where he can give himself away, without meeting any suggestive that shall carry him back into himself—an altar form whose art is so transcendent, so essentially mystic, that all art is concealed, and no occurring thought of working on himself, propels him backward on his old centre. And here it is that the objective view of Christ holds a connection so profound, with all that is freest, most unselfish and most elevated in Christian experience. There may be a Christian experience where it is rejected, but it will be composed, to such a degree, of self-culture and self-watching, as to constitute a legal, restricted, often most uncomfortable, always feeble state of discipleship. Nothing is more painful and discouraging than any style of piety in which the human predominates, and the elements of devotion and divine inspiration are obscured, or subordinated. On the contrary, any experience which drops out self, to be filled, guided, animated by God, is sure to be happy, free, and triumphant.

It must also be noted that there is a beautiful agreement, between the attitude of mind induced by the resting of the soul on an objective and vicarious mercy, and the great truth of the Holy Spirit, as a sanctifying power. In order to the effective working of God within us, we must not be always shaping or molding ourselves by our own art and will. But we need to be wholly pliant to the will of God; so suspended as regards all thought of ourselves, that he shall have us completely in his dominion, and be obstructed by no preconceptions and mere will-works of our own. And exactly this is the state in which we are held, when we are hanging upon Christ as our altar, resting in his sacrifice, yielding up our soul to him as one whom God hath set forth to be a propitiation for our sin. This is the attitude of perfect simplicity—an attitude also of faith, in which we are given trustfully up, to be turned as God will turn us. We are carried off our own centre that God may fix our orbit for us about Himself. And if we consider the infinite love of God to character, how His spirit waits to breathe it, as the air to fill every crevice and pore of matter, we may dare to say that, if He could have the bosoms of our race thus open to His power, He would sweep, as a gale of life and love, through them all.

It is also necessary to say, as a guard against misconception, that reflection or reflective action, must be blended, more or less, with the general course of the Christian life, and especially with its earlier stages. We must advert to ourselves frequently enough to know and correct ourselves. We must form ideals and aims of life. We must subject ourselves to the stern discipline of self-renunciation and the cross. Only we may be confident that, as our spirit becomes more sanctified and assimilated to God, we shall become more spontaneous in good, and have less need to be acting reflectively. But, in order ever to become thus spontaneous, we need, when we are least so, to be exercised objectively, thus to forget and go clear of ourselves; otherwise our piety, so called, settles into a mere dressing of the soul before her mirror. It is millinery substituted for grace. If the soul, then, is ever to get her health and freedom in goodness, she must have the gospel, not as a doctrine only, but as a rite before her, a righteousness, a ransom, a sacrifice, a lamb slain, a blood offered for her cleansing before Jehovah's altar. Then, reclining her broken heart on this, calling it her religion—hers by faith—she receives a grace broader than consciousness, loses herself in a love that is not imparted in the molds of mere self-culture, and, without making folly of Christ by her own vain self-applications, he is made *unto her*, wisdom, righteousness, sanctification, and redemption.

I might speak, also, in this connection, of the sad figure that would be made by the rude masses of the world, in applying a gospel of philosophic causes to their own nature; for they hardly know, as yet, that they have a nature. How manifest is it that they want an altar, set up before them, and if they cannot quite see the blood of Christ sprinkled on it, they must have it as a FORM in their souls; he must be a stock of righteousness before them; he must bear their sins for them, and be, in fact, their religion. Then, taking him, by faith, to be all this before and for them, the Divine Art hid in it transforms their inner life, in the immediate, absolute manner of art; and seeing now their new peace, not in themselves where it is, but in God, they rejoice that God is reconciled, and His anger smoothed away.

However, there is no such difference of class, among men, that the most cultivated and wisest disciple will not often need, and as often rejoice, to get away from all self-handling and self-cherishing cares. To be rid of a reflective and artificial activity, to fall into utter simplicity, and let the soul repose herself in a love and confidence wholly artless, is not only to be desired, but it is necessary, as I have said, even to the quality of true goodness itself. To be ever lifting ourselves by our will, to be hanging round our own works, canvassing our defects, studying the pathology of our own evils, were enough, of itself, to drive one mad. The mind becomes wearied and lost in its own mazes, discouraged and crushed by its frequent defeats, and virtue itself, being only a conscious tug of exertion, takes a look as unbeautiful as the life is unhappy. Therefore we need, all alike, some objective religion; to come and hang ourselves upon the altar of sacrifice sprinkled by the blood of Jesus, to enter into the holiest set open by his death, to quiet our soul in his peace, clothe it in his righteousness, and trust him as the Lamb of God that taketh away our sin. In these simple, unselfish, unreflective exercises, we shall make our closest approach to God.

I have thus endeavored to set forth, in as brief and condensed a form as possible, what may be called an outline view of the doctrine of Christ. That which most especially distinguishes the view presented, is the identification accomplished, or attempted, between the subjective and objective, the speculative and ritual forms of the doctrine. At-one-ment and atonement are shown to be, not antagonistic, but fellow truths answering to each other, and only false when they are separated. May I not regard it, indeed, as a beautiful evidence of the correctness of the view presented, that it finds a central truth, in all the principal forms of doctrine that have hitherto prevailed in the Christian church? Generically speaking, these forms are three :—

First, we have what may be called the Protestant form, which takes the ritualistic side of the gospel, the objective side, turns it into dogma and reasserts it as a theoretic or theologic truth. And then, though it be no longer a truth, the form of a truth, and, so far, a divine power lingers in it. I say a divine power, for this holy form of sacrifice is no child of human art or reason, but the body prepared of God to be the vehicle of His love to men. But, alas! the Protestant world have not been able to content themselves in it, or to think it sufficiently wise, till they have changed it into dogma, and made it *human;* in which they have done what they could to set themselves between God's wisdom and man's want. Still there are beams of light shining by them, and some, I trust, shine through.

Secondly, on the left of this Protestant form, we have the speculative or philosophic form, asserting that Christ only comes into the world to bring men into union with God, to reconcile them unto God. Under this, as one of its varieties, the Unitarian doctrine is included. Nor is there any doubt that we declare a great and real truth, when we say that the reconciliation of man to God is the sole object of Christ's mission. But this truth supposes a power, and that power is, in great part, only the power of an objective religion. If, then, we insist on explaining away, as mere Judaistic figures having no value, the blood, the sacrifice, the offering of Jesus, Jesus the curse, the Lord our righteousness, Christ our passover, the lamb of God that taketh away the sins of the world —if we pump out the contents of these holy forms, which God has offered to faith and feeling, and get them all into the molds of natural language and reason, then we are only found asserting, in our wisdom, that Christ has come to reconcile the world, and taking away, in the same breath, that which is itself a principal vehicle of his reconciling power. Reason is not confused and baffled here, as in the Protestant dogma, but the altar of self-renunciation and faith, she has taken down. She has cleared away the sun that she may see the stars. And, though there be a finer show of reason and of astronomic system in the stars, and though some of them be lighted by the sun itself, there is yet a great defect here of solar warmth—a defect so great that to be saved by star-light, is far less plausible and easy than to bask in the sun of righteousness and live.

Thirdly, on the right hand of the Protestant view, we have the Romish form, or the form of the mass. Here the ritual, objective view, is all in all—nay, somewhat more than all. Instead of a divine ritual for the mind or heart, we go back, we Judaize, or paganize, whichever it be; we set an altar before the eyes, and there we offer up a Christ daily. We deal with blood, not as a symbol to faith and feeling, but as a real and miraculous entity. But here, again, a light will sometimes stream by the miracle, into the worshipper's heart—genuine light, from Christ our peace, and the lamb that taketh away our sin. Reason, meantime, is dead within him. The man, most likely, has no questions, no opinions, no conceptions of character, save those which his superstitions yield him. He can never be a full and proper Christian man, till he knows Christ in the grand aim of his mission—Christ as the manifested Life—and has some account to offer of the reasons why he came into the world.

Seeing thus how at-one-ment and atonement and the mass, all, lie about the Christian truth, receiving something from it which belongs to its verity, rejecting much that is essential to its value and power, is it better to busy ourselves for the next eighteen centuries, in quarreling, each for the particle of truth he has, because it is a particle; or, to come back, in shame and sorrow, and receive enough of God's truth to enlarge our consciousness, universalize our feeling, and make us brothers?

An interesting question remains, which I can only reply to just far enough to save from misapprehension viz., how ought Christ to be preached? Not, certainly, as a theory, nor in the half scholastic manner in which I have here exhibited the Christian doctrine. I only think it will add greatly to the comfort and true self-understanding of the preacher in his work, if he has, in his own mind, some such solution as this. Meantime, he is to preach much as the scriptures themselves speak, blending the two views of Christ together. Sometimes he will be more in one, and sometimes more in the other. Probably the philosophic, or subjective view may be allowed to come into a somewhat more prevalent use, among a cultivated, philosophic people, and in a philosophic age of the world. But it must never exclude and displace the sacrificial or ritual view; for even the Christian philosopher himself will need often to go back to this holy altar of feeling, and hang there, trusting in Christ's offering; there to rest himself in the quietness of faith, getting away from his care and reflection, and his troublesome self-culture, to be cared for and clothed with a righteousness not his own.

To be a little more specific, there are three points which, in preaching Christ, will claim attention. (1.) In setting him forth as a sacrifice; always to hold in view, or often to exhibit, lines of contrast between him and the ritual sacrifice. It will be right to produce an impression similar to that which is given, Heb. x. 5—10, a passage which sketches three or four bold points of contrast between Christ and the sacrifices, seeming almost to say that "sacrifice and offering" are to be no longer; and which, yet, concludes:—"through the offering of the body of Jesus once for all." First, Christ is represented as saying that a "body is prepared" him, because sacrifice and offering are wanted no longer; that he is incarnated, in other words, for the discontinuance of all sacrifice. Next, that since God has "no pleasure in sacrifices for sin," he comes to "do the will of God," and by his own obedience, to displace them. Then that they are actually "taken away," the first removed, and the second established. Then that "by the which will," that is, by the obedience of Christ, "we are sanctified." It is perfectly evident, here, that he has no conception of Christ, as a literal sacrifice, though he goes directly on to speak of the obedience of Christ as testified "through the offering of himself." (2.) Christ must be preached, not as an ambassador of pardon simply, but as justification. The rigor of God's integrity, and the sanctity of his law must be maintained. It is not Christianity, as I view it, to go forth and declare that God is so good, so lenient, such a fatherly being, that he forgives freely. No; God is better than that—so good, so fatherly, that he will not only remit sins, but will so maintain the sanctity of His law as to make us feel them. The let-go system, the overlooking, accommodating, smoothing method of mere leniency, is a virtual surrender of all exactness, order, and law. The law is made void, nothing stands firm. God is a willow, bending to the breath of mortals. There is no throne left, no authority, nothing to move the conscience—therefore, really no goodness. Any doctrine of pardon without justification, must of necessity weaken, at last, the sense of religion, and it is well if it does not even remove the conception of Divine government itself. (3.) Christ must never be preached antinomially, or as a substitute for character. No such impression is to be endured. There must be no such jealousy of self-righteousness produced, that our hearers will hardly dare to be righteous at all. The very object for which Christ comes into the world, nay, the object of justification itself, is character, righteousness in the life. The intention is, that the righteousness of the law itself shall, at last, be fulfilled in us; that our robes shall be washed and made white in the blood of the Lamb. This mercy is mercy because it ends in character,—character renewed, purified, sanctified, made white. Therefore, we are to say, with our Master himself,—" Blessed—blessed only—are ye that hunger and thirst after righteousness."

But the best of all directions that I know for the preaching of Christ, and one that supposes everything right in the preacher, as it does in the disciple, is to live in him. And, when I speak of this, I am almost ashamed to have been spelling out, in syllables, this dull theory, and withholding you so long from the lively doctrine of Jesus and his cross. To know Christ Jesus and him only, to die with him in his death and rise in the likeness of his resurrection, to have Christ living in us, life within life, to have his pure spirit breathing in us, to love with his love, to be consciously and eternally united to God by our union with Him, to know that nothing shall be able to separate us from the love of God in Christ Jesus our Lord, in that confidence to be ready ever to partake joyfully in his passion, and become obedient, with him even unto death—this, I say, is to know how to preach Christ unto men. For it is not a rhetoric, not a doctrine or philosophy ; it is nothing that the schools can teach, or the natural understanding learn, but it is the living, life-giving experience of Christ himself; study cleared by communion, knowledge grounded in faith—this it is which prepares insight, character and love, and forms the true equipment of an earnest, powerful preacher. Having this, a man will preach, not by words only, but sometimes quite as effectively by silence. His very life will be luminous, because there is a Christ in it. And with such abides the Lord's good promise—not in some external, official, occasional manner, as some appear to fancy, but in the heart, in depth of feeling, in clearness of light, in patience, wisdom and power—"Lo I am with you always, even unto the end of the world."

O, how manifest it is, my hearers, as we go over this great subject, that God is full, and His grace free, to us all. What infinite pains does he take, to bring down His love to us. And yet, how does our poor human understanding labor and reel before this great mystery of godliness—height, depth, length, breadth, greater all, than we can measure! God's loftiest work, in fact, that in which He most transcends our human conceptions, is the work in which he is engaged to save us. Creation is a mystery, the universe is a great deep; but, O! the deepest deep, in all the abysses of God's majesty is here—in the work He does to unite us unto Himself. Herein is love. Herein we see that His strongest desire is to have us come unto Himself, and be one with Him forever.

O, let us believe this amazing truth, this truth so full of divinity, that God's bosom is indeed open to us all. Let us hear Him say, "Come and be forgiven." "Come, O, ye darkened and humiliated souls, come up out of your guilt, break your bondage, lay off your shame, and return to your Father.

A

DISCOURSE

ON

DOGMA AND SPIRIT;

OR THE

TRUE REVIVING OF RELIGION:

DELIVERED BEFORE

THE PORTER RHETORICAL SOCIETY,

AT ANDOVER, SEPTEMBER, 1848.

DOGMA AND SPIRIT.

It is a hope, cherished by many of the most thoughtful and earnest Christians of our time, that God is preparing the introduction, at last, of some new religious era. Here and there, in distant places and opposing sects, in private individuals and public bodies of disciples, we note the appearance of a deep longing felt for some true renovation of the religious spirit. As yet, the feeling is indefinite, as probably it will be, till its ideal, or the gift for which it sighs, begins to shape itself to view, under conditions of fact and actual manifestation. In some cases, expectation seems never to go beyond the reproduction of old scenes, familiarly known as revivals of religion, and the reviving of revivals is regarded as the only admissible, or highest possible hope to be entertained. But, more generally, there appears to be a different feeling. A degree of dissatisfaction is felt with benefits of a character so partial, so mixed with defect, and especially so little efficacious in producing the fruits of a deep and thoroughly established piety. Hence there is a secret hope, cherished by all such, that something may transpire of a different character and of far higher moment to the cause of God in the earth—something that will set us on a firmer ground of stability, produce a more acknowledged and visible Christian unity, and develop a more consistent, catholic, permanent, free and living exhibition of the renovating power of Christ and his truth.

This is the subject which I now propose to discuss:—THE TRUE REVIVING OF RELIGION. I meet you here as a body of Christian ministers and candidates for the ministry, proposing, not some theme of a merely occasional interest, but one that is dear above all others, I am persuaded, not to me only, but to the heart of God Himself; therefore one which it is my pleasure to believe will be as much more welcome to you, as it is closer to Christian feeling and the practical reign of Christ in the earth.

I know not how to open the subject proposed, from a better point of view, than to begin where Christianity descends into the world—the point that is given us, for example, in—

1 John, i. 2.—*For the Life was manifested, and we have seen it, and bear witness, and show unto you that Eternal Life, which was with the Father, and was manifested unto us.*

Thus it was that Christianity fell into the world's bosom as a quickening power, as Life and Spirit from God. It came into a world dead in trespasses and sins to make it live again—this, also, by depositing in it and uniting to it, as a regenerative and organific power, the Life of God. At the time when it appeared, death and blindness had enveloped the national religion. A few souls, spiritually enlightened by God, lingered about the temple, waiting like Simeon and Anna the prophetess for the Lord's appearing. In the desert wilds of the Jordan, and the caves of the South, there were also, possibly, a few pious eremites, similarly exercised in the things of the spirit. The religion of faith, that which infuses life, and brings a soul into the light and freedom of God, was, for the most part, a lost idea. The speculations of the Sadducees and the interpretations of the Pharisees had developed so much of human light, that the light of God in the soul, was no longer wanted or thought of. Religion had been fairly interpreted away. Debates, traditions, opinions of doctors and rescripts of schools, in a word, such an immense mass had been accumulated of what an apostle calls *dogmas* (translated "ordinances") and also, "commandments and doctrines of men," that there was no longer any place for faith, and the light of faith in the world. The law was held as letter, and had thus no real power but to discourage and kill; for it was the manner of this Jewish theology and its masters or Rabbis, to practice on words and syllables, trying what wondrous lights of opinion they could produce by their leaned ingenuity; and studied thus, in the letter, and without spiritual illumination, or even a thought of it, Moses and the prophets had become so overlaid with school wisdom, and the rescripts of Rabbis, that no true light of God was visible any longer. Spiritual life was extinct, and only a wearisome drill, under legal rites and fleshly burdens, remained.

Just here Christ makes his appearance, denouncing

the Pharisees and their Rabbis, that they open not, but rather shut the kingdom of heaven against men. Therefore he is obliged to separate himself from their doctrine and from all the learning of his day. It is so perverse, so fortified by numbers, by conceit and the respect of the nation, as to be even hopeless. Giving, therefore, the plain testimony of God against it—"in vain do they worship me, teaching for doctrines the commandments of men"—he turns to the uneducated, humble class of the people, and out of these he takes his apostles; simply because they are able, it would seem, to come into the knowledge of spiritual things, hindered by no learned preconceptions or commandments of men, and with minds ingenuously open to the spiritual teachings of God. The sublime doctrine of the kingdom, which is hid from the wise and prudent, and which no school wisdom, or wisdom of dogma, can ever apprehend, God will be able to reveal to these sons of obscurity, these ingenuous "babes" of Galilee. To them, therefore, he turns, making it his first object to attract their faith by his friendly ministries, and fix it on his person. He gives them to understand that he is such, and such the message he brings, that he can be truly apprehended only by faith—that, as the swine have no capacity to conceive the value of pearls, so the unbelieving of the world will never, out of their mere natural wisdom, receive and appreciate the Christian truth. He declares that he comes as the Life, comes to form a life-connection between the world and God;—"As the Father hath sent me, and I live by the Father, so he that eateth me, even he shall live by me. This is that bread that came down from heaven—he that eateth of this bread shall live forever." And then he goes on immediately, while his disciples are debating his words, to show that his doctrine is not for the flesh or for any mere speculative wisdom; that faith only can so far seize it or enter into it, as to produce it internally, and prove its heavenly verity; that it requires a congenial spirit co-existing or dawning in the soul with it, so that it may flow through the soul as spirit, nay, as God's own Spirit, and not be tried dialectically or scientifically, by mere natural cognitions and judgments—"It is the spirit that quickeneth, the flesh profiteth nothing; *the words that I speak unto you they are spirit and they are life.*"

This is the conception of Christianity, as held by Christ himself. And for this reason it was, as he well understood, that his disciples could get no sufficient apprehension of the Christian truth in his life-time and while he was visibly present among them. Therefore it was expedient that he should go away from before their eyes, and a plan be adjusted for calling their simple faith into exercise. Accordingly, they were to wait at Jerusalem, after his departure, for the descent of the Spirit upon them, and he, taking the things of Christ and shewing them internally, that is, breathing an inspiration of Divine Life through their soul, to quicken them internally to a right apprehension of Christ and his work, would bring them into such a knowledge of the truth of Christ and the new scheme of salvation, that they would be ready to go forth and preach him to mankind.

They did as he commanded—the result is known.

Suffice it to say that just there, Christianity is inaugurated as Life and Spirit in the world. There it bursts in as a gale of Life and a quickening power from God, and we see, in the preaching of Peter and in the whole scene which follows, that a new conception of Christ as the Prince of Life—his death and resurrection, his final exaltation and his present reigning power—is at this moment seized upon. Before Christianity had been dark to them, they knew not what to think of it; now it is light—they have it as spirit and life in their hearts. God, who commanded the light to shine out of darkness, hath shined in their hearts, to give the light of the knowledge of the glory of God, in the face of Jesus Christ.

Accordingly, the first age of the Church, or of Christianity, which opens at this point, is to be distinguished as an age of life and intense spiritual vivacity. It is an age, not of dogmas or speculations, but of gifts, utterances, and mighty works, and, more than all, of inspiration, insight, freedom, and power. Looking back upon it as revealed in the New Testament, and in the first chapters of the subsequent history, this one thing appears, predominant above all others, that the Church is alive—simple, inartificial, partially erratic, but always alive. He that was crucified and rose again, liveth visibly in them—not in their heads, but in their hearts. They have an unction of the Holy One that teaches and leads them. The preaching is testimony, publication, prophesying—not theology. The doctrine has no dialectic or scholastic distribution; it is free, out of the heart, a ministration of the Spirit. It is luminous by a divine light within; it streams through a character congenial to itself, taking its mold, not from any discipline of theory or of rhetoric, but from a nature and working that God has visibly configured to Himself. The effect is known to all. Incredible as it may seem, it is yet indisputable, a fact of history, that, within three centuries, the fire that is thus kindled, catches and spreads, till its light is seen and its sanctifying power is felt, throughout the Roman Empire.

Many speak of this event as a wonder. In one view it is. But something like it will always appear, when religion casts off the incrustations of dogma, and emerges into life. Christianity was, indeed, a new truth, but in nothing so new as in requiring faith of its disciples, insisting that they draw their light from God, and have it, not in their natural reason, but in and through a character that is itself newness of life. Considering the deadness of the religious element in his nation when our Lord came into it, and the utter imbecility of the Rabbinic theories and ordinances, who could have imagined that a man, crucified as a malefactor, was to begin such a reviving of the religious spirit in the world that, within a few generations, he will have the imperial city of the earth under his power, princes and principalities owning his dominion and laying their gods at his feet. But it is done, and something like it will always be done, when men are drawn close enough to God, to be separated from the law of their mere human opinions and judgments, and brought to receive their light from God as an inspiration, or internal realization of faith.

Observe, especially, as regards these first centuries of the faith, that it was a faith. They had no theology at all, in our modern sense of the term. Not even Paul, so much praised as the "dialectic" apostle, was anything of a system maker, and I shall show you, presently, that, if he had any theoretic system, the first and fundamental truth of it was, that spiritual things must be spiritually discerned. Accordingly, if we examine the history of these first ages, we find them speaking, in the utmost simplicity, of the Father, Son, and Holy Ghost; but having still, confessedly, no speculative theory or dogmatic scheme of trinity. The word, in fact, is not yet invented. When they speak of Christ, it is of Christ as the Life,—Emanuel, Saviour, Redeemer, Son of man and Son of God, crucified and risen, wisdom, righteousness, sanctification and redemption. They had not begun, as yet, to busy themselves in setting forth the internal composition of Christ's person. They had no forensic theory of justification, made out in terms of the civil law, and defended by speculative and dialectic judgments—they only saw the law confirmed and sanctified by Christ's death, and a way thus opened to peace with God. They had no theory about regeneration, assigning the parts, determining the how much on one side and on the other, and settling the before and after, as between God's working and man's. They had the word of God in power, but not as yet in science—Christian dogmatics were yet to be invented. If you desire to see the form in which they summed up the Christian truth, you have it in what is called the Apostles' Creed. This beautiful compend was gradually prepared, or accumulated, in the age prior to theology; most of it, probably, in the time of the Apostolic Fathers. It is purely historic, a simple compendium of Christian fact, without a trace of what we sometimes call doctrine; that is, nothing is drawn out into speculative propositions, or propounded as a dogma, in terms of science.

Now begins a change. After Christianity as spirit and life, uttered in words of faith and sealed by the testimony of martyrs in every city, has taken possession of the world, it finds another class of Rabbis, whom Christ never saw, viz., the Rabbis of the Greek philosophy; and these begin to try their hand upon it. Some of the Christian teachers are disciples of the Greek learning, and the scientific instinct of the Greek schools begins to meditate the preparation of some new form, for the Christian truth, that shall finally establish its sway over the world of thought and learning. Thus begins theology. With it, of course, enters controversy, and controversy being wholly out of the Spirit and in the life of nature, whittles and splits the divine truth of the gospel, and shapes it into propositions dialectically nice and scientific, till, at last, the truth of Jesus vanishes, his triumphs are over, and his spirit even begins to die in the world.

The change that is to come is sufficiently indicated by a comparison of the Apostles' Creed and the Athanasian, or the Nicene. Passing from one to the other, we consciously descend from a realm of divine simplicity and life, into a subterranean region, where the smoke of human wisdom, hereafter to stifle the breath of religion, is just beginning to rise, and the feeble cant of dogmatism is trying its first rehearsal. In both, you hear the disciple saying, it is true,—"I believe;"—but in one, he believes the grand, living, life-giving history of Christ; in the other, he believes his own scientific wisdom concerning it—his mental cognitions, judgments, and theories. In one, the faith professed is truly a faith. In the other, it is only such faith as follows sight, or opinion, or scientific reason. The process of descent from the spirit into the flesh is easy, and goes on rapidly. That historical and vital Christianity, which Christ presented in his life, is replaced, ere long, by what some call a doctrinal; that is, by a Christianity made up of propositions and articles. The teachers think they are shedding great light upon the new religion, but we, looking back, perceive a dark age just there gathering in upon Christendom. Dogma has eclipsed the sun. Even the religion of Jesus itself begins to wear the look of a work of darkness. It is as if the discords of hell had broken loose. Councils are called against heretics, and against councils. Bishops levy arms one against another. Excommunications are dealt back and forth. Whole provinces are deluged with the blood of Christian persecution. Princes mingle in the confusion, as exterminators, or patronizers of one or another dogma. The freedom of the spirit and of faith is even ruled out of the church itself, and no disciple is allowed to have any light that comes of spiritual discernment, or even to think a thought which transcends the dogma of his time. Finally, as all bishops have exalted themselves above truth, the bishop of Rome exalts himself above the bishops, and assuming thus the headship of the church, the work, long ago begun, is complete—the church becomes a vast human fabric of forms, offices, institutions, and honors; a store-house of subtleties and scholastic opinions, a den of base intrigues and mercenary crimes, as empty of charity and humanity as of Christian truth itself.

Here it is that Luther appears, bursting up through the incrustations of ages, to assert, once more, Faith, and the rights of faith—justification and salvation by faith in Jesus Christ. A great reformation and reviving of the religious spirit follows, which is felt throughout the Christian world, not excluding the Roman Catholic portions. Many supposed and, I believe, still suppose, that Luther righted everything—that he even set the church back into her original position. Others have had a different impression, among whom I may instance our own immortal Robinson. In the ever memorable address he gave to the Pilgrims, on their departure to the new world, the prophet father of New England had grace given him to "bewail the condition of the reformed churches, in so soon having come to a period in religion," refusing to go beyond "the instruments of their reformation." "Luther and Calvin," he said, "were great and shining lights, in their times, yet they penetrated not into the whole counsel of God. I beseech you, be ready to receive whatever truth shall be made known to you from the written word of God." He was right in these convictions. Luther had made a good beginning, but only a beginning. He left so much undone that the church has not been able to hold the vitality he gave it; but, as if some element of fatal obstruction were still retained in its bosom, has been gradually sinking into such divisions and infirmities, such deadness to truth and faith and spirituality of life, that the truest friends of God, in every part of the Protestant world, burdened by a

25

common sorrow, are sighing, at this moment, for some deeper renovation, some more thorough reviving of religion.

Luther left the church connected with the state, subject to the corrupting influence of courts and of state patronage. Here we have advanced upon him already, and with every reason to rejoice in the results. But the great and most fatal defect of Luther's reformation was, that he left the reign of dogma or speculative theology, untouched. He did not restore the ministration of the Spirit. Opinions were left to rule the church, with just as much of consequence as they had before. He delivered us from the Pope and the councils, but that which made both Pope and councils he saved, viz., the authority of human opinions and of mere speculative theology. The man of sin was removed, but the mystery of iniquity, out of which he was born, was kept. Opinions, speculations, scholastic and theologic formulas, were still regarded as the lights of religion. All judgments of men, as apostate or unchristian, continued, as before, to be determined by their opinions, not as Christ required, by their fruits or their character. Love, mercy, faith, a pure and holy life, was still left a subordinate thing—important, of course, but not the chief thing. Christianity remained in the hands of schools and doctors, and that was called the faith, here and there, which, here or there, was reasoned out as the veritable theologic dogma. Formulas still reigned over faith, as the Pope had done before. The natural reason was the keeper of God's supernatural truth. Indeed, we may say that Aristotle was the doctor still of doctors, and that Christ was dispensed by the

Peripatetic method. The unction of the Holy One was virtually subjected still to the scholastic sentences, and graduated under the predicaments.

In short, the second chapter of the first epistle to the Corinthians was really not restored, and has not been, in the true spirit of it, to this day. We manage, indeed, to say, that the things that are freely given to us of God, in Jesus Christ, are spiritual, and can only be spiritually discerned; sometimes, also, that we speak, not in the words man's wisdom teacheth, but which the Holy Ghost teacheth, comparing spiritual things with spiritual, —we say this, because we have it, as one of our articles, that what the scriptures affirm, must be held by us; but we do not really mean it in the apostolic sense. On the contrary, we judge as the schools judge, speak what the formulas tell us, and will not even tolerate the belief, that God can ever lead a disciple to discern what is different from these. We do not really understand, as Paul here declares, that Christian truth can be *in* our soul only as it is *of* it, begotten there by the indwelling of Christ, and the private rehearsal of the Spirit. We suppose that learning and debate can master the Christian truths, and handle them as it can questions of grammar and archæology. We do not put our theology to school to faith, but our faith to school to theology. The head is to be made wise in formulas, and then the head is to take care of the heart. "Private *judgment*" is the word. The natural man receives the things of the spirit of God, and he that is natural, judgeth all things.

These things I affirm, not in a sense so literal as to imply that we are not Christians. Enough, doubtless, of divine truth leaks into our conceptions to save us, but not enough to feed the true apostolic devotion in our lives. We really have not, and cannot have, the ministration of the Spirit in its power. Four important and most deplorable consequences follow. (1.) Endless divisions, subdivisions, schisms, denunciations, simply because we are living, not in spiritual insight, not in our heart as united to Christ, but in our head; that is, in articles that are only opinions of the head. Not being in the ministration of the Spirit, which is unity, love, gentleness and peace, and would thus melt us into a common circle, through a common brotherhood of character, we are in the ministration of opinion; that is, of formulas, schools, and doctors, who have many heads, and of course can make nothing but diversity and division. (2.) We are unspiritual for the same reason. We do not expect to live momentarily under the immediate guidance of God. As we measure piety by formulas and opinions, and put religion itself under their keeping, so we expect, most of the time, to live in the life of nature. We only expect to relapse, or fall back a little into the dominion of the Spirit, on Sundays, and yet a little further, when there is some special movement called a revival of religion. I desire not to be uncharitable, but it must be evident to all thoughtful observers, that our modern piety, considering especially what works of beneficence we have on hand, is marvelously unspiritual. It has little depth or unction—no real intimacy with God; but an air of lightness and outsideness rather, as if it were wholly of ourselves, not a life of God in the soul. Even in the highest scenes we have of religious attention or excitement, there is a show of rawness and passion, as if we had more of ourselves in exercise than we know how to manage. Then, again, (3.) this subjection to dogma is quite too visibly a subjection, not of ourselves only, but also of the Spirit in us. It is marvelous, that in the highest tides of spiritual exercise we know, our demonstrations are molded still so exactly by our formulas and those of our sect. Thus a Methodist revival will go on visibly in the method of Wesley; a Congregational under the Cambridge, or Saybrook Platform. In both, the Spirit will ere long give way, and Wesley and the Platforms will be all that is left. These will be constant, the Spirit occasional; for to be in the Spirit is not our law, but to be in our school; and it will be this, (not the Spirit,) that will be accepted always to teach us the things that are freely given to us of God. Again, (4.) note as another consequence of mischief, the desolating sweep of scepticism, connected with the Protestant church, and moving in parallel lines with it. If religion is, first of all, a doctrine, a formula, something worked out by the school, then, of course, let the school work, and the doctors manufacture opinions as industriously as possible. Learning, logic, ingenuity, audacity, here is a field for all. Hence rationalism, filling the sky of Germany with darkness, and hiding the sun Luther once looked upon, so that it can scarcely be seen longer. And as the same causes have the same effects, so we are destined to experience the same shade of obscuration here, unless we can let go the reign of dogma and ascend into the life of the Spirit. Then we may dare, with Christ, to declare that our pearls are not for swine, and since we have them in our *heart*, reason can never rob us of the treasure. Natural reason is impotent against a Christianity that is spirit and life. But, if the defenders of the gospel offer it, first of all, as a book of articles, it will not be strange if, when they have separated the Life, it is unable to live.

I bring you thus to the very point where we now are, and where Protestant Christendom is. And here I rejoice to find a great many of our truly Christian ministers and brethren questioning, sighing, praying for the reviving of revivals. Conscious of the mournfully low state of religion, the growth of worldliness, the want of godliness, the decay of ministerial force, and the afflicting signs of a delicate and earthly spirit in the ministry—afflicted by this, as every Christian heart properly should be, they lift their voices in the pulpit, on the platforms, and in the religious newspapers, calling upon us to arise and seek unto God for the renewing of those scenes of fervor and Christian power which they remember in former years. They see no hope, save in the restoration of those operations which have had effect heretofore. They reprove us for the delicate or fastidious spirit we manifest. They tell us, kindly, that God will not do things according to our tastes and fashions, that we must have protracted exercises, and not scruple to enlist evangelists, and set on foot those religious measures which the distinguished operators of former times found to be so effective.

I accept these remonstrances, with that respect which is due to the Christian anxieties in which they emanate, but they seem to propose a remedy quite too slight for our disease. A mere reviving of revivals does not reach our case, and I do not expect that they ever will be revived, unless it be with such modifications of manner and spirit as to produce a different class of manifestations, and fill a different place in the practical dispensations of religion.

God never restores an old thing, or an old state. If he produces something that has resemblance to an old state, it will yet be different. If he brings us up, at last, out of dogma, and sect, and mutual judgments of each other, and worldly living, into the ministration of the Spirit, we shall not be there as the apostles and first Christians were, but we shall carry up all the wealth of our bitter exercise with us. We shall be men of the nineteenth century, not of the first—republicans, men of railroads and commerce, astronomers, chemists, geologists, and even rationalizers in the highest degree; that is, men who have reason enough to discover the insufficiency of reason, the necessity of faith, and the certainty that a soul must die into darkness when it is not in the life and light of God. Let us not expect, then, that God will restore revivals just as we have seen them. It is a dull patient that expects always to be cured by the same medicine.

And why is it that these revivals are so long discontinued? Have we not some evidence, in this fact, that their force is spent? Has not such a conviction come upon us, in spite even of ourselves? Did we not see them go down, by gradations, into lower forms of exercise, and show, both in the means devised to carry them on, and also in their fruits, what we could look upon only as signs of exhaustion?

Besides, they manifestly do not belong to a really ripe and true state of Christian living, but rather to a lower state, which we ought even to hope may, at last, be discontinued. They were throes, in one view, of disease; just as God works a diseased body into health by intermittences of pain or fever. If the church were to abide in the Spirit, as it certainly ought, for the promise of the Comforter is that he shall abide with us, still I suppose there would be changing moods and varieties of exercise, though not any such alternations as these—alternations between death and life, the spirit and the flesh. I make no question that there will always be displayed in the church scenes of variety or diversified impulse, times of social movement and public exaltation, times of stillness and privacy, times when the word preached will have its effect more in one direction or more in another. We must not require that the demonstrations made in religion shall even be unexceptionable; for when we come to that, and are able to act without any symptom of disease, it will be proved that we no longer want medication under any system of exercise. But have we no right to complain of these sharp alternations between vitality and utter deadness? Is it not plain that, under this kind of regimen, we are even instigating disease? Are not the fruits we realize too visibly diseased themselves, and is it not precisely this that we are now bewailing?

What, too, are we declaring, by our very sighs, unless it be the fact that our revivals have brought us no such fruits of character, stability and spirituality, as we may reasonably desire and ought, for the honor of the gospel, to exhibit? Is it wrong to believe that even these sighs themselves are divinely instigated, and that, rightly interpreted, they are yearnings, produced in us, after some better gift which God is preparing to bestow? For what, possibly, has he allowed the long suspension, which many are now deploring, but for this very purpose—to awaken in us higher thoughts and prepare us for a new Christian era? What, possibly, is he now offering, if only we are ready to receive it, but a grand inaugural of the Spirit throughout Christendom—an open day of life and love and spiritual brotherhood, in which our narrow confines of bigotry and prejudice shall be melted away, and all the members of Christ's body, holding visibly the Head, shall visibly own each other; shining in the light, revealing the spirit, co-operating in the works of Christ, and living for the common object of establishing his kingdom?

It is not for me to prophesy, nor do I pretend to publish the secrets of God. But I think I see, by signs which others may inspect as freely as I, that there is a gift waiting for the church, if only she had room to receive it. I can also see what most visibly we want. We want, as the great Robinson believed, "more light to break forth from God's holy word"—not from the formulas, or the catechisms, or the schools, or the doctors, but from God's holy word; and especially from those parts of the word which represent the Christian truth as spirit and life, attainable only as our heart and spirit are configured to it, and able to offer it that sympathy which is the first condition of understanding—attainable only by such as are in the Spirit themselves. This will bring a true reviving of religion—not sporadic manifestations of the Spirit here and there, now in one village or town, now in another; not *revivals,* possibly, in the plural, such as our friends and fathers stir us up to look for, apparently not observing that, in this plural word, they carry the implication that we are to look for successions here and there, in time as well as place, and, of course, that we set out with the expectation of resting ourselves by another relapse into deadness and sin, when it is convenient. No, it will bring us what is more and higher, an era of renovated faith, spreading from circle to circle through the whole church of God on earth; the removal of divisions, the smoothing away of asperities, the realization of love as a bond of perfectness in all the saints. It will bring in such an era as many signs begin to foretoken; for it comes to me publicly, as relating to bodies of Christian ministers, and circles of believers in distant places, that they are longing for some fuller manifestation of grace, and debating the possibility of another and holier order of Christian life. It comes to me also privately, every few days, that ministers of God and Christian brethren, called to be saints, having no concert but in God, are hungering and thirsting after righteousness in a degree that is new to themselves, daring to hope and believe that they may be filled, testifying joyfully that Christ is a more complete Saviour, and the manifestation of God in the heart of faith, a more intense reality than they had before conceived. Meantime, as we all know, a feeling of fraternity is growing up silently, in distant parts of the Christian world. Bigotry is tottering, rigidity growing flexible, and Christian hearts are yearning, everywhere, after a day of universal brotherhood in Christ Jesus. These are the signs we have before us It is in view of these that we are to form our expectations ; also, in part, that we are to shape our plans and settle our Christian aims. Indeed, it is even a great maxim of philosophy, that, when we see men wide asunder, beginning to take up the same thoughts and fall into the same sentiments, and that without concert or communication, we are generally to believe that something decisive, in that direction, is preparing ; for it is the age that is working in them, or the God rather, probably, of all ages ; and, accordingly, what engages so many, at once, is only the quickening in them of that seed, on whose stalk the future is to blossom.

Should we not, therefore, expect a gradual appearing of new life, which years only can prepare ? Shall we not even dare to spread our Christian confidences by the measures of Providence, and, in this manner, take up the hope that, when so many signs and yearnings meet in their fulfillment, we may see a grand reviving of religion, that shall be marked by no village boundaries, no walls of sect or name, but shall penetrate, vivify, and melt into brotherhood, at last, all who love our Lord Jesus Christ on earth ?

In this protracted statement I have set forth what I conceive to be our position, both as related to the past and the future. If, as I have intimated, results of so great consequence are hanging on the reduction or displacement of dogma, it becomes my duty, in the nex place, to verify that conviction. And in order to this I must, first of all, endeavor to distinguish, as accurately as possible, the true idea of dogma.

The word *dogma* literally means an opinion, but it is almost uniformly understood to include something more, viz., an authoritative force. We see this element conspicuous in the word *dogmatize*, and it belongs historically to the word *dogma* itself. Thus it was anciently used to signify a decree, as when Cæsar decreed the taxing. The epistle sent out to quiet the churches, by the council of the brethren at Jerusalem, was also called a dogma, (Acts, XVI. 4.) where the term is used in a milder sense to denote a basis which had been agreed upon for the pacification of difficulties, and which, it was hoped, would be generally respected. Paul uses the word three times in his epistles, where it is translated "ordinances;"—for example, when he speaks of "the law of commandments contained in ordinances"—the reference being, in this and the other cases, to that overgrowth of opinions, speculations, and religious rescripts, under which the doctrine of Moses had been hidden, and in sweeping which away, Christ brought in, as we have seen already, a new era of religious freedom and power. When we speak of Christian dogmatics, or of dogmatic theology, we associate the same idea of authority, in a little milder sense, understanding some scheme or system of religious opinion, propounded as a guide to others, who are theologic pupils or Christian disciples. And when we come to the testing of Christian character, or to terms of fellowship, then it will be seen that our dogma, by whatever name we call it, is taken to be a fixed rule of authority, to all who are concerned.

Two elements, then, as I conceive, enter into the notion of dogma—first an opinion, which is some decision of natural judgment, or some merely theologic conclusion. Secondly, the propounding or holding of that opinion as a rule to the opinions, the faith, or the Christian experience, whether of ourselves or of others.

It is also to be noted, in regard to the first named element, the opinion that enters into dogma, that it holds a decided contrast with faith, heart, spirit, and life; which contrast also belongs, of course, to dogma.

An opinion is some result, which is prepared out of the mere life of nature; some perception, cognition, or judgment, that we produced out of our natural activity, as intelligent beings. But faith carries us above nature, into apprehensions that transcend the reach of mere natural judgments. Being that act in which a man passes off his own centre, to rest himself practically in God, it unites the soul to Him, and becomes, in that manner, an experience of Him. In one view, faith is grounded in evidence, but it also creates evidence, by the realizations it makes of spiritual things. Hence it is declared to be the evidence of things not seen, the substance or substantiator of things hoped for. It is, in this way, more than by all opinions, that we are able to give reality to things invisible.

Opinion, too, is of the head; it is the knowledge gotten by thought and reflection. But there is also a knowledge of God and Christian truth, which is of the heart; for a right sensibility is as truly perceptive as reason, and there are many truths, of the highest moment, that can never find us, save as we offer a congenial sensibility to them. What is loftiest and most transcendent in the character of God. his purity, goodness, beauty, and gentleness, can never be sufficiently apprehended by mere intellect, or by any other power than a heart configured to these divine qualities. And the whole gospel of Christ is subject, in a great degree, to the same conditions. It requires a heart, a good, right-feeling heart, to receive so much of heart as God here opens to us. Indeed, the gospel is, in one view, a magnificent work of art, a manifestation of God which is to find the world, and move it, and change it, through the medium of expression. Hence it requires for an inlet, not reason or logic or a scientific power, so much as a right sensibility. The true and only sufficient interpreter of it is an esthetic talent, viz., the talent of love, or a sensibility exalted and purified by love. The expression is made, in part, to mere natural feeling, such as is common to the race. Hence it has a power to work on man at his lowest point of character, and then, when his heart is engaged and propitiated by the secular charities of Jesus, it is to be transformed, regenerated, carried up into goodness, and there introduced to the higher revelations and knowledges of God, as set forth in his Divine Life. Then it knows him. Blessed are the pure in heart for they shall see God. It is not by opinion, but by love that we most truly know God. If any man love God, He is known of him. And he that loveth not, knoweth not God, for God is love.

Opinion, also, is dark and feeble in the contrast with

spirit and inspiration. Christianity is called "spirit," partly because it can truly enter us and be apprehended by us, only as we are in it and of it, and have its spirit in us. The letter cannot teach it, words cannot tell us what it is. We can never find it, or be found of it, till we come up out of questions and constructions, into the living spirit of Christ himself. It is also called 'spirit,' in part and perhaps chiefly, because it is received and receivable only through some concourse of God, or the Spirit of God. The human soul under sin, or considered simply as unreligious, is necessarily dark, because it is divorced from God, by whose inbeing it was made to have its light. It cannot make light, by opinions gotten up in itself. Revolving God's idea, systematizing external cognitions, derived from his works, investigating the historic evidences of Christ, his life, his doctrine—busied in all such ways, it is rather creating darkness than light, until it receives God, as an inner light, and knows him by that spiritual manifestation within, which Christ promised.

This great truth is continually present in the teachings of Christ and his apostles. If only Peter takes up the belief that he is the Messiah, the Saviour sees a discernment in him which is not of the man himself—a revelation. "Blessed art thou, Simon Bar-jona; for flesh and blood hath not revealed it unto thee, but my Father, which is in heaven." Whenever his doctrine or parable is understood, he sees an inner light of God in that understanding. "Thou hast hid these things from the wise and prudent, and revealed them unto babes." In the same view, he promises the Comforter to his disciples, as an abiding teacher, who shall make what is now dark in respect to him, as viewed by their mere understanding, luminous and clear. They waited for him at Jerusalem according to their Master's direction, and there it would seem as if Christianity first dawned upon their conceptions. Just there, we may say, Christianity, which opinion could not reach, comes into sight, and Christ is known as the Redeemer and Saviour of the race—the Life of God manifested in the world.

Paul is continually setting forth Christianity, as a ministration of the Spirit, in the same way. It is no judgment of the flesh, it is no wisdom of this world, it is not the letter, but it is spirit and life—Christ dwelling in us. In the second chapter of his first epistle to the Corinthians, he is fuller and more definite than elsewhere, asserting the great, and, as it seems to me, universal truth, that in order to be known by us, God must live in us. He does not mean to say that, up to a certain time, we are incapable of knowing God, or understanding Christ, and that then, being converted or having a new function communicated, we are ever after able to understand him. He only means to say that we never do, in fact, receive the true sense of Christianity, save as we are spiritually illuminated, and in the degree of that illumination. Our theologians would have his true meaning, if they took his words as intended for themselves; to show them that they will have the knowledge of Christ, not in debates alone, not in articles, systems, and opinions, such as they get up in the life of nature, but by the constant indwelling, rather, and teaching of God's own Spirit. Would to God he might be thus received! and that we might all be able to say, with Paul, "Now we have received not the spirit of the world, but the spirit which is of God, that we might know the things that are freely given to us of God." If, ceasing to be merely natural, we become spiritual, in the true apostolic sense; we shall discern, I am sure, if not all things, many things that have as yet been hidden from us.

There is yet another remarkable contrast between opinion and life, which is seen in the fact that opinions may be written down, or retained in the memory, while the realizations of faith and love and spirit cease and disappear, as they themselves do, unable either to be retained in the memory, or to be recalled, in any manner, afterwards. Spiritual truth dies with spiritual life. It is vital, it is essential life in its own nature, and therefore must be kept alive as it began to live, by an inward and immediate connection with God. Perhaps I shall come nearest to an exact representation, if I say that spiritual truth is God Himself, dwelling in the soul and manifested there. This, it seems to me, is the clear implication of John, when he represents the same truth just now asserted from Paul, under the figure of an unction. "Ye have an unction from the Holy One, and know all things—but the anointing which ye have received of him, abideth in you, and ye need not that any man teach you, but as the same anointing teacheth you of all things, and is truth, and is no lie, and even as it hath taught you, ye shall abide in him." Here the implication is, that the knowledge will abide, because the unction abides; therefore, no longer than the unction abides. And this, exactly, is the experience of every unfaithful disciple. His light perishes with his love. All his clear perceptions and vivid realizations of God depart, and cannot be recalled. Even the scripture that was light, grows dark again. His opinions remain, but his soul, like a chamber shut up at noon, is forthwith darkened, as soon as the daylight of God is shut away.

It is thus made plain to us that the highest and only true realizations of God are effected, not through opinion, but through faith, right feeling, spirit, and life. With these, mere opinion holds a very clear and distinct contrast, and should manifestly occupy, under them, a very inferior place. Now, opinion is one of the elements of dogma, and therefore, dogma holds the same contrast, and should hold the same place. But the other element is authority, or a ruling power. Conceive opinion, then, exalted to become a rule to faith, to the perceptive power of love, to the teachings of the Spirit, and the realizations of the life,—a measure, a guide, a standard, a rule of judgment, a test of character, a term of fellowship—then you have the proper conception of dogma. This, too, I conceive, to be its proper meaning; also, in common use, its virtual meaning; and, in this view, as it is found exalting itself above faith and the Spirit, it must, in reverence, be rejected.

I said its virtual meaning. Perhaps I ought to raise an express distinction here between its virtual and its conscious or intended meaning; for we certainly speak of scientific and dogmatic theology, when we have no thought of setting human speculations and opinions above the liberty of the Spirit and the light of faith, and when, in fact, we should heartily disclaim any such thought.

Only it will generally turn out, after all, that we actually have it; for so deeply fixed is our traditional impression that systematic divinity, school theology, or whatever we call dogma, is to be the rule of our judgments and the guardian of our purity, that we never hesitate, in the church or in the council, to try all subjects of belief, practice, or character, by this standard—admitting no possibility that divine illumination may have assisted any disciple to transcend it, and really assuming that we want no such illumination ourselves, unless it be in the application of our dogma to the question in hand.

Were it not for this virtual assumption of authority in our school divinity, which makes it dogma, when really no such thing is thought of as the subjection of faith and spirit to the measures of opinion, it would be wholly unnecessary to take any stand as against dogma. Undoubtedly we have a right to investigate and form opinions in matters of religion, as in reference to all other subjects—a right, also, to assert and teach opinions—we only have not a right to make the life of nature and our natural judgments a law to the inspirations of faith and the realizations of God, in the hidden life of the Spirit. Manifestly, opinions, taken as mere actings of our intellectual nature, cannot compass matters of so high a quality. We cannot, by any mere phosphorescence of thought, throw out from within ourselves that daylight which our soul desires, and which, in the manifested radiance of God, it may ever have. Neither is that possible, which is continually assumed without, apparently, even the suspicion of a doubt, that theology, taken as a work of analysis and speculative generalization, is competent to produce a body of judgments that will be a true and proper science of God. If there is ever to be anything produced here that can reasonably be called a science, it will more resemble an experience than the dry judgments and barren generalizations hitherto called theology. To have science of a matter is to know it, and there are many of the humblest babes of faith, in corners of obscurity here and there, who really know more, and have a truer science of God, than some who are most distinguished among the Christian doctors.

Besides, if we are ever to have any sufficient or tolerably comprehensive theology, it can never be matured, save through the medium of an esthetic elevation in the sensibilities of our souls, which only the closest possible union of the life to God can produce. For the scriptures offer us the great truths of religion, not in propositions, and articles of systematic divinity. They only throw out in bold and living figures, often contrary or antagonistic in their forms, the truths to be communicated. Language is itself an instrument, wholly incapable of anything more adequate. Therefore, what we want, in the receiving of light from the scripture, is a living, ingenuous, patient, pure sensibility—a heart so quickened by the Spirit of God, as to be even delicately perceptive of God's meaning in the readings and symbols he gives us. And then, having gotten the truth, we want modesty enough not to take our spiritual discernings into our natural judgment, to be shaped and manipulated there—modesty enough not to assume that we can go beyond the scriptures and body into science and fixed articles of divinity, what they, for want of any sufficient medium, never attempted. So that, after all, our ripe comprehensive theology, when we find it, will be so convoluted with spirit, and so mixed with faith, that it will be as much a life, a holy breadth and catholicity of spirit, as a theory. It will be as far from possible representation, in any of the niggard forms of abstract science, or the debated articles of school divinity, as can be conceived.

It is not my design, then, as you perceive, wholly to discard opinion, science, systematic theology, or even dogma in the best possible sense of the term. I would only set the judgments of the natural life in their proper place—or rather in a place that is not most improper; for, in proper truth, all the thinkings, judgments, analyzings, opinions, and the faculties by which they are wrought, should themselves be filled with the same quickening Spirit, and exalted by the same faith which animates the heart; with that, also, bathed in the radiance and indwelling light of God, so as to be themselves organs and vehicles of essential truth and life. Then every faculty is promoted, and the whole man becomes spirit, acting not as in mere nature, but as in the life of God; without eagerness, partiality, prejudice, or care—acting as in rest. And then it will be, not science, stretching itself as before, to compass the unimaginable and infinite worlds of faith, but science indeed, the quiet reading of God through the heart. The noise and commotion before made, in the busy clatter of opinions, ceases, and the tumult is heard no more. We dwell in the light, in the stillness, so to speak, of the light of God; for light is a silent element—all vivacity, another name for motion, but silent

But it is not in this highest, truest state of spiritual life and union to God, that the gospel finds us. Our faith is imperfect, only initiated, possibly not even that; and since the world we live in, too, is full of false learning, corrupt opinion, and deceitful pretenses of knowledge, we must be allowed to cultivate theology, with what measures of grace we have, and struggle up through our imperfect mixtures of natural judgment and spiritual discernment, into the full day of light and love. Though our theologies and opinions and supposed scientific conclusions, in as far as they are of the mere life of nature, have no more of authority, and are no more entitled to a Christian standing than our speculations in geology, they have yet a far higher consequence, because they are related to matters of graver import, and are sure to be connected with results of deeper consequence.

That I may produce a just impression of my subject, and deliver it of any appearance of partiality or extravagance, let me enumerate, here, some of the uses that are served by Christian theories, and the scientific forms of truth elaborated by the Christian symbols, and teachers.

In the first place, they have an immense pedagogic value. I mean, by this, that, like the old system of Moses, they are schoolmasters to bring us to Christ. Doubtless they often deserve, and with much greater emphasis, to be called "beggarly elements," yet there are uses to be served by them still. The world is not in the spirit, but in the life of nature. There it must be met, and somewhat on its own level. If it were addressed only out of the inner light, and in terms of the highest and purest Christian experience, it would be no better than if it were called in an unknown tongue. But Christian theology comes to it, with a view or theoretic outline of the gospel, which is itself made up, for the most part, speculatively, within the life of nature. It enters into the thinking power, and begins a motion there. If it is lame, in itself, as all systems are, still it will have a value. Probably it will have some connection with the age, and will set forth Christ, in a scheme of thought that has some reference to the present habit and want. In this way, Christianity gets into the mental system of the world, and, through that, into the heart. A good scheme is far better than a bad, but even a bad will be better than none at all; for if Christianity were known and presented only from the point of highest spiritual experience, it would never find a place of contact; therefore, no place to begin its regenerative work. And yet, there is more of the true light of Christ in one hour of highest communion with him, than the best scheme of theological opinions has ever been able to offer.

A similar and very important influence is exerted by the catechetic discipline of children, or their exercise in Christian doctrine. Here might seem, at first view, to be one place, where dogma, in its proper sense of authority, is appropriate. But it will be found, after all, that the soul of a child will not be fastened to Christ by spikes of dogma driven by parental authority. The truest power of discipline is that which is most divine, the fragrance of a divine life filling the house. Still there is wanted a human view of Christ and his truth, a conception of principles, opinions, and, to some extent, of theoretic matter, which, if they are catechetically given, will work in the childish mind as moving powers of thought, and so, as preparatives and grounds of a true Christian faith.

Secondly, there is an instinct of system in our nature, which must have its liberties and opportunities in religion as in all subjects. Our mind adheres to unity, demanding that all events and opinions shall conform to system, and support, as a whole, what we sometimes call the unity of reason. Hence we are continually drawing our knowledges, consciously or unconsciously, toward unity; and if we succeed but poorly in our attempts, the little success we have comforts us, and our endeavor comforts us still more. Manifestly it is wholly impossible for us, in the mere life of nature, and by force of opinion, to grasp the universe of religion, and mold it into the system of a science. Still, if only we set the world pulling at these high themes by guesses and yearnings after knowledge, they may possibly draw themselves up, at last, by God's help, into those higher realizations which are fitly called science. I suppose it has been generally observed, that curiosity abates when faith enters, and that the instinct of system lulls in its activity, as spiritual life quickens in the soul. And the reason seems to be that, when it is connected thus with the life of God, and receives him in his power, it virtually receives all system—even the true system of God Himself, and has it, by a sense deeper than consciousness, or at least, in a manner that is beyond definite conception. It has the sympathetic touch, if I may so speak, of all things, and blesses itself in the sense of a unity vaster than thought can reach

And it will be seen that, in this view, scientific theology stimulates the soul in reaching after God. It is the alphabet in which nature begins to stammer; which exercises and also exasperates her curious impulses, preparatory to a true knowledge of God in His fullness.

Thirdly, there is a value in scientific theology, considered as a speculative equipment, for meeting the assaults of unbelief, false learning and scepticism. I am well aware of the unfruitfulness of mere polemic argumentations with infidels and sceptics. Few are the cases where such argumentations have produced conviction, and led to a hearty embrace of Christ. And yet there is an effect of inestimable value, one remove farther off, and more general, viz., in the impression produced, that Christianity has something to say, that it can take its place on a level even with science, and stand scrutiny there, holding its ground invincibly against all opponents. Were it not for this, had it nothing to speak of but experiences and spiritualities, it would be disrespected by the uninitiated, as a scheme that begins and ends in unintelligible vagaries.

Fourthly, Christianity must be handled under forms of science and speculation, because in that manner only can it form a valid connection with truths of fact and philosophy. Christianity does not come into the world armed against all other knowledge, to destroy it. It claims, on the contrary, its right to possess and appropriate and melt into unity with itself, all other truth; for whatever truth there is in the universe belongs to the Lord of Christianity, and holds a real consistency, both with him and it. Therefore Christianity must open its

27

bosom, bring its holy affinities into play, repel the false, attract the true, and gather to its poles all particles of knowledge and science, as the loadstone gathers the particles of iron. Hence Christianity fell into immediate contact with all human philosophies and opinions, and a process of attrition began, in which it was, at last, to wear itself into union with all real truth. The same process is now going on between Christianity and the revelations of science. Thus, for example, it was seriously apprehended that the modern doctrines of astronomy would make as great havoc of Christianity, as they certainly did of many of the church dogmas. But the God of Calvary and of the firmament, the love of one and the grandeur of the other, are gradually melting into union. We have still immense masses of theologic rubbish on hand, which belong to the Ptolemaic system, huge piles of assumption about angels that have never sinned and angels that have, about other worlds and the reach of Christ's atonement there, which were raised up, evidently, on the world, when it was flat, and must ultimately disappear, as we come into a more true sense of the astronomic universe. So, also, geology, opening to view new conceptions of the cosmogony of the universe, is destined gradually to assimilate with the Christian truth and become a part of it. For, as God is one, he is sure, at last, to be found in agreement with himself. And then we shall know the Christian truth as much more perfectly, as we better conceive the truth of things. Science without, will favor simplicity and rest within. As the idols of superstition or false science are displaced, as the range of intellection is broader and more clear, Christianity will better know her place, her office, and her nature. And if she has many times been corrupted and shackled by the false wisdom of man, she will emerge, at last, in the strength and freedom of her youth, as much more at home in the broad universe of her Lord, as much readier to fulfill a mission of victory and grandeur, as she better knows herself and the orbit in which she moves.

Once more, considering that Christian character is imperfect, liable to the instigation of passion, to be overheated in the flesh and think it the inspiration of God, Christian theology and speculative activity are needed as providing checks and balances for the life, to save it from visionary flights, erratic fancies, and wild hallucinations. It was partly for the want, I suppose, of some such influence as this, that Papias, Tertullian, Irenæus, the sober Clement, even, and a large class of the early teachers ran into so many absurd and fanciful errors. The intellectual life needs to be kept in high action, else, under pretense of living in the Spirit, we are soon found living in our fancies and our passions—just as the kite rises gracefully and sleeps in equipoise on the upper air, only in virtue of a pull upon the cord below; and if it be maintained that the cord only pulls downward, and not upward, it does yet hold the bosom of the paper voyager to the breeze, without which it would soon be pitching in disorderly motions to the ground. It appears, in other words, that we have two distinct methods of knowledge, a lower method in the life of nature, and a higher, in the life of faith. Therefore, we are not to set them in mutual opposition, as has generally been done heretofore, by the rationalists on one side, and the mystic on the other; but we are to assume that a healthy working of our religious nature is that which justifies uses, exercises, all. Regarding the realm of reason, and the realm of faith, as our two Houses of Assembly, we are to consider nothing as enacted into a law, which has not been able to pass both houses. For if a man will reduce all religious truth to the molds and measures of the natural understanding, receiving nothing by faith, which transcends the measures of the understanding, he acts, in fact, upon the assumption that he has no heart; and as he cannot perceive, by the understanding, what is perceivable only by the faith of the heart, he ignores all living truth, and becomes a sceptic or a rationalist. If, on the other hand, what power of reason or science he had is wholly disallowed and renounced, so as to operate a check no longer on the contemplations of faith, or assist in framing into order the announcements of feeling, then faith and feeling are become a land of dreams, and the man who begun as a Christian, ends as a mystic. Faith must learn to be the light of nature, nature to apply her cautions and constraining judgments. The heart and the head must be as two that walk together, never so truly agreed as when they agree to help each other.

Accordingly, it is one of the chief problems of Christianity to settle the true relationship of reason and faith, the truth of reason and the truth of the life; a great and truly magnificent problem, in the working of which all the past ages of the church have, under God, been engaged. To settle this, and bring us out, at last, into a true and healthy conception of the natural and the spiritual, as related one to the other, seems to me to be the real burden of the past history of the church. For if the descent into dogma, of which I have spoken, has been a most sorrowful experience, which few will be able to deny—if it has even been a fall, answering, in one view, to the first fall of the race, still this experience, this fall, it were even wrong not to believe will at last turn out for the furtherance of the gospel. God suffers no barren experience—this will not be such. On the contrary, if we are to return, as I fervently hope, to the simple life-giving truths of the first teachers, we must expect to go back enriched by this dark experience. Indeed, those eminent disciples who have risen up, here and there, to recall us to the simple, original truth of Christ, seem to me to have failed, on this very account, that they have had no sufficient perception of the benefits to be received from this exercise of man upon the Christian truth. And so, beginning an unreasonable war upon the uses of reason, they have failed, of necessity. Contrary to this, it is my hope, that God is about to bring us back to the original, simple age of spirit and life, and yet, in such a way, that we shall have our benefit in what we have suffered, and shall see that all the sorrows we have passed through, and the confusions we have wrought, were necessary, in a sense, to the complete intelligence and final establishment of the church.

Let us turn our thoughts, now, for a few moments, in this direction, inquiring how and why it was that the church made her lapse into dogma, and glancing at some of the happy results that are to follow, when she emerges and resumes her true position.

The discontinuance of the spiritual gifts and prodigies of the apostolic age, necessitated a remarkable change in the action of the church. While those gifts continued, the external life of religion was so strikingly set off by wonders as to hold the mind to itself, and detain it, in a great measure, from speculation, as well as from the more reflective and philosophic forms of thought. Indeed, the church was beginning to regard the outward gifts, not as the signs only of an inward agency, for which purpose they were added, but as being in themselves the substantial import of the Spirit. Hence it was necessary that they should be discontinued. Now, therefore, begins a struggle. Henceforth the disciples know nothing of the Spirit but by his invisible work in the heart. Accordingly, their minds are invaded by endless questions. They begin to reason. They invent opinions. They mix in theories. They draw out propositions. They run the Christian truth, in short, into all the shapes suggested to their thoughts, or gendered by their prurient fancy. It could not well have been otherwise. For a pure doctrine of spirit and life, dropped into the mind of a creature half in the spirit and half in the flesh, manifestly could not, be held, so that nothing from the side of the flesh should mix with the side of the spirit, to corrupt its simplicity and deform its truth.

As the gospel extended its sway and became familiarized to men, a more worldly and less intensely Christian spirit began to appear in the church; and it will always be observed that, as the activity of faith and spirit declines, the activity of the flesh and of dogma increases. When the disciple is filled with love, he hardly knows what to do with dogma; but if the fund of love is spent or exhausted, he wants a large supply of it, and probably some very stiff wars to maintain for it besides; for when the activity of spirit fails, the activity of nature, including the will and the passions and even the muscular parts, is needed to supply the defect.

Just here, too, Christianity was coming into contact with the Greek philosophy, which exasperated the same evil tendency; for the Greek philosophy was a wisdom in the life of nature—all opinion, doctrine, dogma—universally admired, a name for scholarship itself, and all elegant learning. Many persons have wondered why, or in what manner, Christianity became so intensely doctrinal or dogmatic; for they discover no such character in the teachings, whether of Christ or his apostles; but the fact is easily explained, when once it is recollected that the Greek learning or wisdom, which is nothing but a body of natural judgments and opinions, emptied itself into the bosom of the Christian church, and gave it a character. Nothing met the Greek mind which was not doctrine. Opinions, dialectic arguments decided all questions. Christianity, therefore, to meet such a disposition, must take on the Socratic method, draw out her contents into dialectic articles, and set herself before men to be accepted, not as Christ, not as the incarnate Life, but as doctrine.

Precisely here, too, Christianity rises into power, and becomes a state religion. The bishops go up into diocesan eminence, as piety and truth go down. Understandings are formed between them and the civil power, and mutual stipulations are entered into, these to support the state, the state to support their ecclesiastical pretensions, and enforce their favorite dogmas by the civil arm. Christianity, the living words that Jesus spoke to the world's heart, hardened thus into dogmas; the dogmas flashed into swords; and the swords, having each a cutting edge, hewing its way into the necks and the blood of human beings, became fit symbols of the awful transformation that must follow, when the natural life displaces the spiritual, and opinion, sharpened by the stern sanctions of religion, is exalted into law. Thus it was that Christianity became so intensely doctrinal—this was the fall of the church into dogma. It is a melancholy sight; but in what manner it could have been prevented I do not see. Most Christians of our age suppose, I believe, that we are quite cured of this disaster—in which they mistake as badly as it is possible.

But the cure is to come—though as yet quite incomplete. We no more look upon it as Christian to make opinions draw blood, but we hold them still as rules of judgment and terms of fellowship, in a sense almost as absolute as ever. This error also must be cleared, and then, when the church ascends again into the realm of love and life, it will be seen, as I firmly believe, that these long ages of trial and darkness have peaceable fruits of righteousness to yield us at the last.

Most obviously it was necessary, not only that the gospel should be set forth positively, as spirit and life, bu that all the negatives round about should also be set fo t

In order to have an exact, definite conception of the Christian truth, we must know as well what it is not, as what it is—know it in contrast with what it is not. Thus we have, in the first age, not a trinity, but simply Father, Son, and Holy Ghost. But how can we ever conceive, at all, what this means, until we are shown what it does not mean? And then, to show us this, it is necessary that somebody should rise up in the world and assert that it means something which it does not—three metaphysical persons, three beings, for example, existing on terms of society. Then, perhaps, another somebody—some Patripassian, or Arian, for example—not satisfied with this, must be allowed to come forward with his better view. And then, after speculation has fully exhausted her resources, we may be able to come back, and say, Father, Son and Holy Ghost, knowing, not only, that we mean something by the words, but (which is a great deal,) exactly what we do not mean by them And that will be enough, it may be, to steady and comfort us in the great and Holy Three, as the God of our worship, forever. That we can ever exactly measure God, or the divine three, so as to comprehend them in a positive knowledge, is obviously impossible. Therefore, to have settled what is *not* the truth, may quiet our speculative difficulties, and set us, ever after, in a condition of intelligent repose. So, in regard to the doctrine of atonement, of the Holy Spirit, of depravity and regeneration, it is of immense consequence to have found out exactly what is not true. And here it is that rationalism is found to be doing a work of mournful, yet immense practical consequence to religion. It produces continually, new forms of thought—in one view, new religions. These are generally more negative than positive; still, they are claimed to be positive. Then, being set on foot, we are to see what is in them. Thus, if any false doctrine of Christ, or atonement, is advanced, a difficulty will at last be encountered, the machine will not go. It may be a very plausible, very reasonable looking machine, but it will not go. Churches will not live to hold it or ministers to preach it; therefore it dies. Then we know, by experiment—a very important experiment it is—that this is not the living truth. Now, all these knowledges of what the truth is not, were undiscovered to the men of the first age. It was necessary that the human understanding should go to work, try its hand upon the truth, bring out its dogmas or opinions, and let the world see them die. Then it is visible to all men what the truth is not; and then the simple living truth of God, offered to our faith, surrounded by the dead births of folly, looks more divinely clear and lovelier to our hearts.

We receive the same truth, under a somewhat different form, if we contemplate Christianity as ordained of God for the expurgation, at last, of all error—entering the world, therefore, as a power antagonistic to all error, and armed at all points for the deadly grapple. Only, when we speak in these warlike figures, we must not imagine a certain army, called the truth, drawn up fronting a certain army, called error. The battles of truth are not waged in this manner. The difficulty is to find out error—that, in fact, is the war; for when error is once revealed and known, it dies itself. Hence, it was the great problem of God to make all error reveal itself; that is, to make all the oblique and false-seeing opinions of man disclose themselves. And this they would best do, only as we took the gospel into our own hands, to handle it in our own way, and try our own wisdom upon it. First, God reveals the Christian truth; then man, beginning to work upon God's truth, bringing it under his own theories, measuring it in dogmas shaped by his natural understanding, makes the revelation of error. Every infirmity of reason is displayed, every perverse temper colors some opinion to be its visible representative. The ambition, the pride, and even the devilish cruelty of man —all are brought forth into dogma, and are seen assuming, one after another, some theologic shape, ugly enough to represent their detestable origin. And thus it is that all error is to appear and die out in the handling of God's truth. Thus men shall try at the gospel, and try out the poisonous errors by which their human wisdom would mend it. It goes into mixture and solution with all their human thoughts and theories, to form its own nucleus and crystallize, at last, all truth and science about itself. And so, every controversy, council and burning, down to the present moment, has been either the winnowing out, or what is not far different, the revealing and acting out of some error. Heresies are most commonly the counterpoints of heresy, and the resulting motion, generated between them, is an almost certain approach towards the Christian truth. Accordingly, the eyes of men are now being turned, as never before, towards the hope of some new catholic age, where spirit and faith, having gotten their proper realm, clear of adverse possession, shall be able to abide there in God's simple light, to range it in liberty, and fill it with love.

Nor let any one doubt the possibility of such an issue to the agonies of the church. All such distrust is carnal, and pusillanimous. Truth is omnipotence—a slow omnipotence, I grant, but yet omnipotence. It runs through churches, men, and empires, with a galvanic current, only with a different celerity—sometimes, too, as we have seen of late, with an almost galvanic celerity. No power of man can raise an impassable barrier against it, or do anything more than to offer some false argument, whose point shall receive the charge, and be shivered in its passage. Bayonets it will as easily shiver. Some think despairingly of truth, because she seems, at times, to have been so long disarmed and trampled on. Never was she disarmed, never was there an hour in which she has not been hastening to victory. Her dark ages, as we call them, were only her dark arguments. Her penal fires and dungeons have been the victory of her patience. And now she is coming forth, I trust, out of her tribulation, to speak to a world, whose centuries of woe have, at last, opened its ears. The long night we have passed was itself but the death-scene of error, in which truth, behind her veil, stood jubilant, in the brightness of an angel.

Such, I conceive, are some of the uses that have been served by Christian dogmatism. Most bitterly has the church suffered, and yet her pains have been salutary—pains, I may say, of birth. She forsook her simplicity, and went after wisdom; she tried to get the spirit into the letter; she asked the natural man to tell her of Christ, and explain the life of faith in the terms of reason. Dreadful was the confusion that followed. She took hell into her bosom, and fanned the fire with her prayers, till the fuel was exhausted. And now, at last, when the fires are going out, and she begins to find herself encrusted all over, in the cooling, with a dry cinder of dogma, she thinks again of the Life, and the times of her first liberty, and hears a gentle voice of chiding at her heart,—" O, foolish Galatians, who hath bewitched you! Having begun in the spirit, are ye now made perfect by the flesh!"

Reviewing, now, the ground over which we have passed, you will see that in the opening of my discourse, I set forth the hope of a new religious era, or great and true reviving of religion, to be produced by a general displacement of dogma and the restoration of the church to the simple, life-giving spirit of the apostolic age. Next, I endeavored to exhibit the distinction existing between dogma and spirit, or science and faith. Then I spoke of the uses of religious opinions and systems, or of theological science. Lastly, to fill out the true theoretic conception of the subject, I spoke of the causes under which the church lapsed into dogma, and the advantages she will have gained when she emerges from it. It now remains, neglecting logical distribution, to offer some thoughts on a series of promiscuous topics, practically related to the subject; such as will show us where we now are, also by what method we may best escape the oppressive dominion of dogma, and find our way back into the genuine apostolic liberty of spirit and life. And—

1. It needs, at the present time, to be a leading topic of inquiry among religious teachers, and especially in our schools of theology, what are the capacities of scientific or propositional theology, which, for the sake of brevity, and without any reference to the matter of authority, we will call dogma? There is no other point in the whole field of Christian inquiry, where so much light is to be expected, and so much impulse given to the cause of Christ in the earth, as here. The questions, too, that are here at hand, waiting for light, are some of the deepest and gravest ever offered to human consideration. They are such as these:—

(1.) Whether the scriptures embody any proper system of dogmatic theology; and, if not, whether it is because this particular work, regarded now as a work of highest moment, was necessarily reserved, or kept back from inspiration, that it might be more adequately done by the science of the natural understanding, and the higher constructive wisdom of Christian philosophy? (2.) Whether human language is an instrument capable of embodying, in propositions and forms of definition, any proper system of Christian truth? (3.) How far religion is poetic, addressing itself to the imagination, in distinction from the understanding—requiring, of course, a sanctified and spiritually elevated imagination, to conceive it? (4.) How far it is a matter of feeling, addressing itself to an esthetic power in the soul—perceived and perceivable only through a heart of regenerated sensibility; one that is quickened into vitality, and even rendered delicately pure, by a life of protracted, secret intimacy with God? (5.) Whether truths that come to us in the realms of imagination and feeling, and so enter as powers of life into our religion, can be presented in the forms of logic, or in speculative propositions? (6.) Why dogma has hitherto been so remarkably unsuccessful, and whether, if we admit some progress in theological science, it has not been very exactly proportioned to the relaxations of dogmatic rigor, and the approaches made toward spiritual freedom in the church at large? (7.) How much dogma is worth as a test of character? (8.) Whether true science is not experimental, whether prayer is not more experimental than speculation, and whether it is so because we are most logical and most dogmatic in prayer? (9.) Whether dogma has been, as we continually hear, a bond of unity, and a safeguard of purity in religion? (10.) Whether it is not possible to be very much distinguished in systematic theology, and yet know very little, have but a very faint conception of Christ and Christian truth? Other questions of equal pertinence and importance will be found lying in the same field. But in the proper handling of these ten, there is work prepared for a life. And if any young candidate for the ministry could sufficiently answer these questions, I am free to confess that I should take it as a better proof of his fitness to preach Christ to men, than I should if he were fluently prepared in almost any scheme of school divinity.

2. It appears evident to me that we embrace a very great and truly unchristian error, in holding the relative estimate we do of the head and the heart. When we

speak of talent, ministerial talent for example, how generally is it estimated by the head. How extensively is our judgment of Christian character itself suspended on the question of mere opinions and theoretic beliefs. We seem also to imagine, which is worse than all, that the head is to take care of the heart, the opinions to regulate the faith—that we are first to fill the head or natural understanding with articles and dogmas, and then that the head is to shape the experience of the life, and even to be a law to the working of the Spirit. Exactly this, indeed, when baldly stated, is the theory of Christian education held by many parents. True Christianity holds a very different opinion. It teaches that out of the heart are the issues of life; that God hath given us light in the face of his Son, by shining into our heart; that heresies themselves belong to the natural understanding; and that only the pure in heart can behold the face of God. Let the second chapter also of the first epistle to the Corinthians be studied, and it will open a deeper and vaster revelation still. Holding these representations in view, it is very clear, I think, that there is something great in the world besides understanding—another talent, a higher and more Christian. And so much is there in this, I am free to say, that if I were to choose a preacher for myself, holding the question as a mere question of talent, I should first of all inquire into the talent of his heart, whether that light is in him which shines only into the heart; and then, a long time after, I would begin to inquire after his capacities of science, speculation, understanding, in a word, his head.

In this matter of head and heart, you may figure the

head or understanding, it seems to me, as being that little plate of wood hung upon the stern of the vessel, that very small helm by which the ship is turned about whithersoever the governor listeth. But the heart is the full deep body of the ship itself, with its sails lifted to the breath of a divine inspiration, containing in itself the wealth, the joy, and all the adventuring passions, wants, and fears of the soul. In a certain superficial sense, you may say that the helm is everything, because, by that, so great a body is so bravely steered and turned about in the sea. And the man at the helm may fancy, too, that he is the moving and directing cause of all. But look again, and you shall see how foolish a thing this little piece of wood may be; for when the wind sleeps, when the great heart of the ship receives no inspiring breath, then how idly does it swing from side to side, as a vain and silly thing. It is by the love of the heart only that we know God. Here is all inspiration, all true motion and power. And when the great heart of faith is not parting the waves of life before it, and rushing on to its haven, the busy understanding is but a vain and idle thing, swinging round and round with an addled motion, whose actions and reactions are equal, and which, therefore, profit nothing.

O, what momentum, and power, and grandeur will Christianity reveal when a true Pauline devotion to God is kindled in the whole church, when the opinions of the head cease to be supreme, when the petty tyranny of formulas and dogmas falls back, dethroned, and the full living heart of the church is offered, without subtraction, to the occupancy of Christ and the power of his cross! Every thing Christ-like is made little in us now—chilled, straitened, pinched by the usurpations of the head; or, what is the same, by the debating, judging, rationalizing industry of our human wisdom, which, in God's opinion, is only foolishness. This brings me to speak—

3. Of insufficient views now held concerning the Christian ministry, which manifestly need to be corrected, and must be, before the full power of preaching can be realized. It is not to be disguised, that, with the immense benefits resulting from theological seminaries, and from none more emphatically than from this, there have also been connected some pernicious results, which time only could develop. They are such, in great part, as result from the assembling of a large body of young men in a society of their own, where they mingle, exhibit their powers one to another, debate opinions, criticise performances, measure capacities, applaud demonstrations of genius, talk of places filled by others, and conjecture, of course, not seldom, what places they may be called to fill themselves. They are thus prepared to exhibit Christ scholastically, rhetorically, dogmatically—too often ambitiously, too seldom as spirit and life. Perhaps it is only by sore mortification and the stern discipline of defeat or diminishing repute, that they will, at last, be humbled into the true knowledge of Christ, and prepared to bear his cross.

I may speak the more freely on this subject here, because there is no reason to suspect that what I may say has any special application. I am also moved by the conviction that, if any great reviving of religion is to be prepared, any more fruitful era of Christian piety introduced, it will be seen, first of all, as I trust it begins to be already, in the kindling of a new fire in our schools of theology. Rejoicing, also, as I do, in the more perfect intellectual discipline, the more elevated scholarship, the personal refinements of taste and character produced in our schools of theology, and deeming these improvements necessary even to the advancing wants of American society, I am the more encouraged to speak of defects that appear in connection with these benefits.

Two great truths of the highest practical import, need to be set in the mind of all students of theology and all preachers of Christ, as probably they never have been, since theology began to be attempted.

First, that no man really knows Christ, or can learn, or be taught the Christian truth, who is not in the spirit of Christ. If he cannot say, "Christ liveth in me," not even a thousand years of study will give him any proper conception of the Christian plan. Words cannot bring it into the heart, dogma cannot give it in the dry light of reason. The mere natural understanding, fruitful as it may be in formulas about God, can as little see Him, as a telescope can overtake Him in the sky, or a microscope detect His retreating into the mites of the world. He must be in the soul, in His own self-evidence; present to faith, embraced by love. Or, if we speak of Christ more especially, or his work, here again, he that believeth hath the witness in himself—only he. We must be crucified with him, rise with him, abide in his peace, feed upon him as our bread, or else we know him not. All these high matters belong to the life, and it is the pure heart only, the simple, believing, divinely illuminated heart, that can ever know them. Spiritual things must be spiritually discerned. We can know the things that are freely given to us of God, only as Paul knew them—by the Spirit that is of God. Therefore it is not in lectures or in books, not in exegetic or dogmatic discipline, not in any and all other methods, so truly as in the elevations of prayer, and the inbreathings or inspirations of God, that a human soul may be truly initiated into the life and doctrine of Christ. Theology, so called, can really import into the soul none of the things of Christ, or anything more than simply the shadows and images of them.

Instead, therefore, of spending the time, or so great a part of it, in collecting knowledges, trying opinions, and storing the mind with cognitions and judgments, it would often be far better, as a mere point of economy, to occupy many hours in contesting with the sins that make a Saviour necessary, and in those sublime realizations of his power, which reveal him as the inner light and peace of the soul. Nay, it were better, if necessary to forego all instruction, shut up the libraries, give the weeks to prayer, shave the crown, put on hair girdles, ordain a year of silence—better, I would say, to practice any severity, rather than to attempt the knowledge of God by the mere natural understanding. Or if it be wise in teaching the military art to spend a full three months each year in the encampment, or service of the field, would it be wider of reason, in the training of a

Christian ministry, to spend as long a time, each year, in the holy drill of charity, patience, and devotion?

Inspirations are wanted to prepare the Christian preacher, as truly as the gymnastics of study. And is there nothing here to be learned from the schools of the prophets? In these we see the youthful candidates for prophecy led into retirement; practiced there in songs, processions, and impassioned acts of devotion; exercised in symbols and the senses of mystic forms; kindled by the lofty improvisings of the seers and prophet fathers—all that they, too, may be brought into the free intuition of God, and become seers themselves. They had no dogmatics. The plan was simply to bring them up out of nature into the "Spirit of the Lord," and open, within their souls, original sources of knowledge; immediate and free visions of light. True, the Christian minister, who is the prophet of Christianity, has books to receive and interpret, secondary knowledges to study and digest, but he can never take the senses of these holy documents, till the inner light of the seer, that is, of true insight, is kindled in him—on which account he needs to be trained in a holy element, and be led along as a pupil of the Spirit, into that deep knowledge of the secrets of God, that pure and hallowed union of spirit with Jesus himself, which is the fountain of all Christian light.

Another and second suggestion, which I proposed to offer, is that we need to distinguish more accurately than is generally done, between the idea of a Christian minister and that of a Christian preacher. A preacher is a public speaker, and a public speaker in the pulpit is estimated in much the same way as a speaker at the bar. Has he a well-trained understanding, a good rhetoric, a well-toned, flexible voice, a capacity of fire and a graceful action ?—these are the questions raised. And it seems to be supposed that a man will carry effect, and be a powerful minister of the New Testament, just in proportion to the degree of his personal talents and accomplishments, when judged in this manner. Contrary to this, how often do we see that a very ordinary preacher, as regards what men call eloquence, is yet a great and powerful minister of God. I cannot tell how it is, but a few plain words, spoken out of a present living faith and union to God, gently spoken, mere child's words in the form, equally distant from ambition on one side, and cant on the other—these will have more of true power to awaken thoughts of God and stir up desires after Him, than the most eloquent harangues. Here is a something which no drill in rhetoric can teach, no talent execute. Paul tells how it is done, when he sets forth his conception of the Christian teacher, as a minister of God :—"Whereof I am made a minister," [how ? by his skill in exegesis, his power in dogmatic theology, his rhetoric, his fine speaking, his human eloquence? no, but] "according to the dispensation which is given to me for you." Again, we have terms yet more precise and significant: "Whereof I was made a minister, *according to* the gift of the grace of God given unto me, by the effectual working of his power." Again—"Whereunto I also labor, striving according to his working that worketh in me mightily." And again—"But I labored more abundantly than they all—yet not I, but the grace of God which was with me." I believe it is common to resolve these striking declarations into a mere assertion of spiritual aid or co-operation. I do not so understand them. On the contrary, it is their precise design to represent that the man, in his human person, is to be the organ or vehicle of God; thus to have his power, not under the laws of mere natural effect, but as an expression of God's own Spirit. He is to be luminous by the suffusion of a divine light, thus a minister of God. The treasure is not to be the earthly vessel itself, but in the earthly vessel. The man is to be so united to God, so occupied and possessed by the Eternal Life, that his acts and words shall be outgoings of a divine power. And exactly this Paul himself declares, when he says—"And my speech and my preaching was not with persuasive words of man's wisdom, but in demonstration [αποδεἰξει] of the spirit and of power." And this is the proper, the truly sublime conception of the minister of God. He is not a mere preacher occupying some pulpit, as a stand of natural eloquence; but he is a man whose nature is possessed of God in such a manner that the light of God is seen upon him; a man whose life and words are apodictic—a demonstration of the Spirit.

To make us ministers of God, in this high and truly Christian sense, is the object of all theological training. It is to be a spiritual cultus in the things of Christ, wherein we are to learn the life of faith, the meekness and patience of Jesus, die unto ourselves, drink the spirit of Christ's passion, become pure as he is pure, learn to walk as he also walked, and receive the unction of the Holy One. In a word, we are to acquire that knowledge of Christ which is immediate, and which only the Father and the Son, manifested in us, can impart; the only true and really vital knowledge. And then we are to go forth and testify of him as they that have beer with him, to be a demonstration of him and his spirit.

O, if we had such a ministry, if we who now are serv· ing in this gospel, and all who are to join us, ceasing to be system-makers and preachers and place holders, and becoming ministers of God, were to go forth thus, and prove our fellowship with God and his Son, how soon would that great reviving of which I have spoken begin to appear. Doctrine would no more be the same as dogma. We should not preach a catechism, but a gospel. Dialectic quarrels would subside, or be drowned, rather, in the freedom of spirit and life. Panics raised over misspelt syllables, excommunications dealt upon those who venture on some disagreement with the church, in matters that belong only to the natural understanding, would be heard of no more. Then it will be something to love God, to walk in the Spirit, and bear the fruits of righteousness. And, as the scandals of past ages are wiped away, the word will run swiftly again, as in the days of the apostles, and be fulfilled with power.

4. There needs to be a revision of our current impressions, in reference to the value of doctrinal platforms and articles of scientific divinity, taken as bonds of unity and defences of purity. Christ and his apostles manifestly had no such conception of unity, as that any external ligament of opinion or science may compass it and fasten it. Christian unity, in their view, is not a fascicle, but a tree, vitalized by a common life—"I in them and thou in me, that they may be made perfect in one." It is

"holding the head," and, under it, being "fitly joined together." It is moral, not logical; of the heart, not of the head. It is precisely what an apostle means when he speaks of "*the unity of the Spirit;*" under which there is, of course, one body or embodiment as there is "one Spirit,"—"one Lord" above, "one faith" in the heart to embrace him, "one baptism" as the outward profession of that faith, and then, as the soul, the internal, vivifying principle of all, "one God and Father of all, who is above all, and through all, and in all." Discarding this magnificent view of internal brotherhood in the life, dogma early undertook to build an external, scientific unity; and then exactly that followed which only could follow, viz., that, as the heads which propagate dogma are many, not one, so the church, ceasing to be one, became, externally viewed, as many as the heads. Manifestly no human opinion could have scope and force to unify all thought or belief under it, and the more stringently it insists on containing the world in its human measures, the more certain is it that dissent, disruption, and all manner of discord will follow. So it has been, so it ever will be. These attempts to settle the world into unity under the external bonds of opinion, continually defeated, have been continually insisted on, and so the divisions and subdivisions have been constantly growing finer, till now, at last, the imposture is discovered—the articles of opinion that were to be the bonds and bases of a unity externally constructed, in place of the vital unity of the Spirit, have fretted away, at last, even the appearance of unity.

Nothing is plainer, whether as a matter of theory, or

of fact, than that dogmatism is and should be the most fruitful of all causes of division. If faith has to do with the infinite, if life is the presence in the soul of the infinite, how clear is it that opinions can compass no such matter. And then how evident is the reason why opinions divide, and sects arise, and wars rage. O, this wretched babble of opinions, this mutual barricading of opinions, by which Christian souls are fenced away from each other, and, if possible, from the Life of God!—as if the known, acknowledged fact, that God is manifested in the world, and wants the world's love, were nothing; to receive it, nothing; to meet in receiving it, no unity! Therefore, we must bring this astounding, untheorizable fact into theory, install it, in consequence, under the name of some school, or in some article of theology, and then, to unite in it, we fancy, makes a brotherhood. And thus we go on to talk, debate, measure and judge one another, and quarrel religion, from age to age, without so much, it may be, as one spiritual apprehension of God or of Christ as the life of the world! Opinions, deductions of mere logic, dogmas impotent and dry, discussed, debated, stood for by some, rejected by others, yielding to none the true food of life—these, with such intermixtures of strife and fire as are naturally to be expected, constitute the history of religion.

The manner in which dogmatism necessitates division may be well enough illustrated by the mournful separation which has taken place in the New England churches. Had we been embodied in the simple love of God under some such badge, for example, as the Apostles' Creed, it is very probable to me that the causes of the division would never have existed. But we had an article which asserted a metaphysical trinity, and this made the assertion of a metaphysical unity inevitable; nay, more, even desirable. So we had a theory of atonement, another of depravity, another of regeneration, or the ingeneration of character, which required the appearance, so to speak, of antagonistic theories. Our theologic culture, meantime, was so limited, on one side, that we took what was really our own opinion only, to be the unalterable truth of God; on the other, the side of the revolt, too limited to perceive the insufficiency of dogma as a fruit of the mere understanding, too limited not to take the opposite, with the same seriousness and totality of conviction. On this side they assumed the sufficiency of opinions and of speculative comprehension, in a more unrestrained sense than had been done before. They even fell to the work of constructing a religion wholly within the molds of natural reason itself, admitting nothing transcendent in the reach of faith, or the manifestation of the Life of God. They asserted liberty, as they must to vindicate their revolt, producing, however, meantime, the most intensely human, and in that sense, the most intensely opinionative religion ever invented, under the name of Christianity.

Have they no reason, together with us, to take up now, at last, some suspicion of the insufficiency of dogma and of all mere speculative opinions formed within the life of nature? May we not all begin to see that the ministration of life is somewhat broader, deeper, more sufficient, more divine? And what if we all, feeling our deep want, and sorrowing over the shame our human wisdom has cost us, should come back together to the simple Father, Son, and Holy Ghost, one God, there to enter into peace through the blood of Jesus, and there to abide in the fullness of love and brotherhood. Or if we should kneel down together before Him, and say—"I believe in God the Father Almighty, Maker of heaven and earth," and go on thus, to—"the life everlasting," what invisible minister of God, hanging as a listener about us, would not join us, at the close, and say "AMEN."

Perhaps it may be too soon to look for any so beautiful result as this. But it is not too soon for us to be setting the human in the place of the human, the divine in the place of the divine; to be drawing, all, towards simplicity; to pray more, and expect more light to come of the Life; to be more in love, and less in opinion; oftener to bless, and as much less often to judge.

One limit, I rejoice to believe, is already reached, as regards this process of division, and a consequent reaction may, accordingly, be hoped for. No longer is it possible for any man to think it a matter of ambition to become the founder of a sect. For this business of sect-making is already quite overdone, and the products turned out, in later times, are so indifferently small, because of the number, that when the busy leader gets his name stuck upon a small platoon of adherents, it seems to be a judgment of God upon him thus to expose him to ridicule. Henceforth the once powerful motives of ambition are taken away from the activities of dogmatism, and now there is nothing left us, in fact, but to strive after the Head; to draw the bleeding members, if we may, of Christ's lacerated body together, and have it for our most blessed and pure reward, to see them coa esce and live.

And to hasten such a result, we must disallow, as unchristian, all human schools and names of men. The time was when it was a somewhat brave demonstration for a man to declare that he was not a Calvinist, or not the disciple of some other human name. Possibly there are men who would think it a little heroic to do so now. But the day is at hand, I trust, when men will want their courage on the other side; when their conscience will forbid, and they themselves will not dare to be called by any other name than the name of God and of his Christ; when that pungent, cutting question of the word, "Is Christ divided?" or that other, "Who is Paul, and who is Apollos?" will be something more than a turn of rhetoric. The sin, the idolatry of man, that suffers any name but the blessed name of the Crucified, will be felt, forsaken, and, I hope, forever displaced from the world.

Do I then propose, it may be asked, to make nothing of opinions, to abolish all our platforms and articles, and embrace every person who pretends to be a disciple? Far from this. The recent experience of the Unitarians themselves may yield us a lesson of caution here. I propose no violent or abrupt change whatever. That our platforms and church Articles are generally too minute and theoretical, I certainly believe; but we must feel our way in the preparing of changes. It will suffice to relax, in a gradual manner, the exact and literal interpretation of our standards; to lean more and more, as we have been doing for the fifty years past, towards the side of accommodation, or easy construction. This, too, in the hope, which we may lawfully cherish, that it will, at last, be found amply sufficient as a term of fellowship, to unite in formulas far more simple and untheoretic, than any which we have at present.

I will go farther; I will venture to suggest the doubt, whether a state of spiritual elevation, light, sobriety, and freedom from passion, may not finally be reached, in which the "unity of the Spirit" will suffice, without any human formulas, to preserve the purity of the church. Manifestly we preserve no true semblance of purity now, by our formal standards; for the worst kind of impurity is practical, not theoretic, the impurity of a selfish, unspiritual, undevout life; and this will shelter itself as quietly under the platforms of orthodoxy, as if it were even acceptable to God. How often, indeed, is it the shame of religion, that a confessedly true disciple is hunted out of the church, for some gentle aberration of opinion, when many are endured in it, who neglect every duty, and are known to live in a manner that disavows every spiritual relation, whether to God or man,—simply because there are so many persons assuming to be pillars in the churches, who make a religion of orthodoxy, and find it so much easier to be exceedingly mad for this, than to be humble, gentle, and patient for Christ's sake.

Is it not possible, under the double action of a twofold process, named by the Apostle John, to have a pure church kept in preservation by mere spiritual affinities? First, in virtue of the fact that those who are not of the church, will go out from it themselves, because they are not of it? And, secondly, by the intuitive discerning of spirits, enabling those who are truly in the Spirit, and who, according to another apostle, "judge all things," to perceive the spirit of other minds? It certainly was not the design of John to affirm that every one is of God who "confesseth that Jesus Christ is come in the flesh," regarding him simply as receiving this mere formula. He gives the test as practical, and relating to the existing state of things. He goes on, accordingly, occupying the whole chapter that follows, as I understand him, with an exposition of the signs by which a true heir of God may be distinguished. Much ridicule has been heaped, in modern times, on human attempts to judge spiritual character. But however presumptuous, in one view, it may be, a far better and truer judgment, I am confident, may be formed of character than of opinions. We do, in fact, judge character more truly than we do opinions. It is more palpable. We are accustomed to read character. We do it almost unconsciously, and by an affinity deeper than we understand ourselves. It only requires a truly simple, unprejudiced heart; and, having that to offer to any character, it is drawn or repelled as by a certain divine polarity in us. Should that true reviving of the religious spirit, of which I have spoken, come to pass, and a heart spiritually enlightened and purified be found in the Christian body generally, may it not then be found also that the Life of God, in the Christian brotherhood, will sufficiently separate them from the unbelieving and unspiritual by its own transcendent affinities? Again—

5. I must call your attention more directly to the mournful effects of dogma, as a limitation upon piety

itself. It is so much easier to think than to slay our sins, to judge others than to live to God ourselves, to be orthodox than to be holy, that we are very prone to set one kind of activity in place of the other, and please ourselves in the pious and respectable look of it. If, too, we once pass into dogma and become active in it, we begin, at once, to over-value it, mixing our pride with it, adding to our pride our will, to this our passions, and to these our prayers, till, finally, we become at once thoroughly religious in our way, and, at the same time, thoroughly abominable and wicked in our spirit. This class of characters are about the worst and most mischievous that are ever to be found in the church.

I know of no illustration of the effect of dogmatism, taken as a limit upon piety, which needs to be pursued, at this time, with more attention than that which is furnished by the theory, extensively held, of Christ's work: He is regarded not as a power, in the manner of the New Testament, but more as a paymaster; not as coming to bring us life, and take us to his bosom, but in literal dogmatic verity, to suffer God's displeasure in our stead, and so to reconcile God to us. Taken as he stands, theologically represented, there is nothing given to us of Christ, which is closer to feeling, often, than that he fills out a judicial machinery, and is good as a legal tender for our sins. Diminished thus, by dogma, Christ ceases to be the Life. We only look to see how he brings us by the law. He is a mere forensic entity. Then follows what only could ;—a doctrine of justification by faith, is held by many so literal and forensic in its form, that the gospel of heaven's love and light is narrowed almost to a superstition. They scarcely dare entertain the thought of a personal righteousness, or to look upon any such hope as permissible. It implies, they fear, some expectations of being saved, not wholly by the merits of Christ. They cannot even read or hear, without a little jealousy or disturbance of mind, those texts of scripture that speak of assurance, liberty, a conscience void of offence, victory over sin, a pure heart, a blameless life, and a perfected love. They are so jealous of merit that they make a merit of not having any. They are so resolved on magnifying the grace of God, as almost to think it a crime to believe that the grace of God can make them any better. They come before God in confessions of sin, so extravagant, so wide of their own consciousness, that if a fellow man were to charge upon them what they confess, they would be mortally offended. And though there be no sincerity, no real verity in such confessions, they think it altogether safe to include enough, because it strips them of merit! Meantime their standards are let down to the lowest point of attainment; for if they deem it an essential part of their piety to keep up their confessions, it will be somewhat natural, at least, to live in a manner to do them some tolerable degree of justice. And, if an air of falsity or affectation is thus thrown over their piety, what, meantime, becomes of Jesus the Saviour—God in Christ reconciling the world to himself? What element of life and divine eloquence is left? Where is Christ, the wisdom and the power?

But you will best understand the stringent power of dogma as a limit upon spiritual character, if you advert to the common fact, everywhere visible, of a dogmatic piety. What a picture do I call up by these two words—'dogmatic piety'! It rises clear before you, and your heart sickens at the view of it. You behold, not a Calvinistic confession, but a Calvinistic piety; rigid, stern, standing for the letter, inflexible as the decrees of God—an Episcopal piety; moderate, complaisant, unaccommodating only in that which human opinion and custom have sanctified—a Presbyterian piety, a Quaker, a Methodist, all wearing a stamp from their human origin and polity so distinct that you could tell the religious communion of a stranger, under any one of these names, by a half hour's presence with him. You would see his dogma pricking through his skin, setting his postures, turning the angle of his motions, or tattooing itself in his face. What sight more sad than to behold these poor, unsuspecting disciples labeled off in this fantastic fashion, and standing up before both God and man, as illustrations of the extent to which mere human notions and conceits of the human understanding may limit the freedom of grace, and distort the beauty even of spiritual life.

I cannot pursue this topic further, save to suggest one simple remedy that seems to be provided, in a certain degree, out of the mischief itself, viz., that in every school and sect, the disciples give themselves to an attentive study of the best and most deeply devotional Christian writers in different ages, and under forms of worship and opinion most remote from their own. Let them read for instruction, not for criticism. Here they will see the Life struggling out through other forms of dogma, and while these other forms are meeting, and, perhaps, neutralizing their own, the image of Christ will shine out more clear and simple than they ever saw it before. They will see him as he lives in all his followers, and loving them with a new spirit of catholicity, will worship him with a new sense of oneness with him and his redeemed. And I anticipate no danger in this free communing with the devotional spirit of the disciples of our Lord, under other and repugnant forms of opinion. To behold the inner light with a Fox and a Gurnall, and with them to be in the Spirit; to look into that deep well ot spiritual thought, which God has uncovered in the sainted pages of Tersteegen; to steal into the cell of the old monk Thomas á Kempis, and weep with him; to follow to his exile the great archbishop of Cambray, that most luminous and loveliest of teachers, that most beautiful, most Christ-like, and, to human judgment, purest of all living characters since the days of the apostles—O, if this be dangerous, likely to unsettle our opinions, or dissolve our formulas, still may God grant that the effects of such kind of license may appear as soon as possible, and in the largest possible measure.

I would even go so far as to recommend, especially to Christian ministers and students of theology in New England, that they make a study, to some extent, of the mystic and quietistic writers; inquiring, at the same time, how far Christ and Christianity partake in these elements—also, whether it be not a fault of our own piety and character, that it partakes of neither? We have no reason, at present, to cherish any fears of mysticism. It can do us no harm until we are much farther off from the busy, speculative, dry, and almost total rule of dogma than we ever yet have been, or than it is, at present, in our nature to be. And as to quietism, it will be soon enough to apprehend ill consequences from that in New England, when the bees are found sleeping in summer shades, or the lightnings stagnate in the sky. In fact, there is nothing but spiritual life itself that is so much wanted in our American piety, as a larger infusion of the quiet spirit—to be less in commotion, and more in God, to learn the grace of silence and of secret alms, to acquaint ourselves with God, and be at peace.

6. It remains to be suggested, that our modern piety appears to have been limited and partially dwarfed, almost universally, by the admission of certain opinions or impressions of the Holy Spirit, which are referable wholly to scientific theology, and which need to be revised.

It has been remarked, I think by others, and truly nothing is more remarkable, than that individuals and communities are often deeply moved, as in revivals of religion, by the Spirit of God, and yet that the sect-spirit is, in general, rather exasperated than softened. There is visibly more of love, and yet the antagonisms of sect appear to be more active. A result, manifestly, which is not of God, but rather of some bad limitations, which are really hostile to the proper unity of the Spirit in us. Nor have we any doubt where this limitation is to be sought. Our own consciousness tells us where it is; for what man ever finds it in him to expect that the Spirit of God will melt down a platform, or dissolve one dogma? It is even taken for granted, that he will let alone our opinions and disturb no articles we have adopted! We secretly, though doubtless unconsciously, impose our dogma as a limitation of the Spirit.

What a revelation, then, have we here! Were there no other cause to differ our piety from that of the apostles, this would suffice. The Pauline character can never appear again till we are so disencumbered of restrictions, that we can offer our whole being up to the pure and total guidance of God. This is the first condition of a complete Christian life, that God shall have free course in us. We cannot wall him about with our wisdom, and then require of him to finish the spirit of Christ in us.

The reality and power of this limitation is displayed in other methods. In how many minds is the Spirit viewed or received, through their speculative theology, not as maintaining any social, moral, endearing relations in us, but simply as an abstract and dry agency—mere efficiency, running out from God's decrees, to execute them in us by an ictic force; or, at best, as an effluence or influence streaming through us, which does not shape itself, has no social consciousness, but only works in the way of mere causation, like a stimulant or an opiate. This, manifestly, is not the Holy Spirit of the scriptures, but the Holy Spirit, rather, of the schools. And the difference is the more remarkable, that our dogma even goes beyond the scriptures in asserting the metaphysical personality of the Spirit. We call him a person, insist on his personality, raising, at the same time, a scheme of dogma, which reduces him to a something literally purchased for us, and dispensed as a gift to us; or to a mere causative agency that works in us without feeling sociality, character, or anything which properly distinguishes personality. Hence, there is scarcely produced in us at all, the sense of mutuality, love, or inwardly abiding friendship.

In the scriptures, on the other hand, he is even represented as being the spirit of Christ—nay, Christ himself. This also by Christ himself; for he says, in his promise of the Comforter, "*I* will come to you,"—and to his apostles, "Lo *I* am with you always." And this is said, evidently, that we may conceive the Spirit socially, as being in some proper sense Christ himself, with us always, in all the feeling of Jesus—breathing his feeling as love and life into every fibre of our inner man. The word is nigh us, even in our mouth and heart. The Christ of the garden and the cross is with us, suing at our heart, and striving to communicate all that we could hope from the love of Gethsemane and Calvary socially present in us. If, then, we can give up our soul to his occupancy, and let him abide in us, according to his promise, what attainments, what elevation, what purity and peace of spirit may we not believe he will work in us!

We have also raised a theologic distinction, under the word *inspiration*, which, it is very clear to me, is operating a sad depression in our modern piety, even if originally there was nothing false in the distinction; for we have now taken it, practically, in such a sense as cuts us off from the holy men of scripture times, and works a feeling in us that God is now more remote, and, of course, that it is no longer permissible to realize the same graces, and expect the same intense union of the life with God.

Thus, out of our own opinion we judge, and from our pulpits declare that there is no inspiration in these latter times. It was confined, we say, to the times previous to the canon of scripture. At that time it was discontinued. True, it may only be intended that prophetic inspirations, or the inspirations of evangelists and apostles was discontinued, and yet, by thus appropriating the word, we carry a deeper impression, which is certainly untrue; for all the workings of the Spirit are inspirations as truly as these. Christian character itself, and all its graces, are forms of inspiration. It requires an inspiration, according to the second chapter of the first epistle to the Corinthians, to understand or really to come into the truth of Christ at all. Nay, it is even required of us that we shall, as disciples, be led of the Spirit, so that he shall be the practical guide of life; which is nothing less than to say that there is an inspiration for everything right in life—as there was for the good goldsmith Bezaleel, when "filled with the Spirit of God, in wisdom, and in understanding," "to devise cunning works, to work in gold, and in silver, and in brass, and in cutting of stones." In short, the true idea of Christianity, as a ministration of the Spirit, is that the disciple shall be led out of one moment into the next, through all his life, by a present union to God and a constant guidance—that he shall be the child of the Spirit. Thus, whether he be a cultivator of the soil, an artisan, a teacher, a magistrate, or a minister of God's truth, he shall live, not in himself, but in God, and have just that kind and degree of inspiration or guidance which his calling demands.

Rectifying thus, and enlarging our ideas of the Spirit

and his relations to us, how clear is it that a new intimacy of faith and love will be visible between the church and God—that the old incrustation, or dogmatic shell of our piety will be melted away, and that, ceasing to see in the sparks of our own kindling, looking to God in the whole course of life, there will be unfolded a style of piety wholly unknown, at present, in the world. Then the church of God will be again, what an apostle said it was, the inhabitation of Christ—his body, the fullness of him that filleth all in all.

There are, still, many things waiting to be said, in connection with this very momentous subject, but I must draw my remarks to a conclusion. I have spoken of dogma as a limitation upon piety; or, rather, even as a lapse in the Christian spirit itself. This I most firmly believe to be true, and, I think, I have given you sufficient reason, if not to embrace, at least, to consider with profound deliberation, the view I have stated. If I am right, nothing is wanted now, in order to realize a grand renovation of the religious spirit throughout Christendom, more glorious, probably, than the Reformation itself, but simply to recover from this ancient lapse into dogma—not to uproot opinions, not to stop the intellectual and scientific activity of the church, but simply to invert the relations of dogma and spirit, so as to subordinate everything in the nature of science and opinion to the spirit, and thus to elevate everything in the nature of science and opinion into the region of spirit and life.

As regards revivals of religion, it is not any purpose of my discourse to object against them. I only have a conviction that God is calling us to look farther, and comprehend more. To do so is, in fact, the best method of preparing revivals, if that were our object—the only method in which it can be done effectually. The true doctrine seems to be that we are to labor, not for a reviving of revivals, but for a reviving of the real life and deepest and most earnest power of religion itself. And then, if it please God to bring us into some state that we may call by the ordinary name revival, we shall be in it healthily, in it as being in religion, permanently given to God, and not as in some casual flame that is got up, in part, by the friction of human effort and expectation. We certainly cannot miss of revivals, if they are wanted, by means of a new spirit of piety from God, such as we have never before realized. If we are after the most spiritual habit, the most complete devotion, the deepest union to God, the fullest liberty and the most established and permanent life of religion, we shall not miss, I am confident, of any casual blessings on our way. What do we require, in fact, but that every disciple shall be revived for his whole life—that he shall undertake, not for a scene, but for a life; that he shall die to self, come into the true liberty and rest of faith, achieve his victory, live the secret life, and prove the fullness and sufficiency of Christ as a Saviour. This I am sure will be, in the truest, fullest sense, a reviving of religion; only it cannot come up in a night, in some social meeting, but must come gradually, as the day dawns. It will require patience, holy application, and a capacity, I think, to bear some reproach from disciples who cannot enter at once into a view so remote from their apprehensions, or opposite to their prejudices.

One thing is clear, that the highest form of piety can never appear on earth until the disciples of Chiist are able to be in the Spirit, in some broader and more permanent sense than simply to suffer those local and casual fervors that may be kindled within the walls of a church, or the boundaries of a village. The Spirit of God is a catholic spirit, and there needs to be a grand catholic reviving; a universal movement, penetrating gradually and quickening into power the whole church of Christ on earth. Then and then only, in the spiritual momentum of such a day, when the Spirit of God is breathing inspirations into all believing souls, and working graces in them that are measured, no longer by the dogmas of sect, but by the breadth of his own character—then, I say, feeling the contact, every man, of a universal fellowship, and rising with the flood that is lifting the whole church into freedom and power, it will be seen what possible heights of attainment—hitherto scarcely imagined—what spiritual completeness and fullness of life the gospel and grace of Christ are able to effect, in our sinful race. Partiality of movement involves a limitation of power. By this cause Christianity has hitherto been dwarfed in all its results and manifestations. Nothing better can ever be realized, till, ascending into Christianity as spirit and life, in the fullest and freest sense, we submit our souls to God's universal movement. We are to receive the Spirit in his own measures, not any more in ours, and prepare ourselves, gradually, for an outspreading era of life, that shall be as the manifested Life of God.

It is also to be noted, that we are the only people who are prepared to lead in so great a work; for the manifest reason that, in every other Protestant nation, dogma remains, even to this hour, intermixed with and supported by civil statutes. From these we have made our escape, and now it remains to use the advantage gained—to assume the work Luther left incomplete, and go forward to re-inaugurate that ministration of the Spirit which Christ ordained for the world.

If any apprehend that, in such a movement for the reduction of dogma as I have proposed, we are likely to fall into confusion and run loose into all the wild extravagances of the mystics, let them observe that the apprehensions they suffer are excited by the experience of past ages; which experience will avail to make other men cautious, as it does to make them apprehensive, and will thus operate as a check to extravagance; also, that I give ample room for a strong theological activity, raising a demand for it even by requiring that nothing shall be accepted as truth, which is contrary to reason or true learning, as exercised on the scripture; also, that I propose no abrupt change—no change at all, in fact, but such as consists in being more simply and absolutely united to God.

If I have suggested the possibility of a reunion of the separated churches of New England, who can estimate the effects that would follow such an event, the influence it would exert on the religious well-being of the nation, and also of the world? If, then, we surrender to our adversaries no truth, if we simply cast out repugnant forms of opinion that are human, and disencumber the words of spirit of those loads of unwisdom which the past ages have heaped upon the truth, should we not for Christ's sake do it? And, if we meet them in the Father, Son, and Holy Ghost—one God; if we meet them in Gethsemane, or on the hill of Calvary, there to kneel and weep away our sins together—which we do, or else we meet them nowhere—who shall suffer, who will be offended? Shall we not, rather, stand ready to meet the world here also? And what if we all, in every name and kindred and family, relaxing, a little, the bondage we are under to our dogmas, should come up into spirit and life as the freemen of the Lord, and begin to claim our common property together in the old Apostles' Creed. Most sure, I am, that no spectacle more sublime, or more truly pleasing to God, will ever be witnessed on earth, than if taking up this holy confession, sanctified by the faith and consecrated by the uses of so many ages, all the disciples of Jesus on earth, may be heard answering in it together, sect to sect, and people to people, and rolling it, as a hymn of love and brotherhood, round the world:—

I believe in God the Father Almighty, Maker of heaven and earth: And in Jesus Christ, his only Son, our Lord; Who was conceived by the Holy Ghost, born of the Virgin Mary, suffered under Pontius Pilate, was crucified, dead, and buried. The third day he rose from the dead; He ascended into Heaven, and sitteth on the right hand of God the Father Almighty; From thence he shall come to judge the quick and the dead.

I believe in the Holy Ghost; the Holy Catholic Church; the communion of Saints; the forgiveness of sins; the resurrection of the body, and the life everlasting. Amen.

www.ingramcontent.com/pod-product-compliance
Lightning Source LLC
LaVergne TN
LVHW010153110826
845151LV00002B/509

* 9 7 8 1 4 2 5 5 3 7 2 7 2 *